VOLUME 614

NOVEMBER 2007

THE ANNALS

of The American Academy of Political
and Social Science

PHYLLIS KANISS, *Executive Editor*

The Biology of Political Behavior

Special Editors of this Volume

JOHN R. HIBBING
University of Nebraska–Lincoln

KEVIN B. SMITH
University of Nebraska–Lincoln

SAGE Publications
Los Angeles • London • New Delhi • Singapore

Origin and Purpose. The Academy was organized December 14, 1889, to promote the progress of political and social science, especially through publications and meetings. The Academy does not take sides in controverted questions, but seeks to gather and present reliable information to assist the public in forming an intelligent and accurate judgment.

Meetings. The Academy occasionally holds a meeting in the spring extending over two days.

Publications. THE ANNALS of The American Academy of Political and Social Science is the bimonthly publication of the Academy. Each issue contains articles on some prominent social or political problem, written at the invitation of the editors. Also, monographs are published from time to time, numbers of which are distributed to pertinent professional organizations. These volumes constitute important reference works on the topics with which they deal, and they are extensively cited by authorities throughout the United States and abroad. The papers presented at the meetings of the Academy are included in THE ANNALS.

Membership. Each member of the Academy receives THE ANNALS and may attend the meetings of the Academy. Membership is open only to individuals. Annual dues: $84.00 for the regular paperbound edition (clothbound, $121.00). Members may also purchase single issues of THE ANNALS for $17.00 each (clothbound, $26.00). Student memberships are available for $53.00.

Subscriptions. THE ANNALS of The American Academy of Political and Social Science (ISSN 0002-7162) (J295) is published six times annually—in January, March, May, July, September, and November—by Sage Publications, 2455 Teller Road, Thousand Oaks, CA 91320. Telephone: (800) 818-SAGE (7243) and (805) 499-9774; Fax/Order line: (805) 499-0871; e-mail: journals@sagepub.com. Copyright © 2007 by The American Academy of Political and Social Science. Institutions may subscribe to THE ANNALS at the annual rate: $612.00 (clothbound, $692.00). Single issues of THE ANNALS may be obtained by individuals who are not members of the Academy for $34.00 each (clothbound, $47.00). Single issues of THE ANNALS have proven to be excellent supplementary texts for classroom use. Direct inquiries regarding adoptions to THE ANNALS c/o Sage Publications (address below). Periodicals postage paid at Thousand Oaks, California, and at additional mailing offices.

All correspondence concerning membership in the Academy, dues renewals, inquiries about membership status, and/or purchase of single issues of THE ANNALS should be sent to THE ANNALS c/o Sage Publications, 2455 Teller Road, Thousand Oaks, CA 91320.Telephone: (800) 818-SAGE (7243) and (805) 499-9774; Fax/Order line: (805) 499-0871; e-mail: journals@sagepub.com. *Please note that orders under $30 must be prepaid.* Sage affiliates in London and India will assist institutional subscribers abroad with regard to orders, claims, and inquiries for both subscriptions and single issues.

Printed on acid-free paper

THE ANNALS

© 2007 by The American Academy of Political and Social Science

Editorial Office: 3814 Walnut Street, Fels Institute for Government, University of Pennsylvania, Philadelphia, PA 19104-6197.
For information about membership* (individuals only) and subscriptions (institutions), address:
Sage Publications
2455 Teller Road
Thousand Oaks, CA 91320

For Sage Publications: Rachel Mayer (Production) and Sandra Hopps (Marketing)

From India and South Asia, write to:
SAGE PUBLICATIONS INDIA Pvt Ltd
B-42 Panchsheel Enclave, P.O. Box 4109
New Delhi 110 017
INDIA

From Europe, the Middle East, and Africa, write to:
SAGE PUBLICATIONS LTD
1 Oliver's Yard, 55 City Road
London EC1Y 1SP
UNITED KINGDOM

*Please note that members of the Academy receive THE ANNALS with their membership.
International Standard Serial Number ISSN 0002-7162
International Standard Book Number ISBN 978-1-4129-6404-3 (Vol. 614, 2007) paper
International Standard Book Number ISBN 978-1-4129-6405-0 (Vol. 614, 2007) cloth
Manufactured in the United States of America. First printing, November 2007.

The articles appearing in *The Annals* are abstracted or indexed in Academic Abstracts, Academic Search, America: History and Life, Asia Pacific Database, Book Review Index,CABAbstracts Database, Central Asia: Abstracts &Index, Communication Abstracts, Corporate ResourceNET, Criminal Justice Abstracts, Current Citations Express, Current Contents: Social & Behavioral Sciences, Documentation in Public Administration, e-JEL, EconLit, Expanded Academic Index, Guide to Social Science & Religion in Periodical Literature, Health Business FullTEXT, HealthSTAR FullTEXT, Historical Abstracts, International Bibliography of the Social Sciences, International Political Science Abstracts, ISI Basic Social Sciences Index, Journal of Economic Literature on CD, LEXIS-NEXIS, MasterFILE FullTEXT, Middle East: Abstracts&Index, North Africa: Abstracts&Index, PAIS International, Periodical Abstracts, Political Science Abstracts, Psychological Abstracts, PsycINFO, Sage Public Administration Abstracts, Scopus, Social Science Source, Social Sciences Citation Index, Social Sciences Index Full Text, Social Services Abstracts, SocialWork Abstracts, Sociological Abstracts, Southeast Asia: Abstracts& Index, Standard Periodical Directory (SPD), TOPICsearch, Wilson OmniFileV, and⋅ Wilson Social Sciences Index/Abstracts, and are available on microfilm from ProQuest, Ann Arbor, Michigan.

Information about membership rates, institutional subscriptions, and back issue prices may be found on the facing page.

Advertising. Current rates and specifications may be obtained by writing to The Annals Advertising and Promotion Manager at the Thousand Oaks office (address above).

Claims. Claims for undelivered copies must be made no later than six months following month of publication. The publisher will supply missing copies when losses have been sustained in transit and when the reserve stock will permit.

Change of Address. Six weeks' advance notice must be given when notifying of change of address to ensure proper identification. Please specify name of journal. POSTMASTER: Send address changes to The Annals of The American Academy of Political and Social Science, c/o Sage Publications, 2455 Teller Road, Thousand Oaks, CA 91320.

THE ANNALS

OF THE AMERICAN ACADEMY OF POLITICAL AND SOCIAL SCIENCE

Volume 614   November 2007

IN THIS ISSUE:

The Biology of Political Behavior

Special Editors: JOHN R. HIBBING
KEVIN B. SMITH

FORTHCOMING

The Epidemic of Childhood Overweight
Special Editor: AMY JORDAN
Volume 615, January 2008

The Politics of History in Comparative Perspective
Special Editor: MARTIN O. HEISLER
Volume 616, March 2008

Public Diplomacy in a Changing World
Special Editors: GEOFFREY COWAN and NICHOLAS CULL
Volume 617, May 2008

The Biology of Political Behavior: An Introduction

A broad cross-section of the social sciences is increasingly turning to biology and evolutionary theory to help explain human behavior. Political science is a notable exception to this trend, even though there are sound conceptual reasons for expecting biological processes to play an important role in explaining political behavior. While agreeing with the conceptual arguments, the authors believe original empirical research is the most persuasive means of convincing political science to incorporate biology in explanations of political behavior. Techniques developed in neuroscience, behavioral genetics, agent-based simulation, experimental economics, and other fields offer exciting research opportunities to explore questions of central interest to political scientists. The research presented in this volume provides examples of replicable, empirical evidence that political beliefs and behavior are a product of biological as well as environmental factors.

Keywords: neuroscience; genetics; neurotransmitter; evolution; interdisciplinary

By
JOHN R. HIBBING
and
KEVIN B. SMITH

Who we are and what we do is the product of environmental *and* biological factors. In the life sciences, this simple statement would be regarded as painfully obvious. In many parts of the social sciences, especially in political science, it is seen as peculiar, wrong, and even dangerous. As a result, virtually the entire research agenda in political science is isolated from the vast biological knowledge base that has built up over the course of the past fifty years. Most

John R. Hibbing is the Foundation Regents University Professor of Political Science at the University of Nebraska–Lincoln. With Elizabeth Theiss-Morse, he is the author of Congress as Public Enemy *as well as* Stealth Democracy, *both dealing with public attitudes toward government, governors, and governing. His recent work, primarily with John Alford but also with Kevin Smith and others, attempts to integrate biological concepts and the social sciences.*

Kevin B. Smith is a professor of political science at the University of Nebraska–Lincoln. His research focuses on the application of evolutionary and biological models to political behavior.

DOI: 10.1177/0002716207305471

political scientists continue to be environmental determinists, believing that
human behavior is entirely the product of environmental forces. From this perspective, political attitudes and political behavior are driven by parental socialization, campaign messages, conversations at work, and idiosyncratic experiences.
Political science gives biology virtually no role in answering the questions it seeks
to address. In the extant literature of mainstream political science, biological
independent variables are extremely rare, and biological theory rarely is used to
generate hypotheses and insights.

Why political science continues to ignore biology is unclear. In other social sciences, biology is given a useful and expanding explanatory role. In psychology, personal traits such as risk-taking, harm avoidance, attention deficit hyperactivity
disorder (ADHD), depression, and extroversion have been connected to biological
variables including neurotransmitter levels and even genetics (see Bouchard and
McGue 1990; Pickering and Gray 1999; Plomin et al. 2001; Harpending and
Cochran 2002; Ding et al. 2002). Evolutionary psychology explicitly merges cognitive psychology with evolutionary biology to demonstrate that universal human
tendencies such as strong reciprocity and altruistic punishment are products of evolutionary pressures (see Tooby and Cosmides 1992; Buss 1999; Pinker 2002). In
economics, behavioral economics and neuroeconomics both draw heavily from biological concepts, and both have been growing rapidly in number of practitioners,
contributions made, and public visibility (for reviews, see Camerer, Loewenstein,
and Rabin 2004; Camerer, Loewenstein, and Prelec 2005). In anthropology, the
Human Behavior and Evolution Society is also growing, and many of its members
use evidence from a variety of societies, including hunter-gatherer groups, to test
hypotheses drawn from evolutionary and biological principles (see, for example,
Henrich et al. 2001). And in sociology, a long-established research tradition has
attempted to connect neurotransmitters and hormones to social behavior (see,
for example, Archer 1991; Booth and Dabbs 1993); a recent address by the then-
president of the American Sociological Association (Massey 2002) sounded a clarion
call for that discipline to take biological concepts more seriously.

In contrast, the movement to incorporate biology into political science seems
to be making considerably less progress. Biopolitics, the original movement to get
political science to take biology seriously, traces its roots back more than thirty
years and even has a professional organization: the Association for Politics and the
Life Sciences (APLS). Political science's central disciplinary organization, the
American Political Science Association (APSA), once included a biopolitics group
as one of its official sections, but the movement has encountered problems.
Membership in the section fell below APSA's threshold requirements, so the
group is no longer recognized. APLS and its core of biologically oriented political
scientists now host a small conference independent of the discipline's primary professional society, leaving biopolitics outside the mainstream of political science.

Why does political science lag behind when it comes to incorporating biology
into its research? Part of the reason may be a sop to political correctness and the
associated fear of openly recognizing innate human differences. It seems unlikely,
however, that political scientists' devotion to political correctness exceeds that of,

say, sociologists. A more likely reason pertains to the subject matter of mass-scale politics, which, more than other subject areas, may seem to be environmental rather than biological. Behavior can be usefully placed in three categories: personal, social, and political. Personal behavior is behavior that is a characteristic of the individual; it requires no social interaction to manifest itself. This includes risk-taking, depressive symptomatology, and similar behavioral characteristics that can be in evidence either with or without other people. Social behavior requires the presence of at least one other human being in the immediate environment and might involve altruism, revenge, or trust. Political behavior is different from social behavior in that it pertains to preferences for the structure and organization of mass-scale social life even if this structure and organization might not directly affect an individual's immediate social environment. Gay marriage, for example, may not affect a given individual, or have an impact upon anyone in his or her family or social circle, yet that individual still may have extremely strong preferences about the manner in which society should regulate (ban, allow, or something in between) intimate relationships between members of the same gender.

Why does political science lag behind when it comes to incorporating biology into its research? Part of the reason may be a sop to political correctness and the associated fear of openly recognizing innate human differences.

While numerous animal species display observable personal (see Gosling and John 1999) and social (see de Waal 1982, 1996) behavior, only humans have preferences for the organization of large-scale group life. Animals may care about the hierarchy of their immediate, small-scale group, but such issues relate to small-scale dominance hierarchies and not to large-scale politics. Perhaps because mass-scale politics seems so uniquely human, so cerebral, and so rational, scholars of politics are prone to conclude that it somehow transcends biology.

Whatever the reason, political scientists have grown comfortable ignoring biology. The biological underpinnings of behavior has virtually no presence in the curriculum of political science graduate programs, has very little presence in the leading scholarly journals, and is largely ignored in undergraduate instruction. The notion seems to be that even though many other aspects of human behavior are shaped by genetics and biology, politics is sui generis and therefore incapable of being informed by biological insights. The prevailing assumption is that, if biology matters at all, its effects are trivial. Though widely held, this assumption is bereft of supporting empirical evidence. If biological variables are never employed, it is impossible to support *any* claim of their impact on behavior, including a claim that they have no impact. Given the influence of biology on other aspects of the human condition, the onus would seem to be on the environmental determinists to demonstrate that they are correct in ignoring biological variables. Otherwise, the suspicion has to be voiced that biology is ignored partly because doing so absolves political scientists of the need to become familiar with modern biology.

We believe ignoring biology is a mistake. The uniqueness of human politics does not mean it is divorced from biological processes any more than it is likely that human politics are completely divorced from human personal and social tendencies. And those personal and social tendencies themselves undoubtedly have biological origins (see the works cited earlier). The "theories" claimed in political science are usually just collections of relationships, little more than recapitulations of time tested correlations, rather than assertions of ultimate causes. Little in the political science literature even acknowledges that any two people subjected to identical environmental stimuli over the course of their lifetimes could still possess dramatically different behavioral predispositions. Until political scientists incorporate biology into their theoretical and empirical models they will risk being labeled "incoherent environmentalists" (Tooby and Cosmides 1992).

In an effort to promote the application of biological principles to political science, in October 2006 we hosted a conference on the campus of the University of Nebraska–Lincoln. Our goal was to bring together political scientists doing work informed by biology with scholars in other disciplines who are investigating questions of interest to political scientists. This conference was made possible by a generous gift from a Nebraska alumnus named G. E. Hendricks with additional support from the Department of Political Science, and we were extremely pleased with the quality and diversity of the two dozen scholars from at least half a dozen different disciplines who attended the conference. Scores of people besides those giving presentations came to the conference sessions where they witnessed the following reports on research.

Neuroscientist Michael L. Spezio of Cal Tech, on behalf of coauthors R. Michael Alvarez, Kyle Mattes, Alexander Todorov, Hackjin Kim, and Ralph Adolphs, demonstrated the neural pathways involved when subjects view candidate photos for the purpose of discerning character traits. Jennifer Wolak of the University of Colorado and George E. Marcus of Williams College tested for the possibility that subjects with different personality traits would display predictable emotional responses to political stimuli. Diana Mutz of the University of Pennsylvania showed that television is atypical in that it exposes people to close-up conflict between disagreeing parties; she then documented the physiological consequences of this situation. Rose McDermott of the University of California, Santa Barbara, along with coauthors Dominic Johnson, Jonathan Cowden, and Stephen Rosen, using an imaginative simulation, suggested that levels of testosterone may influence the degree to which aggressive decisions are made. Peter K. Hatemi of the University of Nebraska–Lincoln, along with geneticist Nicholas Martin of the Queensland Institute of Medical Research, employed modern structural equation models to show the connection between genes and voting behavior. Ira H. Carmen of the University of Illinois offered a detailed account of the specific genes that have been identified as relevant to personal temperament and speculated on the manner in which these same genes are likely to bear on political behavior. James H. Fowler of the University of California, San Diego, in combination with coauthors Christopher T. Dawes and psychologist Laura A. Baker, provided additional evidence on the relevance of genes to politics—in this case on the tendency of individuals to either turn out to vote or not.

Economist Paul Zak of the Claremont Graduate School documented the importance of trust to social behavior and discussed recent research on the biological bases of trust, particularly the correlation of trust with the hormone oxytocin. Using a computer simulation based on the logic of biological evolution, Paul E. Johnson of the University of Kansas modeled the changes likely to occur in political organizations such as interest groups. Christopher W. Larimer of the University of Northern Iowa, working with Rebecca Hannagan and Kevin B. Smith, observed the tendency of experimental subjects to prefer certain types of decision makers and traced these preferences to evolutionary sources. John R. Alford of Rice University, along with coauthor John R. Hibbing, investigated the potential connection between personality traits (known to be partially genetic) on one hand and social and political traits on the other. Thomas Craemer of the University of Connecticut provided evidence that people's racial attitudes, perhaps for evolutionarily sensible reasons, are different depending upon whether personal idiosyncratic attitudes or socially shared attitudes are being reflected. Leonie Huddy, Stanley Feldman, and Christopher Weber of the State University of New York at Stony Brook showed that some people simply feel more secure than other people and that this variation mediates the manner in which people respond to external threats. Darren Schreiber of the University of California, San Diego, used modern neuroimaging techniques to demonstrate the manner in which race is processed by the human brain. Arthur Lupia, working with Jesse O. Menning, modeled politicians employing fear in an attempt to stimulate support for policy preferences that may not be optimal.

Anthropologist Michael Price of Brunel University in the United Kingdom, using data collected in personal observations of Shuar hunter-horticulturalists, found interesting patterns in preferences for individuals who cooperate as opposed to individuals who benefit. Psychologist Robert Kurzban of the University of Pennsylvania, working with coauthors Peter DeScioli and Erin O'Brien, investigated the intriguing phenomenon of moralistic punishment and discussed both the conditions under which it surfaces and the evolutionary pressures from which it likely derives. Law student John Sautter of the University of Vermont identified some individuals as more empathetic than others and predicted that these individuals will behave differently in the prisoner's dilemma game. John Orbell of the University of Oregon, with coauthors Oleg Smirnov,

Holly Arrow, and Doug Kennet, employed computer simulations to show the advantages derived when some individuals make sacrifices in the face of out-group threats and others make sacrifices in the face of threats coming from within the group. And anthropologist John Tooby detailed the essential role of "outrages" in intergroup conflict.

We took the time to list each of these topics and approaches to demonstrate the many different ways in which biology can be applied to the study of political phenomena. As can be seen, the range of topics is virtually endless; the methodological approaches include computer simulations, laboratory experiments, survey data, formal models, evolutionary theorizing, behavioral genetics, hormonal assays, psychophysiological measurements, and neuroimaging techniques such as functional magnetic resonance imaging (fMRI). A second reason for providing this full list of presentations is to indicate that it is not necessary to hold an advanced degree in either molecular biology or neuroscience to apply biology to politics. By thinking carefully about the role of emotions, decision making, human similarities and differences, experimental design, and group life; by paying attention to work being done in other disciplines; and by forming teams with scientists possessing different areas of expertise, it is possible to make significant advances without spending a lifetime retooling. We owe it to potential collaborators to become familiar enough with biology to understand generally and to be able to converse intelligently, but division of labor is the order of the day in the sciences, and this is the most sensible approach for applying natural science techniques to social science questions.

We owe it to potential collaborators to become familiar enough with biology to understand generally and to be able to converse intelligently, but division of labor is the order of the day in the sciences, and this is the most sensible approach for applying natural science techniques to social science questions.

Many of the presenters at the conference, particularly the non–political scientists, had already committed their research for publication elsewhere, but when Phyllis Kaniss and Julie Odland suggested the possibility of placing revisions of the conference papers in a volume of *The Annals*, we prevailed upon the other presenters to revise their conference presentations into publishable articles, and we solicited one additional article from conference attendee William T. Anderson of the University of South Dakota and his colleague Cliff H. Summers. The result is this collection of nine original articles all touching in some fashion on the salience of biology to political behavior and all illustrating the fruitful directions that the study of biology and politics can be taken.

The acid test is not that there exist good conceptual reasons for political scientists to pay attention to biology, but that there is testable, replicable empirical evidence that biology helps explain political behavior.

If biology is to make important contributions to answering the questions that interest political science, then research must be empirical and not just conceptual. The handful of political scientists that have published in high-profile journals using biological variables and/or theory are generally distinguished by empirical work with original data. Examples of such productive, ongoing research agendas include those of John Orbell on the evolutionary basis for behavior and Machiavellian intelligence in social groups (see Orbell et al. 2004), Milton Lodge on hot cognition (see Lodge and Taber 2005), George Marcus on affective intelligence (see Marcus, Newman, and Mackuen 2000), as well as earlier work by Douglas Madsen (1986) on serotonin and Roger Masters (Sullivan and Masters 1993) on the facial appearance of leaders. We strongly believe that it is this sort of research that will best make the case that biology deserves important consideration by political scientists. We are sympathetic to pleas for more biologically related research as well as to biologically based theoretical accounts that do not include original empirical findings (e.g., Wahlke 1979; Somit and Peterson 1997). However, original empirical research ultimately has to carry the argument. The acid test is not that there exist good conceptual reasons for political scientists to pay attention to biology, but that there is testable, replicable empirical evidence that biology helps explain political behavior. It is the latter that is more likely to energize other scholars, especially graduate students, to construct a lasting research agenda on the foundation laid down so ably by the earlier biopolitics movement. If biology is going to play a significant role in political science research, the time for exhortations is past and the time for data and analyses is present.

It is our hope that this collection of articles, all but a couple of which rely on original empirical findings, will help to provide inspiration for further empirical investigations of the manner in which biology interacts with environmental forces to produce social and political beliefs and behavior. Thanks to the river of evolution and thanks to the remarkable variation in genes, politics is much more than the product of environmental forces. Biology can help to account both for central behavioral tendencies and also for the astounding variation around these central tendencies.

The research possibilities are arrayed before us. Fascinating questions regarding the origins of politics and the causes of human political variation now rest beside the remarkable techniques developed in neuroscience, experimental economics, computer simulations, psychophysiology, behavioral genetics, and molecular biology. Applying these techniques to the fundamental questions that have bedeviled political scientists for centuries will be thrilling. Human behavior, whether personal or political, does not transcend biology even as it is not determined by biology. We hope this volume will encourage social science scholars to investigate more concertedly the rich dynamic interplay of environmental *and* biological variables that makes us who we are and makes the political system what it is. When it comes to human behavior, evolutionary theory is more than a metaphor for societal change, and biology is more than an interesting but irrelevant discipline.

References

Archer, J. 1991. The influence of testosterone on human aggression. *British Journal of Psychology* 82:1-28.

Booth, A., and J. Dabbs. 1993. Testosterone and men's marriages. *Social Forces* 72:463-77.

Bouchard, T. J., and M. McGue. 1990. Genetic and rearing environmental influences on adult personality: An analysis of adopted twins reared apart. *Journal of Personality* 58:263-92.

Buss, David M. 1999. Human nature and individual differences: The evolution of human personality. In *Handbook of personality*, 2nd ed., ed. Lawrence A. Pervin and Oliver P. John. New York: Guilford.

Camerer, Colin, George Loewenstein, and Drazen Prelec. 2005. Neuroeconomics: How neuroscience can inform economics. *Journal of Economic Literature* 34:9-55.

Camerer, Colin, George Loewenstein, and Matthew Rabin. 2004. *Advances in behavioral economics*. Princeton, NJ: Princeton University Press.

de Waal, Frans B. M. 1982. *Chimpanzee politics: Power and sex among apes*. London: Jonathan Cape.

———. 1996. *Good natured: The origins and right and wrong in humans and other animals*. Cambridge, MA: Harvard University Press.

Ding, Yuan-Chun, Han-Chang Chi, Deborah L. Grady, Atsuyuki Morishima, Judith R. Kidd, Kenneth K. Kidd, Pamela Flodman, M. Anne Spence, Sabrina Schuck, James M. Swanson, Ya-Ping Zhang, and Robert K. Moyzis. 2002. Evidence of positive selection acting at the human dopamine receptor D4 gene locus. *Proceedings of the National Academy of Sciences* 99 (8): 309-14.

Gosling, S. D., and O. P. John. 1999. Personality dimensions in non-human animals: A cross-species perspective. *Current Directions in Psychological Science* 8:69-75.

Harpending, Henry, and Gregory Cochran. 2002. In our genes. *Proceedings of the National Academy of Sciences* 99 (8): 10-12.

Henrich, J., R. Boyd, S. Bowles, C. Camerer, E. Fehr, H. Gintis, and R. McElreath. 2001. Cooperation, reciprocity, and punishment in fifteen small-scale societies. *American Economic Review* 91:73-78.

Lodge, Milton, and Charles Taber. 2005. The automaticity of affect for political candidates, parties, and issues. *Political Psychology* 26:455-82.

Madsen, Douglas. 1986. Power seekers are different: Further biochemical evidence. *American Political Science Review* 80:261-69.

Marcus, George E., W. Russell Neuman, and Michael Mackuen. 2000. *Affective intelligence and political judgment*. Chicago: University of Chicago Press.

Massey, Douglas S. 2002. Emotion and the history of human society. *American Sociological Review* 67:1-29.

Orbell, John, Tomonori Morikawa, Jason Hartwig, James Hanley, and Nicholas Allen. 2004. Machiavellian intelligence as a basis for the evolution of cooperative dispositions. *American Political Science Review* 98:1-16.

Pickering, Alan D., and Jeffrey A. Gray. 1999. The neuroscience of personality. In *Handbook of personality*, 2nd ed., ed. Lawrence A. Pervin and Oliver P. John. New York: Guilford.

Pinker, Steven. 2002. *The blank slate*. New York: Viking.

Plomin, R., J. C. DeFries, G. E. McClearn, and P. McGuffin. 2001. *Behavioral genetics*. 4th ed. New York: Worth.

Somit, Albert, and Steven A. Peterson. 1997. *Darwinism, dominance, and democracy*. Westport, CT: Praeger.

Sullivan, D. G., and R. D. Masters. 1993. Nonverbal behavior, emotions, and democratic leadership. In *Reconsidering the democratic polity*, ed. G. Marcus and R. Hanson. University Park: Pennsylvania State University Press.

Tooby, John, and Leda Cosmides. 1992. The psychological foundations of culture. In *The adapted mind: Evolutionary psychology and the development of culture*, ed. Jerome H. Barkow, Leda Cosmides, and John Tooby. New York: Oxford University Press.

Wahlke, John C. 1979. Pre-behavioralism in political science. *American Political Science Review* 73:9-31.

Testosterone and Aggression in a Simulated Crisis Game

By
ROSE McDERMOTT,
DOMINIC JOHNSON,
JONATHAN COWDEN,
and
STEPHEN ROSEN

This study investigated the impact of testosterone on aggression in a crisis simulation game. We found a significant positive relationship between levels of testosterone and aggression. Men were much more likely to engage in aggressive action than women. They were more likely to lose their fights as well. Since testosterone was around five times higher among men, and men engage in such fights more than women, there is an automatic statistical link between testosterone and aggression that is hard to separate from other possible gender-based causes.

Keywords: testosterone; experiment; aggression; crisis; gender differences

Over the years, there has been a great deal of debate about the problem of nature versus nurture in causality: is it genetics or environment that accounts for specific behaviors? One of the behaviors that people have been most interested in is aggression and its many manifestations, including war. The implications of the proper origin of aggression suggest different strategies for intervention; if social conditions are responsible for violence, then changing certain situational or institutional factors can reduce the incidence of death and destruction. However, if genetic predispositions and biochemical hormones play a decisive role, ethical intervention becomes more difficult to imagine.

Previous scholars have suggested that testosterone can lead to aggression directly. Others posit that testosterone really represents a catalyst to respond in the face of challenge; it constitutes the potential for action more than action itself. Cognitive and social attributions and mediators remain decisive in whether challenge leads to actual physical aggression. Critical among these factors is whether there is

NOTE: We would like to thank Emily Barrett, Renat Lumpau, and Richard Wrangham for help in planning and conducting this research. We also gratefully acknowledge support from Andrew Marshall in the Office of Net Assessment, Department of Defense, for generous funding of this research.

DOI: 10.1177/0002716207305268

a face-to-face challenge over status; such dominance strivings appear to present particularly conducive circumstances for the emergence of violence between male foes. In this experiment, we begin to test the impact of testosterone on aggressive action in a simulated crisis game.

Literature Review and Hypotheses

Testosterone exists in both men and women. In both sexes, it exerts the same effects of building muscle and increasing libido. However, male testosterone tends to run about five to ten times higher than the levels in women, on average. Testosterone has been shown to be stable over time within individuals but to vary with a predictable circadian rhythm, such that levels are highest in the mornings (Dai et al. 1981). Social factors can help explain some of the difference in testosterone levels between individuals, but not within a given individual (Gray et al. 2004). More than 40 percent of the variance in individual levels of testosterone derives from heredity (Meikle et al. 1988). This finding supports the old adage of "like father, like son."

Testosterone and age

The relationship between age and testosterone has been well established in both animal and human males. Most significantly, levels of serum testosterone peak in late adolescence and early adulthood and decline precipitously after that (Dabbs 1990). In fact, the most significant relationships between testosterone and life history appears to be with age and obesity. Other factors, including physical activity and alcohol use, do not appear related. Smoking relates to testosterone

Rose McDermott is an associate professor of political science at the University of California, Santa Barbara. She is the author of two books published by the University of Michigan press titled Risk Taking in International Politics *and* Political Psychology in International Relations. *She has also published numerous articles on experimentation.*

Dominic Johnson is a lecturer in international relations at the University of Edinburgh, UK. He has two books with Harvard University Press: Overconfidence and War: The Havoc and Glory of Positive Illusions *(2004) and, with Dominic Tierney,* Failing to Win: Perceptions of Victory and Defeat in International Politics *(2006).*

Jonathan Cowden is a lecturer at the University of California, Santa Barbara, in American politics and public opinion.

Stephen Rosen is the Beton Michael Kaneb Professor of National Security and Military Affairs and the director of the Olin Institute for Strategic Studies at Harvard University. He was the civilian assistant to the director, Net Assessment in the Office of the Secretary of Defense, and the director of Political-Military Affairs on the staff of the National Security Council. He is the author of Winning the Next War: Innovation and the Modern Military, *which won the 1992 Furniss Prize for best first book on national security affairs, and of* Societies and Military Power: India and Its Armies. *His latest book, titled* War and Human Nature, *was published by Princeton University Press in 2005.*

levels only through its correlation with age (Dai et al. 1981). The one time that age-adjusted testosterone appears to vary, and increase, over time, involves the years surrounding divorce (Mazur and Michalek 1998). This correlates with well-documented increases in domestic abuse during the time surrounding divorce (Mazur and Michalek 1998; Wilson and Daly 1993). Among females, by contrast, testosterone tends to *increase* with age (and estrogen *decrease*) as a result of contraceptive pill use among young women, aging processes, and menopause. As a result of these previous studies, we test the following hypotheses:

> *Hypothesis 1a: Younger* males will have higher testosterone and show greater aggression.
> *Hypothesis 1b: Older* females will have higher testosterone and show greater aggression.

Testosterone and aggressive action

Testosterone levels have been linked with aggression (for a review, see Meyer-Bahlberg 1981); dominance (Gray, Jackson, and McKenry 1991); antisocial behavior, including fighting, drug abuse, and nontraffic arrests (Dabbs and Morris 1990); and sensation seeking (Daitzman and Zuckerman 1980). Indeed, a great debate about the relationship between testosterone and aggression has raged in the psychological, anthropological, and sociological literatures. Clear evidence exists that testosterone correlates with dominance rank in male chimpanzees (Muller and Wrangham 2001), and heightened testosterone increases aggression in various other species (Monaghan and Glickman 1992; Svare 1983).

[A] great debate about the relationship between testosterone and aggression has raged in the psychological, anthropological, and sociological literatures.

Some primate models suggest two different forms of aggression, defensive and offensive. Kalin (1999) suggested that a unique neural mechanism underlies each type. He posited that defensive aggression is fear-based, controlled by the right frontal lobe of the brain, and correlated with high cortisol levels. On the other hand, offensive or impulsive forms of aggression are associated with lower levels of serotonin and cortisol and higher levels of testosterone. He argued that all forms of aggression are affected by environmental factors and, as with humans, the greatest risk is conferred by serious disruptions in the mother–child bond.

Some studies have found a direct relationship between higher levels of testosterone and higher levels of aggressiveness in humans as well, even within normal ranges (Gerra et al. 1997). For example, some researchers report that testosterone correlates with anger and verbal aggression in men (Von Der Phalen et al. 2002). Others find that testosterone significantly relates to levels of both verbal and physical aggression (Soler, Vinayak, and Quadagno 2000). We found that a low second-to-fourth digit ratio, which is a marker of high levels of early life testosterone exposure, predicted aggression in our war game experiments (McIntyre et al. 2007). Experimentally inducing increased testosterone levels seems to confirm these overall patterns. While an additional dose of 300 mg per week appears not to exert an effect on behavior, dosages in excess of 500 mg per week induce noticeable increases in psychiatric symptoms, including increased manic and aggressive behaviors (Pope, Kouri, and Hudson 2000). In a nice twist on the old Milgram paradigm, subjects with higher levels of testosterone showed greater willingness to engage in physical aggressiveness by giving electric shocks to an increasingly challenging fictitious opponent (Berman, Gladue, and Taylor 1993).

Testosterone clearly has an impact in competitive settings. Male judo competitors, for example, displayed a direct relationship between levels of testosterone and the number of threats, fights, and attacks (Salvador et al. 1999). In further studies with this same population, Salvador et al. (2003, 364) found that the group with higher testosterone also performed better in competition; the authors suggested that testosterone provides "an adaptive neurobiological response to competition." The evidence for the impact of testosterone on competition in women is less well explored. One study found that women with higher testosterone were more likely to express their competitive feelings through verbal aggression. Interestingly, women with higher levels of estrogen were less likely to compete with others over athletics than their lower-estrogen counterparts (Cashdan 2003). This might suggest that pill use, which artificially affects estrogen levels, could alter female competitive athletic performance.

Others claim, however, that few studies have found a direct link between testosterone levels and direct aggression in primates and humans (Albert, Walsh, and Jonik 1993; Archer 1991). They suggest that the most accurate way to conceptualize the relationship between testosterone and behavior involves the manifestation of dominance, especially in one-on-one, face-to-face status-based interactions (Mazur 1985; Dabbs and Hargrove 1997). In one study of social dominance in boys, for example, Rowe et al. (2004) found that DSM-IV symptoms of conduct disorder increased around the time of adolescence, and that these age trends were driven, at least in part, by increasing levels of circulating testosterone. He found no relationship between physical violence and high testosterone levels. Oftentimes, however, these grabs for dominance manifest in the form of direct aggression. One large study, involving 1,709 men, demonstrated a relationship between personality profiles of dominance with some aggression and elevated levels of androgens, including testosterone (Gray, Jackson, and McKenry 1991).

On a larger sociological level, there remains absolutely no question that men commit violent crimes in hugely greater numbers than women. In one systematic sample of homicides in Chicago and Detroit, for example, more than 85 percent of homicides were committed by men. Interestingly, more than 80 percent of the victims were also male (Daly and Wilson 1988). This pattern of vastly higher rates of same-sex male homicide seems to hold in all cultures over time (Buss and Shackelford 1997).

While it may be difficult to prove a direct relationship between testosterone and criminality, behavior that can be exacerbated by high levels of testosterone tends to get men in trouble with the law. Prison studies, for example, show that high-testosterone men commit more violent crimes against other people, as opposed to property crimes, and act out more than lower-testosterone men (Dabbs et al. 1995). This remains consistent with the notion that face-to-face status interactions among high-testosterone males elicit greater chances for violence to erupt. Furthermore, men convicted of domestic violence also possess higher levels of testosterone and display greater physical violence than healthy controls (George et al. 2001).

While it may be difficult to prove a direct relationship between testosterone and criminality, behavior that can be exacerbated by high levels of testosterone tends to get men in trouble with the law.

Testosterone also correlates with sensation seeking. Testosterone appears to correlate with high disinhibitory instincts, which is a sensation-seeking subscale. In one study, testosterone related to personality profiles including stable extroversion. It also correlated with impulsivity and high levels of heterosexual contact. Indeed, high testosterone remains significantly correlated with antisocial behavior, high-risk behavior, unemployment and low-paying jobs, and being unmarried (Booth, Johnson, and Granger 1999).

On the other hand, lower levels of testosterone correlate with self-control and social conformity (Daitzman and Zuckerman 1980). In fact, lower levels of testosterone appear to correlate with several kinds of prosocial behavior. Specifically, low-testosterone men have a more pleasant and friendly manner, including smiling more (Dabbs and Hargrove 1997), and maintain much more positive relationships with their families (Julian and McKenry 1989; Booth and Dabbs 1993).

Social and personality factors appear to be able to mediate at least some of the effects of testosterone on behavior. In one study of seventeen professional basketball players, subjects who attributed their victory more to luck than skill showed lower levels of salivary testosterone than their more egotistical counterparts (Gonzalez-Bono et al. 2000). Furthermore, high-hostility subjects who were harassed during their performance of a solvable experimental task demonstrated higher blood pressure, heart rate, testosterone, and cortisol relative to their low-hostility counterparts or those who were not harassed (Suarez et al. 1998).

Why should humans, and men in particular, have evolved in such a way as to be predisposed toward dominance and its sequelae of aggression? One explanation suggests that testosterone—while it may promote dominance—also provides some immunity against illness (Granger, Booth, and Johnson 2000). Another suggests that it might prove advantageous in combat or military conflict, enhancing the chances of winning in battle (Johnson, Wrangham, and Rosen 2002; Wrangham 1999; Johnson 2004). Buss and Shackelford (1997) argued for an evolutionary understanding of human aggression. They suggested that aggression is context-sensitive and that human males evolved to respond adaptively to different social interactions. In particular, they posited that aggression may have emerged as a solution to at least seven such problems, including stealing other's resources, defending oneself, competing with same-sex rivals for attractive mates, negotiating power and status hierarchies, deterring others from future attacks, preventing mates from engaging in sexual infidelity, and limiting resources spent on raising someone else's children. Given that testosterone appears to be related to aggression and dominance behaviors, we hypothesize that

Hypothesis 2: Individuals with higher levels of testosterone will be more likely to engage in aggressive action than those who possess relatively lower levels of testosterone.

Testosterone and relationship-status

Age is not the only factor that has been shown to exert a dramatic impact on testosterone levels. Marriage and parenthood lower testosterone as well, at least in men. In the most systematic and careful investigation of this phenomenon, Gray et al. (2002) found that married men had significantly lower testosterone than unmarried men. Even among married men, those with greater involvement, interaction, and time spent with their wives had lower testosterone levels than their less engaged married counterparts. Fathers also had lower testosterone levels than their single counterparts. In fact, Gray et al. (2002) found that the only significant predictor of testosterone levels in their evening sample was relationship status. Other factors they examined, including body mass index, exercise, and stress, did not achieve significance. They argued that their findings support theories (Lancaster and Kaplan 1992; Wingfield et al. 1990) that suggest a direct trade-off in males between competitive behaviors, supported by higher testosterone, and mating and parenting behaviors, which appear to precipitate drops in testosterone.

These results find support in other areas of the literature as well. Mazur and Michalek (1998) found that age-adjusted testosterone rates were lower in married men than in those who were single and divorced. In fact, testosterone levels appeared to peak four to eight years prior to marriage, and declined beginning shortly after marriage. In another study of 4,462 male military personnel, Booth and Dabbs (1993) found that those men with higher testosterone levels were less likely to marry and more likely to divorce if married. If married, men with high testosterone proved more likely to leave the marriage because of trouble in the marriage involving their own infidelity, hitting or throwing things at their wives, and a lower quality of marital interaction.

Marriage clearly exerts an impact on criminality as well, possibly through the mechanism of decreased testosterone in married men. For example, Daly and Wilson (1990) found that married men were less likely than their single counterparts of the same age to kill an unrelated male. In an earlier study, Wilson and Daly (1985) found that in Detroit, 73 percent of male murderers and 69 percent of male victims were unmarried, although the base rate of same-age unmarried men in Detroit at the time was 43 percent. In a larger study examining same-sex murder of unrelated people from Canada (1974–1993), England (1977–1986), Chicago (1965–1981), and Detroit (1972), Daly and Wilson (1990) again found both that murder rates drastically declined as men aged (peak murder rates in all samples were early twenties) and that married men were much less likely to commit murder than unmarried men. Divorced men, as the data from Mazur and Michalek (1998) would suggest, possess homicide rates that are most similar to single men. In another study of criminal behavior and deviance over the life cycle, Sampson and Laub (1990) found that strong marital attachments inhibited adult criminal and deviant behavior.

Therefore, we hypothesize that

Hypothesis 3: Men in long-term relationships will be less likely to engage in aggressive action than their unmarried or divorced counterparts.

Methods

This study used an experimental laboratory simulation methodology to investigate these hypotheses.

Subjects

This study involved 186 subjects who were recruited from the Harvard Business School experimental subject pool. We were able to obtain usable testosterone samples from 180 subjects prior to the game, 78 women and 102 men. We had 134 samples from the middle round of the game, 59 women and 75 men. And we had 179 samples from the final round of the game, 77 women and 102 men. The sample sizes vary because (1) some testosterone samples did not provide valid data and (2) samples taken when the game ended before all six possible rounds had occurred were treated as final, not middle round, samples. Our sample had

TABLE 1
SUMMARY STATISTICS ON (RAW) TESTOSTERONE AND AGE

	Females					Males				
	N	Mean	SD	Min	Max	N	Mean	SD	Min	Max
Age	79	22.99	5.37	18	48	107	21.80	5.58	18	65
T1	78	77.72	60.29	14	323	102	341.50	202.08	45	1208
T2	59	50.19	58.56	14	304	75	241.75	140.32	28	708
T3	77	45.16	40.33	14	217	102	244.75	145.44	32	710

the following racial composition: 60.8 percent Caucasian, 19.4 percent Asian, 11.3 percent African American, 3.2 percent Hispanic, 1.1 percent Native American, and 4.3 percent Other. Ages ranged between 18 and 65, with a mean of 22.31. The oldest woman was 48, while the oldest man was 65. Only 2 subjects had children, and so we were not able to conduct any analysis on the relationship between parenthood and testosterone levels. Table 1 provides the summary statistics for subjects in the analysis.

We received human subjects permission for this experiment from the Harvard Institutional Review Board. There was absolutely no deception in this experiment. All participants signed informed consent forms prior to their participation and were told they could leave the study at any time without penalty. All subjects were volunteers who received cash payments of either $20 or $30, depending on how well they performed during the game.

Procedure

This simulation game was complex in nature. When subjects arrived, they were given informed consent forms to read and sign. After they had done so, they were given Extra original flavor chewing gum to stimulate salivation. They then spit into a 15 ml collection vial pretreated with sodium azide, an antibacterial agent. Samples were temporarily stored at room temperature, after which they were frozen, and thawed twenty-four hours before being assayed. Samples were assayed at the Harvard University Reproductive Ecology laboratory, following a modified version of an ^{125}I-based, double-antibody radioimmunoassay kit (DSL-4100) produced by Diagnostic Systems Laboratory, Inc. (Webster, Texas). This protocol is described in detail in Gray et al. (2004). Subject samples were assigned to eight different assay groups; assays 1 through 3 were exactly sex-balanced, whereas 4 through 8 had slightly more males than females. Every effort was made to measure testosterone levels of both partners in a dyad within the same assay to make their results more directly comparable. The interassay coefficients of variation for low and high pools were 20.2 and 5.3 percent, respectively.

When they had filled one vial, subjects were seated before a computer terminal. Before the actual game began, subjects filled out a number of questionnaires, including demographic information, and several mood inventories. Subjects filled out scales that included a depression inventory; a self-esteem scale; a narcissism questionnaire; measures of stress, fear, anger; and a social dominance orientation survey. Once subjects had completed these inventories, the actual game began.

In this game, subjects were paired in either same-sex or mixed-sex dyads. These dyads were created through formal random number assignment protocols. Once the real-time game began, subjects read instructions that asked them to role-play the leader of a country in conflict with a neighbor over newly discovered diamond mines on disputed territory. Mine workers had been ambushed and killed and subject-leaders were told to handle this crisis.

This game ran for six rounds, but subjects remained unaware of how many rounds the game would last until after they had finished. In each round, subjects undertook a number of different tasks. In the starting round, each person was given $100 million, which was also given at the start of each successive new round. The subjects could keep that money as cash, they could buy army battalions with them for $10 million apiece, or they could allocate their money into industrial production. The winner of the game was the one who ended up with the most industrial production in their account at the end of the game. Subjects could dismantle army battalions for cash or industry assets at a discounted rate of 50 percent; for example, a person who bought one battalion for $10 million would get $5 million if she chose to disarm. The game was structured in such a way that it was possible to win the game either by negotiating or by going to war and winning. However, there was an inherently greater risk in going to war because the probability of losing always existed, realistically.

After making these choices, each subject had to take an action that included doing nothing, negotiating, making a threat, going to or continuing war, or surrendering. Only one subject surrendered—an older man in the latest experiment we ran. At 8:45 p.m., it became clear that he would rather surrender, and go home, than continue to engage with an unknown probability of earning an additional $10. If subjects chose to negotiate, they had to make allocation decisions about how to divide up the money from the diamond mines. If they went to war, the computer calculated who won and who lost based on a consistent set of probabilities that depended on the balance of military power and experimental condition. After a victory, the loser lost all his battalions, and an equal amount of money (each battalion cost $10 million) was transferred from his industrial production account into that of the winner. If a player lost all of his resources in a war, then the game ended. In addition, if players put all their money into their army without putting any money into industrial production, there was a 10 percent chance, which they were informed of prior to the game, of a coup that would overthrow their government. This eventuality did not take place in this running of the game.

Each round, subjects also had to write a message to the other side and, in later rounds, read a message their opponent had sent the previous round. They were required to tell their partners how many battalions they had acquired, but they were allowed to bluff ±30 percent of their true value if they wished. In addition, subjects filled out subjective assessments of their own and their partners' levels of aggressiveness, hostility, trustworthiness, competitiveness, intelligence, and skill. Finally, students wrote notes, seen only by the experimenters, about why they had taken the actions and made the choices they did. They were required to do all these things in five minutes per round, to simulate the time pressure of real-life decision making.

Midway through the game, we took a second testosterone sample from all subjects. At the end of the game, subjects found out whether they won or lost the game, after which a third saliva sample was taken (unless the game had already ended, in which case the second testosterone sample was the final one). Those who won received an additional $10 in payment (on top of the $20 earnings that all subjects received for participating in the experiment), which they knew about in advance. They also filled out some final questionnaires about the game.

Measures

As noted above, many of the measures were designed specifically for use in this experiment, including most of the measures of decision making and action during the game. However, the initial personality inventories came from established questionnaires. The Beck Depression Inventory was used. We administered the Rosenberg Self-Esteem measure, as well as a standard narcissism measure. We used a measure of fear and anger given to us by Paul Ekman. We used a standard stress measure, and the short version of the Social Dominance Orientation scale (Pratto et al. 1994). All scales are available from the authors upon request.

Results

All raw testosterone data were positively skewed. We therefore transformed them to their natural logarithm, which produced much more satisfactory normally distributed variables allowing a greater range of statistical procedures. One subject's initial testosterone reading was eliminated from the data set because it reached the maximum on the scale ($>> 3$ SD above the mean) and is suspected to have been contaminated.

Overall testosterone levels

Figure 1 shows overall levels of testosterone in our subjects across all three samples, divided into male and female groups. There were no significant differences between the three testosterone samples (in either sex).

Testosterone and age

We found a significant negative relationship between age and all three testosterone samples (Spearman's rank correlations for lnt1, $r = -0.15$, $n = 179$, $p = .04$; lnt2, $r = -2.00$, $n = 134$, $p = .02$; lnt3, $r = -1.8$, $n = 179$, $p = .02$). However, there

FIGURE 1
LOG (LN) TESTOSTERONE LEVELS SAMPLED BEFORE (INT1),
DURING (INT2), AND AFTER (INT3) THE WAR GAME

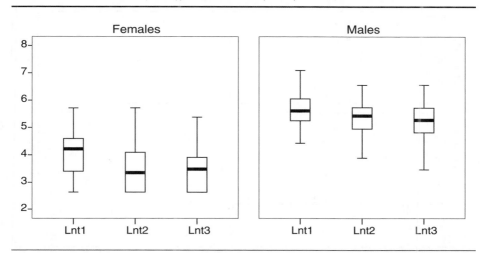

NOTE: For each sex, medians (lines), interquartile ranges (boxes), and highest and lowest values (whiskers; excluding outliers) are shown.

were more older women in the sample than there were older men (see histograms in Figure 2), such that a disproportionate number of young men (who typically have high testosterone levels) and a disproportionate number of older women (who typically have low testosterone levels, compared to men) may have driven these correlations (we found no within-sex correlations). These conclusions were corroborated when using a normalized age variable (given a very heavy skew in raw age data, this required transformation using the third reciprocal root: $-1/[(age)^3]$). A general linear model, which controlled for gender, found no significant relationship between age and level of testosterone (whether using raw age or normalized age).

More belligerent older women

The sample size of women who attacked their opponents is small, but even using a conservative test of raw age and a Mann-Whitney U-test (which makes few assumptions about distribution), those women who made unprovoked attacks were significantly older than women who did not attack ($Z = -2.21$, $p = .027$). This was not true for men (see Figure 3).

Repeating this test using normalized age and a t-test, the result is of borderline significance ($t = -1.98$, $df = 76$, $p = .051$). Older women also were more "hawkish" (meaning that they either made unprovoked attacks *or* retaliated), but this trend did not reach significance ($Z = -1.74$, $p = .08$). There was no difference at all among men (see Figure 4).

FIGURE 2
HISTOGRAM SHOWING AGES OF SUBJECTS

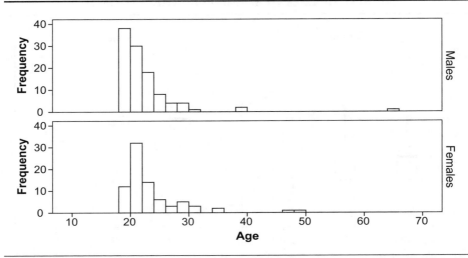

NOTE: There were more younger males than females in the sample, and more males overall.

FIGURE 3
OLDER FEMALES WERE SIGNIFICANTLY MORE LIKELY
TO MAKE UNPROVOKED ATTACKS (NO EFFECT AMONG MALES)

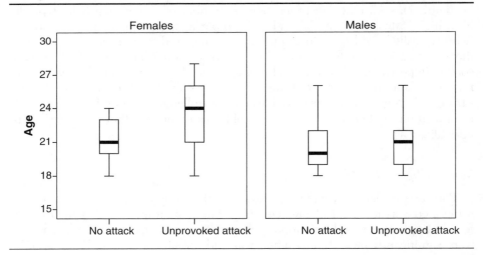

Testosterone and winning

In examining the winners among those who fought, males who fought and lost had higher initial testosterone than males who fought and won ($t = -2.27$, $df = 36$, $p = .029$). There was no such effect among females (see Figure 5).

FIGURE 4
**OLDER FEMALES WERE MORE LIKELY (THOUGH NOT
SIGNIFICANTLY) TO MAKE UNPROVOKED ATTACKS OR
RETALIATE (NO EFFECT AMONG MALES)**

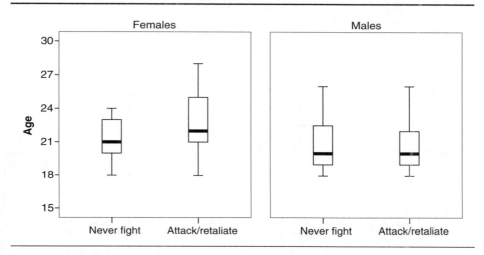

FIGURE 5
**MALES WHO FOUGHT AND LOST HAD SIGNIFICANTLY HIGHER
INITIAL TESTOSTERONE LEVELS THAN THOSE WHO FOUGHT AND
WON (NO EFFECT AMONG FEMALES)**

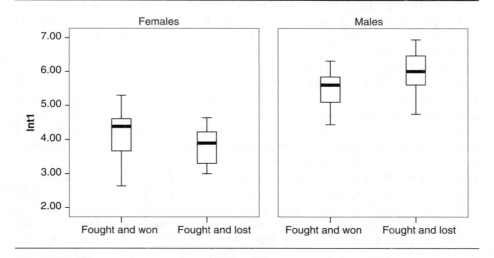

Testosterone and aggressive action

We used unprovoked attacks on an opponent as our dependent variable
for aggression (retaliation *in response* to others' aggression may be mediated by

FIGURE 6
SUBJECTS WITH HIGHER INITIAL LEVELS OF TESTOSTERONE WERE SIGNIFICANTLY MORE LIKELY TO MAKE UNPROVOKED ATTACKS ON THEIR OPPONENTS

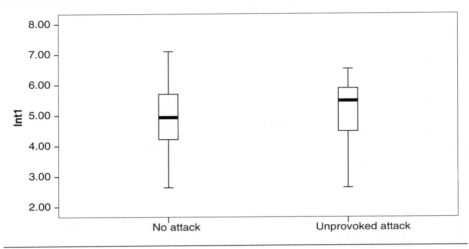

NOTE: There was no such effect within either sex alone, suggesting this relationship is driven by male–female differences: males have higher testosterone and attack more.

various processes and therefore implies a weaker measure of aggressive intent). Individuals with higher levels of testosterone (from the initial pregame sample) were more likely to make an unprovoked attack on their opponent (independent samples t-test: $t = -1.79$, $df = 152$, $p = .037$, one-tailed test; Figure 6). There were no within-sex differences in (ln) testosterone between unprovoked attackers and nonattackers (t-values < 0.5, $p > .6$).

We next used binary logistic regression to examine the effect of (ln) testosterone on the probability of an unprovoked attack (a yes-or-no variable), while controlling for gender, age, and use of oral contraception (the pill) among female subjects (which elevates estrogen levels). This procedure produced a model that was statistically significant in comparison to a null model containing a constant term only (chi-squared = 9.86, $df = 4$, $p = .043$; Cox and Snell R-squared = .062). The model correctly assigned 77.4 percent of the cases. Table 2 details the variables in the model equation and their *partial* effects (that is, their independent effect on the model given the simultaneous influence of all the other included variables), none of which are individually significant. B is the effect size of each variable on the dependent variable. Exp(B) is the odds ratio, which is interpreted, in the case of GENDER, for example, as meaning that a male is .324 times more likely to be an unprovoked attacker than a female. The lack of significance of these variables means they should not be overinterpreted in this model.

TABLE 2
VARIABLES IN THE LOGISTIC REGRESSION WITH UNPROVOKED
ATTACK AS THE DEPENDENT VARIABLE

	B	SE	p	Exp (B)
LnT1	−0.295	0.304	.333	0.745
Age	0.005	0.036	.898	1.005
Gender	−1.126	0.675	.095	0.324
Pill	1.632	1.113	.143	5.112
Constant	−0.957	2.059	.642	0.384

A simple chi-square test showed that males are significantly more likely to make unprovoked attacks than females (chi-squared = 4.77, df = 1, p = .029). (Ln) testosterone was already shown above to have significant effects on unprovoked attacks.

Long-term relationships and aggressive acts

We found no relationship between subjects' type of relationship and unprovoked aggression (chi-squared tests all nonsignificant for both sexes, or when pooled). As Figure 7 shows, the proportion of unprovoked attackers was approximately equally represented in all classes of relationship (however, the sample sizes of married and cohabiting subjects were very small, so the hypothesis is hard to assess).

Discussion and Conclusions

The findings in this study confirm several of our original hypotheses. We did find the expected negative correlation between age and testosterone. Since this was probably driven by the relatively higher number of young men and older women in the sample, it is possible that this finding is secondary to a basic sex difference, since men possessed about five times greater levels of testosterone in this sample than women, on average. This notion is supported by the finding that age did not exert a significant effect on testosterone once we controlled for gender.

Women clearly display a contrary dynamic to that of young men (who appear to be more belligerent); older women are much more likely to engage in unprovoked attacks than younger women. This is almost a direct linear relationship in women between age and likelihood of aggression. We suggest two interrelated reasons for this finding. First, younger women are more likely to be on the pill, thus artificially elevating their levels of estrogen (and perhaps decreasing their competitiveness as a result). Second, older women are more likely to be menopausal, thus lowering their natural estrogen levels, while raising their relative levels of testosterone.

We find strong support for the hypothesis of a relationship between testosterone and aggressive action. In particular, high-testosterone subjects are much

FIGURE 7
THERE WAS NO SIGNIFICANT DIFFERENCE IN THE PROPORTION OF
ATTACKS AND SUBJECTS' PERSONAL RELATIONSHIP STATUS

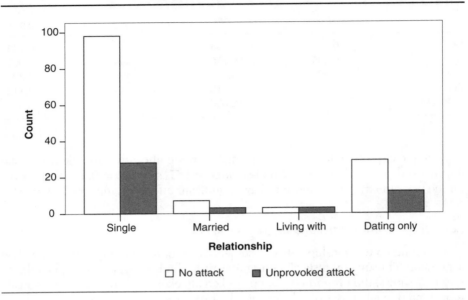

more likely to engage in unprovoked attacks against their opponents than their lower-testosterone counterparts. This result is apparently driven by the fact that males, who have much higher levels of testosterone, attacked more than females did (since we found no significant relationship between testosterone and aggression *within* either sex).

*[H]igh-testosterone subjects are much
more likely to engage in unprovoked attacks
against their opponents than their
lower-testosterone counterparts.*

However, we did not find our expected relationship between long-term relationships and aggressive acts. In our sample, there was no significant difference between those who were and those who were not in a long-term relationship and the propensity for unprovoked attack. This may be because the vast majority of our sample was single, thus making meaningful comparisons difficult because of a lack of sufficient variation on this independent variable. Similarly, because only two of our subjects had any children, we were unable to explore statistically the previously reported relationship between fatherhood and lowered levels of testosterone in this study (Gray et al. 2002).

The strongest and clearest finding that this study generates is that high-testosterone individuals are more likely to engage in unprovoked attacks against their opponents. Since testosterone is about five times higher in men, and men engage in such fights more than women, there is an automatic statistical link between testosterone and aggression that is hard to separate from other possible gender-based causes. We hope to explore these links in future studies. And because such fights often lead to big losses, costs that all subjects are made well aware of prior to play, men tend to lose more than women. Although it should be said that big wins were possible, and did occur, through military conflict, such victories were not common.

After conducting these studies, it appears that the best analogy for the male–female divide in testosterone is that of a car. Men are accelerators and women are brakes. This is particularly true for younger members of each sex. In a contest between two accelerators with no brake, the possibility of collision remains high. In a game between two brakes, there is no accelerator to spark action, and so conflict is unlikely to occur. But in a competition between a brake and an accelerator, only one accelerator is needed to cause conflict: women fight back exactly like men once they are provoked. Women are just highly unlikely to start up the engine of conflict in the first place. In such a competition, the odds favor brakes over accelerators, because the latter will simply try to drive the car off the cliff if left to their own devices. Indeed, other data from this war game experiment show significant correlations between men, narcissistic personality scores, confidence of success, and making unprovoked attacks on opponents (Johnson et al. 2006). Clearly, the biological mechanisms behind aggression evolved in a very different environment to that of today, with very different cues, stimuli, and triggers. In modern political and military decision-making, increasingly novel and complex technology, and ever more distant, both physically and psychologically, command, control, and communications systems make these biological responses far more likely to wreak disaster.

References

Albert, D., M. Walsh, and R. Jonik. 1993. Aggression in humans: What is its biological foundation? *Neuroscience Biobehavioral Review* 17:405-25.

Archer, J. 1991. The influence of testosterone on human aggression. *British Journal of Psychology* 82:1-28.

Berman, M., B. Gladue, and S. Taylor. 1993. The effects of hormones, Type A behavior pattern, and provocation on aggression in men. *Motivation and Emotion* 17:125-38.

Booth, A., and J. Dabbs. 1993. Testosterone and men's marriages. *Social Forces* 72:463-77.

Booth, A., D. R. Johnson, and D. A. Granger. 1999. Testosterone and men's depression: The role of social behavior. *Journal of Health and Social Behavior* 40:130-40.

Buss, D., and T. Shackelford. 1997. Human aggression in evolutionary psychological perspective. *Clinical Psychology Review* 17:605-19.

Cashdan, E. 2003. Hormones and competitive behavior in women. *Aggressive Behavior* 29:107-15.

Dabbs, J. 1990. Age and seasonal variation in serum T concentration among men. *Chronobiology International* 7:245-49.

Dabbs, J., T. Carr, R. Frady, and J. K. Reid. 1995. Testosterone, crime and misbehavior among 692 male prison inmates. *Personality and Individual Differences* 18:627-33.

Dabbs, J., and M. Hargrove. 1997. Age, testosterone, and behavior among female prison inmates. *Psychosomatic Medicine* 59:477-80.

Dabbs, J., and R. Morris. 1990. T and antisocial behavior in a sample of 4462 men. *Psychological Science* 9:269-75.

Dai, W., L. Kuller, R. LaPorte, J. Gutai, L. Falma, and A. Gagguela. 1981. Epidemiology of plasma T levels in middle age men. *American Journal of Epidemiology* 114:804-16.

Daitzman, R., and M. Zuckerman. 1980. Disinhibitory sensation-seeking, personality and gonadal hormones. *Personality and Individual Differences* 1:103-10.

Daly, M., and M. Wilson. 1988. *Homicide.* Hawthorne, NY: Aldine de Gruyter.

———. 1990. Killing the competition: Female/female and male/male homicide. *Human Nature* 1:81-107.

George, D., J. Umhau, M. Phillips, D. Emmela, P. Ragan, S. Shoaf, and R. Rawlings. 2001. Serotonin, testosterone and alcohol in the etiology of domestic violence. *Psychiatry Research* 104:27-37.

Gerra, G., A. Zaimovic, P. Avanzini, B. Chittolini, G. Givcastro, R. Caccovari, M. Palladino, D. Maestri, C. Monica, R. Designore, and F. Brambilla. 1997. Neurotransmitter-neuroendrocrine responses to experimentally induced aggression in humans: Influence of personality variable. *Psychiatry Research* 66:33-43.

Gonzalez-Bono, E., A. Salvador, J. Ricarte, M. Serrano, and M. Arnedo. 2000. Testosterone and attribution of successful competition. *Aggressive Behavior* 26:235-40.

Granger, D., A. Booth, and D. Johnson. 2000. Human aggression and enumerative measures of immunity. *Psychosomatic Medicine* 62:583-90.

Gray, A., O. Jackson, and J. McKenry. 1991. Relationship between dominance, anger and hormones in normally aging men: Results from the Massachusetts male aging study. *Psychosomatic Medicine* 53:375-85.

Gray, P., B. Campbell, F. Marlowe, S. Lipson, and P. Ellison. 2004. Social variables predict between-subject but not day-to-day variation in testosterone of US men. *Psychoneuroendocrinology* 29:1153-62.

Gray, P., S. Kahlenberg, E. Barrett, S. Lipson, and P. Ellison. 2002. Marriage and fatherhood are associated with lower testosterone in males. *Evolution and Human Behavior* 23:1-9.

Johnson, D. D. P. 2004. *Overconfidence and war: The havoc and glory of positive illusions.* Cambridge, MA: Harvard University Press.

Johnson, D. D. P., R. McDermott, E. S. Barrett, J. Cowden, R. Wrangham, M. H. McIntyre, and S. P. Rosen. 2006. Overconfidence in wargames: Experimental evidence on expectations, aggression, gender and testosterone. *Proceedings of the Royal Society (B)* 273 (1600): 2513-20.

Johnson, D. D. P., R. Wrangham, and S. Rosen. 2002. Is military incompetence adaptive? An empirical test with risk-taking behaviour in modern warfare. *Evolution and Human Behaviour* 23:245-64.

Julian, T., and J. McKenry. 1989. Relationship of T to men's family functioning at mid life: Research Note. *Aggressive Behavior* 15:281-89.

Kalin, N. 1999. Primate models to understand human aggression. *Journal of Clinical Psychiatry* 60:29-32.

Lancaster, J., and H. Kaplan. 1992. Human mating and family formation strategies: The effects of variability among males in quality and the allocation of mating effort and parental investment. In *Topics in primatology*, vol. 1, ed. T. Nishida, E. McGrew, P. Marler, M. Pickford, and F. deWaal, 21-33. Tokyo: University of Tokyo Press.

Mazur, A. 1985. A biosocial model of status in face-to-face primate groups. *Social Forces* 64:377-402.

Mazur, A., and J. Michalek. 1998. Marriage, divorce and male testosterone. *Social Forces* 77:315-30.

McIntyre, M. H., E. S. Barrett, R. McDermott, D. D. P. Johnson, J. Cowden, and S. P. Rosen. 2007. Finger length ratio (2D:4D) and sex differences in aggression during a simulated wargame. *Personality and Individual Differences* 42:755-64.

Meikle, A., J. Stringham, D. Bishop, and D. West. 1988. Quantitating genetic and nongenetic factors influencing androgen production and clearing rates in men. *Journal of Clinical Endocrinology and Metabolism* 67:104-9.

Meyer-Bahlberg, H. F. L. 1981. Androgens and human aggression. In *Biology of aggression*, ed. P. Brain and D. Benton. Alphen ann der Rijn, the Netherlands: Sijhofft Noordhoff.

Monaghan, E., and S. Glickman. 1992. Hormones and aggressive behavior. In *Behavioral endocrinology*, ed. J. Becker, S. Breedlove, and D. Crews, 262-86. Cambridge, MA: MIT Press.

Muller, M., and R. Wrangham. 2001. The reproductive ecology of male hominids. In *Reproductive ecology and human evolution*, ed. P. Ellison. New York: Aldine de Gruyter.

Pope, H., E. Kouri, and J. Hudson. 2000. Effects of supraphysicologic doses of testosterone on mood and aggression in normal men: A randomized controlled trial. *Archives of General Psychiatry* 57:133-40.

Pratto, F., J. Sidanius, L. Stallworth, and B. Malle. 1994. Social dominance orientation: A personality variable predicting social and political attitudes. *Journal of Personality and Social Psychology* 67:741-63.

Rowe, R., B. Maughan, C. Worthman, E. Costello, and A. Angold. 2004. Testosterone, antisocial behavior, and social dominance in boys: Pubertal development and biosocial interaction. *Biological Psychiatry* 55:546-52.

Salvador, A., F. Suay, E. Gonzalez-Bono, and M. Serrano. 2003. Anticipatory cortisol, testosterone, and psychological responses to judo competition in young men. *Psychoneuroendocrinology* 28:364-75.

Salvador, A., F. Suay, S. Martinez-Sanchis, V. Simon, and P. Brain. 1999. Correlating testosterone and fighting in male participants in judo contests. *Physiology and Behavior* 68:205-9.

Sampson, R., and J. Laub. 1990. Crime and deviance over the life course: The salience of adult social bonds. *American Sociological Review* 55:609-27.

Soler, H., P. Vinayak, and D. Quadagno. 2000. Biosocial aspects of domestic violence. *Psychoneuroendocrinology* 25:721-39.

Suarez, E., C. Kuhn, S. Schanberg, R. Williams, and E. Zimmerman. 1998. Neuroendocrine, cardiovascular, and emotional responses of hostile men: The role of interpersonal challenge. *Psychosomatic Medicine* 60:78-88.

Svare, B. 1983. *Hormones and aggressive behavior*. New York: Plenum.

Von Der Phalen, B., T. Sarkola, K. Seppae, and P. Eriksson. 2002. Testosterone, 5alpha-dihydrotestosterone and cortisol in men with and without alcohol related aggression. *Journal of Studies on Alcohol* 63:518-26.

Wilson, M., and M. Daly. 1985. Competitiveness, risk-taking and violence: The young male syndrome. *Ethology and Sociobiology* 6:59-73.

———. 1993. Spousal homicide risk and estrangement. *Violence and Victims* 8:3-16.

Wingfield, J., R. Hegner, A. Duffy, and F. Ball. 1990. The "challenge hypothesis": Theoretical implications for patterns of testosterone secretion, mating systems, breeding strategies. *American Naturalist* 136:829-46.

Wrangham, R. 1999. Is military incompetence adaptive? *Evolution and Human Behavior* 20:3-17.

Genetic Configurations of Political Phenomena: New Theories, New Methods

By
IRA H. CARMEN

Recent research by E. O. Wilson, Alford-Hibbing, Carmen, and others indicates that the competing social science paradigms of behavioralism and rational choice are in their last throes. Their salient weakness is insensitivity, bordering on ignorance, to politics as a biologically orchestrated phenomenon. More specifically, political scientists know precious little about either genetics or evolutionary dynamics. In this article, the author presents a new theory—sociogenomics—to replace the shopworn conceptions of yesterday's political science. The author then demonstrates how social scientists can employ the tools of molecular biology to flesh out the genes coding for baseline political attitudes and behaviors. The theory and methods of sociogenomics will serve to synthesize the social sciences with the natural sciences in a broader consilient framework, so that the laboratory of Darwinian investigation can become the laboratory of Aristotelian investigation.

Keywords: genetics; twin studies; magnetic resonance imaging; sociogenomics; consilience

Political science is a discipline in need of a paradigm. What else is new?

Fifty years ago, our predecessors could not even agree on what to call their academic domiciles: did we live in departments of government, of politics, or of political science? Were we institutionalists or behavioralists? Did we believe in natural laws or natural rights? If we were in the business of theory construction, could "theory" also mean normative theory?

Today, the waters are as murky as ever. The empiricism of behavioralism—steeped in the premises and biases of social psychology and attitudinal inference—has long since come under challenge from the deductivism of rational

Ira H. Carmen, Ph.D., University of Michigan, is a professor of political science and a member of the Institute for Genomic Biology at the University of Illinois. He is the author of Cloning and the Constitution *(1986) and* Politics in the Laboratory *(2004), both with the University of Wisconsin Press. He was elected to membership in the Human Genome Organization in 1996, and he served as a member of the NIH's Recombinant DNA Advisory Committee from 1990 to 1994.*

DOI: 10.1177/0002716207305271

choice—steeped in the premises and biases of the economic marketplace and Rawlsian philosophy. Those who hold dear to the preachments of the Enlightenment must fend off the rapacious deconstructionists who argue not only against scripture but against science.

This article will not engage those who do not believe in science; it will not even engage those who do not believe in political science. As E. O. Wilson (1999, 269) has implied, in each and every bona fide competition between the theory and practice of science and the theory and practice of some other calling, science has won out. This article will engage the central question at issue for political science in our time: how can we construct an overarching paradigm for the grand purpose of at long last ending the internecine squabbles among those of us who believe in the scientific pursuit of things political?

[Behavioralists and rational choicers] eschew a study of the human political species as a species, which means they have nothing whatever to say about the driving force of all other species' attitudinal and behavioral repertoires: genetics.

The principle "squabble" continues to be between behavioralists and rational choicers (Alford and Hibbing 2004 [hereinafter A-H], 707), with each side elegantly dissecting the weaknesses of the opposition. Behavioralists emphasize their commitment to investigating the attitudes and actions of real people jousting for influence and power; rational actor models, they claim, are effective only in illuminating the politics of "unreal" people wallowing in acultural preferences. Social choice advocates counter with proofs that humans are fully capable of knowing what is good for them politically and acting accordingly; they scoff at the behavioralists' reliance upon socialization and group identification as result-oriented conditioning agencies. Moreover, both sides find themselves under fire from New Institutionalists who contend that politics cannot be ripped from the contexts of formal and informal decision-making trappings.

The core thesis of this article is simply that these competing paradigms fail because they are not scientific *enough*. Put succinctly, they eschew a study of the human political species as a species, which means they have nothing whatever to say about the driving force of all other species' attitudinal and behavioral repertoires: genetics. The years 2004 and 2005 have seen the dawn of a new subfield, a new focus for political science: "genetics and politics." During that two-year period, Alford and Hibbing published two salient reports developing the genetics/politics nexus, while Carmen published a monograph staking out the broader lineaments of the new subfield. Taken together, these writings do far more than provide a new emphasis on human DNA as precursor of things political. They inspire a fleshing out of those tools of the natural science trade that beg for adoption by our discipline if it hopes to achieve full-blown status as an empirical angle of scholarly vision.

Twin Studies

Social psychologists have been gathering voluminous data on identical and fraternal twins for at least thirty years, both in the United States and abroad. These findings have been seized upon only recently by political scientists, and they constitute the first building block for sociogenomics investigation. Identical twins are virtually congruent genetically as respects their nuclear DNA, while fraternal twins are no more genetically related than any other two brothers or sisters sharing the same biological parents. Twin study specialists have published detailed reports documenting the "heritability quotients" (HQs) arising from comparisons between the two cohorts. By HQ is meant the variation between them that can be ascribed to genetic differences. Of especial concern to us are heritabilities in the context of behavioral propensity. "Behavioral" is defined broadly to include personality and ideology. The conventional wisdom is that when comparing identicals (monozygotes) and fraternals (dizygotes), the heritability score for an array of behavioral traits is about .50 (Robins 2005). This means that, on average, the variation between cluster members is .50; that is, 50 percent of these behavioral differences can be attributed to genetics (for the computational method, see Wilson 1999, 151). The other 50 percent is largely a function of unshared experiences. (For a study implicitly challenging the high HQs recited here, see Hughes et al. 2005.) Even political scientists who eschew an overt "genetics and politics" commitment have spotted the implications of these data for their own scholarship. Take the public law research agenda. In his early work on jurimetrics, Schubert (1965) relied on "attitudes" as the key independent variable, and by attitudes he meant what the authors of The American Voter (Campbell et al. 1964) meant—social psychological affinities. Today's attitudinalists sound a somewhat different note.

> Although genetic explanations of behavior may not be "politically correct" . . . the evidence from the . . . studies of identical twins reared apart is compelling: About half of the variance in personality traits, including several that tie closely to political attitudes, can be attributed to genetic diversity. (Segal and Spaeth 1993, 234)

The most oft-cited twin study data are drawn from repositories in Minnesota and Virginia. Reported below are some of the major findings relevant to political science. By a "politically relevant" repertoire or variable is meant a behavioral propensity which social scientists have associated through their conventional scholarship with some political dynamic. The extent to which particular genes singly or collectively play a causal role in determining the expression of such propensities is the overriding long-term question before us.

Alford, Funk, and Hibbing (2005 [hereinafter A-F-H]) were provided access to Eaves et al.'s (1999) Virginia data set. The salient heritabilities they have published are all statistically significant at the .01 level. They essentially track respondents' support for issue positions, and virtually all significant policy items on the contemporary agenda are represented. The highest quotient (.51) is for the death penalty (cited in A-H), and the lowest (.27) is for segregation. Taken at face value and given our discipline's bias in favor of environmental/cultural determinants, these results should send shock waves through our ranks. But we need to dig deeper. For the Virginia sample, "socialism" elicits a .36 HQ, yet it could do no better than a .14 in an Australian study. Does the term mean such different things in these two universes? More important, the aggregate score for "conservatism" across a number of studies is approximately .45 (A-F-H; Eaves et al. 1999; Martin et al. 1986; Tellegen et al. 1988); however, the term "liberalism" achieves an underwhelming .18. We would certainly expect the concepts of "conservatism" and "liberalism" to trigger about the same level of acceptance, if we have defined them in the same way so that each is the obverse of the other. As I shall show in a moment, this was not the case here.

Needless to say, there is no "death penalty gene." Responses to policy positions or culturally loaded words and phrases (e.g., "Moral Majority," which achieved a .40), to the extent that they implicate heritability, must link to some larger attitudinal/behavioral configuration(s) that is/are genetically influenced. There is an ongoing, noteworthy debate as to the parameters of this larger phenomenon. Some commentators argue for a strong relationship between political ideology and psychological profiles (Tetlock 1983, 1984; Jost et al. 2003); others disagree (Greenberg and Jonas 2003; Alford and Hibbing 2006). Most of the data come from the Minnesota studies and were cited in Carmen (2004). Others are included for the first time in the political science literature with this writing. They range from baseline happiness (.80) to anxiety (.32) (Lemery and Doelger 2005; Lykken and Tellegen 1996). Both of these have been tied directly to U.S. presidential behavior (Barber 1972); so also has novelty-seeking (.40) (Hamer and Copeland 1998). Political scientists who study cooperation/defection would certainly want to know that the HQ for altruism is .50 (Rushton, Littlefield, and Lumsden 1986), and those who investigate rationality ought to benefit from the knowledge that the HQ for general intelligence is .52 (Plomin et al. 1994). Heritability scores for radicalism and right-wing authoritarianism are robust (Eaves and Eysenck 1974; McCourt et al. 1999). Taken together, the statistically significant HQs for issue positions and theoretically relevant psychological indices would seem to establish a prima facie case of linkage.

The presumption, at this stage of the dialogue, is rebuttable. The HQ for the Big Five (neuroticism, extraversion, conscientiousness, agreeableness, and openness) may be .50 (Bouchard and McGue 2003); however, taken as a whole, the set is unrelated to political ideology (Alford and Hibbing 2006). And so, the argument runs, "the political realm may have unique biological substrates (and perhaps genetic markers)"; in any event, much work needs to be done to flesh out the heritabilities not only of personal temperament but also of social tempera- ment (responses triggered by "small-scale social situations") and political tem- perament ("preferences for the structure and conduct of group life") (Alford and Hibbing 2006, 6). It is the latter constellation of values that returns us to consid- eration of the conservative–liberal dimension.

The conservative–liberal dichotomy is the most commonly probed ideological affinity in our literature. Untutored in that literature, twin study specialists not only show little interest in developing standardized tests to flesh out its dynamics but sometimes provide precious little guidance for respondents. Both the Virginia and Australia research studies included the following instruction: "Here is a list of various topics. *Please indicate whether or not you agree with each topic by circling Yes or No as appropriate. If you are uncertain, please circle* ?" And yet the HQs for conservatism are fairly consistent and high. This is the case even when "conservatism" means "aggregate of policy preferences" (A-F-H). What we need are two uniform questionnaire rosters, one administered to conservatives and the other to liberals. These clusters would be identified via pretests. The items should de-emphasize policy preferences; they should be predicated on per- ceptions and dispositions for and against political change and inequality which theory informs us (Jost et al. 2003) are the critical underlying variables. The Survey Research Center (Ann Arbor, Michigan) has developed inquiries of this kind, though they require fine-tuning and none have been employed of late. Rossiter (1962, 16-17, 74, 168) argued that conservative legions are divided between "traditionalists," who are constitutionalists, and "pure traditionalists," who are "enemies of change as well as reform [and who] live in a state of acute cultural schizophrenia." Liberals, presumably, display a corresponding dichotomy. In fact, years ago many observers noted that a substantial number of ex-communists sat on the editorial board of the *National Review*. Can there be genetic antecedents linking hard-core conservatism and hard-core liberalism, wherein the particular ideological predisposition is the .40 to .65 cultural contri- bution? Applying properly constructed sets of questionnaire items to genetically organized cohorts would separate out various types of conservatives and liberals and then penetrate the heritability dimension. That study is now under way (Carmen 2007).

Genetic Procedures, Genetic Precursors

Presumably skeptics are now prepared to give the notion of "genetics and pol- itics" half a chance: twin study data may have pockmarks but their central mes- sage is too clear simply to ignore. The fallback position for those remaining unconvinced is not difficult to imagine: show us the genes. Scientists have been here before. Twenty years ago, when entomologists and lower-order mammalian experimentalists began the quest for behavioral genetic antecendents, "doubting Thomases" expressed the same reservations. They have been proven wrong.

Twenty years ago, when entomologists and lower-order mammalian experimentalists began the quest for behavioral genetic antecendents, "doubting Thomases" expressed the same reservations. They have been proven wrong.

Approximately thirty genes have been isolated in nonhuman species that, if isolated in *Homo sapiens*, would provide important information as to our political behavior repertoires. Researchers have determined the structure and function of each gene. Our colleagues are learning more each year about how to shed light on the sociality of life forms, and our knowledge of insect, mouse, and primate politics has grown enormously. It is common knowledge among molecular biologists that the fundamental genes responsible for human action are conserved up and down the phylogenetic tree. Each and every recent discovery— genes influencing stress vulnerability in rats (Francis et al. 1999), foraging in honeybees (Ben-Shahar et al. 2002), social feeding in nematodes (Sokolowski 2002), aggressiveness in Old World monkeys (cited in Gibbons 2004), and faithfulness in male prairie voles (Hammock and Young 2005)—has its counterpart in the human. All are either orthologs or homologs of DNA found on every double helix of every cell in our bodies. The exact workings of these genes in our species is a front-and-center concern of our biological science peers.

Insight into some of the methodological tools available for analyzing genes is indispensable. The idea is either to insert a gene of interest into the DNA of some other species and assess its impact in behavioral contexts or delete a gene of interest from a species' DNA to assess how that organism will manage in behavioral contexts without it. Again, precision is the order of the day: experimentalists must be able to chart which allele (version) is to be manipulated (genes come in different versions as with blue/brown eyes), what protein will be triggered by that allele, and, of course, the hypothesized, and later proved, behavioral repertoire resulting therefrom. Again, the genes employed have human counterparts, and the action patterns resulting from their expression have clear political implications if the terms "power" and "influence" mean anything in the context of life form scrutiny. To illustrate: geneticists bred a "fierce" strain of

mice and then inserted into its embryos a human gene matching the missing
sociality rodent gene. Viola! The superaggressive mice returned to normal
(Abrahams et al. 2005). Putting human DNA into lower-order creatures will be
commonplace in years to come.

Those who believe that investigating behavioral genes in lower-order organisms is acceptable but that investigating them in the human constitutes some
qualitative, unbridgeable leap are in for a rude awakening. While research
reports are widely scattered and, incredibly, have never been appropriately organized, collated, and contrasted, Table 1 attempts to convey to a political science
audience the basics of what needs to be said. Proceeding in chronological order
of discovery, Table 1 shows fifteen gene-related sequences with clear political
implications. Some of these fall in a twilight zone area between disease genes and
personality genes. How does one classify clinical depression, bipolarism, and
attention-deficit disorder? There are thousands of Americans and many thousands of non-Americans who exercise free speech, vote, contribute money to
political causes, and "play political games" each and every day who could slide
conveniently into one of these behavioral categories. People who are clinically
depressed handle stress far less satisfactorily than others, and there ought to be
a high correlation between stress overload and various strains of political orientation and participation (Carmen 2004). It used to be that scholars bandied about
such wastebasket terms as "psychopathic personality" and "manic depression."
Genetics has rendered those terms obsolete and will render at least some of the
terminology we employ today as obsolete. The more refined the distinction, the
better the opportunity to link one of these configurations to some political mind-
set or action-set.

---

*It used to be that scholars bandied about such
wastebasket terms as "psychopathic
personality" and "manic depression." Genetics
has rendered those terms obsolete and will
render at least some of the terminology we
employ today as obsolete.*

As one glances down the Table 1 list, it is easy to spot the importance of the
neurotransmitters serotonin and dopamine in influencing sociality. Consider the

TABLE 1
HUMAN GENETIC PRECURSORS OF POLITICALLY RELEVANT REPERTOIRES

Gene	Chromosome	Allelic Configuration	Protein Reaction	Behavioral Propensity	Primary Literature Source	Political Science Literature Source
5 markers	X	Presence of markers	Unknown	Male homosexual orientation	Hamer et al. (1993)	Carmen (2004)
5-HTT promoter	17	One/two short versions	Serotonin overload	Neuroticism; anxiety; hostility; harm-avoidance	Lesch et al. (1996)	Ibid.
D4DR	11	One/two long-form versions (eight to eleven 48-letter repeats)	Dopamine overload	Risk-taking; novelty seeking	Hamer and Copeland (1998)	Carmen (2004); Alford and Hibbing (2004)
DAT1	5	Frequency of 10-repeat 40-BP allele	Dopamine overload	Generalized anxiety; obsessive compulsiveness; depression (subjects: children)	Rowe et al. (1998)	Current study
DAT1	5	Homozygous for 10-repeat allele	Dopamine overload	Attention-deficit disorder	Jacobsen et al. (2000)	Ibid.
COMT	22	Diallelic (met/val) polymorphism	Dopamine catabolism	High (or low) executive cognition	Egan et al. (2001)	Ibid.
MAOA promoter	X	Shorter versions of 30 BP repeats (2–3 copies)	Neurotransmitter deficit plus childhood physical abuse	Inappropriate aggressiveness; impulsiveness; violence	Caspi et al. (2002)	Carmen (2004); Alford and Hibbing (2004)

(continued)

TABLE 1 (CONTINUED)

Gene	Chromosome	Allelic Configuration	Protein Reaction	Behavioral Propensity	Primary Literature Source	Political Science Literature Source
5-HTT promoter	17	Homozygous for short version (44 missing base pairs)	Serotonin overload plus high-stress events	Clinical depression	Caspi et al. (2003)	Carmen (2004); Alford and Hibbing (2004)
D4DR	11	Long-form allele plus promoter SNP C allele	Dopamine overload	Novelty seeking in young females	Lee et al. (2003)	Current study
D4DR	11	Absence of allele 2 in 48-letter polymorphism repeat of exon 3	Dopamine overload	Obsessive compulsive disorder	Millet et al. (2003)	Ibid.
CRH marker gene	8	Presence of the 173-BP SNP	Hormonal overexpression	Inhibition to unfamiliarity; proneness to anxiety in novel situations	Smoller et al. (2003)	Ibid.
GRK3	22	P-5 prometer variant	Altered reception signaling	Bipolarism	Barrett et al. (2003)	Ibid.
Tph2	12	Recessive allele	Diminished serotonin in the brain	Unipolar depression	Zhang et al. (2005)	Alford, Funk, and Hibbing (2005)
VMAT2	10	Polymorphism A33050C presents at least one C	Enhanced monoamine packaging	Self-transcendence (spirituality)	Hamer (2004)	Current study
DCDC2	6	Missing sequences in an SNP	Damaged neuronal circuits	Dyslexia	Meng et al. (2005)	Ibid.
MAOA	X	2, 3, or 5 repeats	Serotonin overload caused by ACC shrinkage	Risk for violence and impulsiveness	Meyer-Lindenberg et al. (2006)	Ibid.

5-HTT promoter on chromosome 17. The gene in question controls the serotonin transporter function. Initially, scientists were unable to associate that gene with a whole battery of behavioral characteristics. What they eventually did discover was that a critical difference lay not in the gene coding sequences but in the promoter regions located "upstream" on the double helix. This system can display a "long" version and a "short" version. The long, or normal, system (a mere 32 percent of the general population) effectively clears serotonin deposits; the short mutational system (68 percent), which is dominant, permits serotonin accrual (the percentages provided in Carmen [2004, 178] are incorrect). (Note: most deleterious alleles are recessive as with, say, the cystic fibrosis mutation; others, such as the Huntington's chorea killer, are dominant.) What is the genetic disparity? The normal version contains sixteen sequence repeats approximately twenty base pairs per repeat (a base pair is either A-C or T-G), while the shorter version contains fourteen of these repeats, a difference, then, of forty-four nucleotide sequences. There is a high correlation between the "short" version regime and neuroticism, and further tests showed that three particular manifestations of neuroticism—anxiety, angry hostility, and impulsiveness—are significantly related to the short version. Yet another high correlation was reported for harm avoidance, especially worry, pessimism, fear of uncertainty, and fatigability. Neuroticism has an HQ of .50 (Carmen 2004), and geneticists have concluded that the short version allele (whether in homozygous or heterozygous form) accounts for as much as 50 percent of that differential. Should political scientists synthesize twin study data on neuroticism and its subtraits with 5-HTT promoter configurations of subject leaders–followers or winners–losers, the discipline would be taking a bold step forward in defining political behavior.

Now consider dopamine. Hamer has investigated the dynamics of what he calls the "novelty" or thrill-seeking syndrome. High scorers on questionnaire items enjoy the play of new ideas; they are predisposed to openness in thought and often action. Low scorers are cautious and conventional, prudent and orderly. Novelty-seeking is .40 heritable. Hamer did not inquire—*we need to inquire*—if high scorers correlate with liberalism and if low scorers correlate with conservatism when we square off monozygotes against dizygotes. The misnamed "novelty gene," actually the D4DR gene, is located on chromosome 11. This gene makes a dopamine receptor protein. Rather like serotonin, dopamine is one of those brain chemicals that needs to be at equilibrium in the typical case, or personality problems and worse arise. Dopamine overload correlates with highly risky behavior: too much gambling, too much sex, too much drinking. What about too much politics? How would one define "too much politics"? The D4DR gene contains a series of forty-eight letter repeats. The average number of repeats runs from four to seven; those with two or three are extraordinarily effective in clearing dopamine, whereas those with eight or more (the ceiling is eleven) are not very effective at all. If a subject has two "longs" (one from the father, one from the mother) or a "long" and a "short," the correlation with novelty seeking is far greater than for a subject exhibiting two "shorts." That is, people with less acute pleasure centers have a genetic impetus to develop compensating behavioral propensities. Hamer concludes modestly that the D4DR gene accounts for only 4 percent of the .40 HQ (Hamer and Copeland 1998; Ridley 2000). Of course, it would be wrong to assume that "pure types" are forever gene-driven, that they can do nothing to counterbalance their firmly established mind-sets. We take action contrary to our genetic pulls and pushes all the time. Still, these efforts are corollary to the fundamental role of genetics in politics.

Table 1 highlights further instances of dopamine circulation as politically relevant antecedent. Note that in these cases either the critical gene or its allelic configuration varies. For example, the D4DR precursor displays a strong association with obsessive compulsiveness. Here, the critical genetic structure is not a question of "long" versus "short" occurrence; it is the absence of allele 2 in the forty-eight-letter polymorphism located in exon 3 of this gene (coding regions are called exons; DNA sequences that do not code for proteins are called introns). In another instance, the DAT1 gene on chromosome 5, the only dopamine transporter, enhances in children—adults have yet to be tested—what is called "generalized anxiety." The key parameter is the frequency of a forty-base pair repeat, namely, where the governing allele features ten as opposed to nine copies. And where subjects are homozygous for the ten-repeat allele in DAT1, attention-deficit disorders emerge; again, the line is not bright between personality and hygienic properties. Finally, the COMT gene on chromosome 22 (see Table 1) metabolizes released dopamine. It exhibits a diallelic polymorphism: *met* and *val*. Executive cognition, as demonstrated through Wisconsin Card Sorting Test facility, is enhanced significantly in subjects displaying two *mets*; the contrary occurs in subjects displaying two *vals*. In other words, increased dopamine circulation detracts from mental acuity. As the genes coding for intellectual gifts are deciphered, the keys to political perspicacity should become ever clearer.

As the genes coding for intellectual gifts are deciphered, the keys to political perspicacity should become ever clearer.

Perhaps the oddest, and certainly one of the most controversial, DNA sequences itemized in Table 1 is Hamer's inaptly dubbed "God gene" (Hamer 2004). Questionnaire returns have indicated that some people display a greater sense of "self-transcendence" than others, what Hamer called a sense of spirituality. Spirituality, he said, "provides a numerical measure of people's capacity to reach out beyond themselves." Australian twin study findings had pegged self-transcendence as .48 heritable. Could spirituality be, in considerable component, a genetic artifact? Hamer attempted to correlate self-transcendence with the D4DR. Result: negative. He then tried to correlate self-transcendence with serotonin DNA precursors. Result: negative. But Hamer hit the jackpot when he sought association between self-transcendence and the VMAT2 gene on chromosome 10. This is a less specialized gene than the others responsible for neurotransmitter function. Its protein packages all of the many monoamines into secretory vector units, bundles the brain uses to store signaling molecules. A certain polymorphism can present two alleles, one in which a key letter is an A and a second in which that letter is a C. If subjects carry a C on either of the two inherited 10s, then they will score much higher on a spirituality index than those carrying two As. The C configuration apparently occurs in about 28 percent of our species. Query: Is this a gene also highly indicative of altruism? To what extent do spirituality and cooperation overlap? Are there ethnic differences in these DNA carriages?

Ultimately, "The challenge is to link genes and their products into functional pathways, circuits, and networks" (Loomis and Sternberg 1995, 649). A proliferating literature in political science stresses the need to address decision making as a neuroscientific phenomenon (McDermott 2004). Table 1 addresses part of the challenge—but only part—by pinpointing protein reactions and behavioral repertoires. Table 2 presents data on the missing connection: the neurophysiological rules and processes that capture the brain's several structures as action systems during the play of political contests. Virtually all these data were recruited by employing the functional magnetic resonance imaging (MRI) technology as subjects participated in a wide variety of these contests. Table 2 takes note of the format or game being played, the identities of the competitors, the object or result of the contest, and the winners and losers broadly defined.

Of optimal value would be experiments conjoining genetic and cranial parameters. Only three Table 2 investigations qualify, unfortunately. One should keep in mind that this is a very new field; all Table 2 studies are post-2000. Table 1 reported a strong correlation between those carrying the "short" version of the 5-HTT promoter and anxiety. This finding received a powerful boost when researchers demonstrated a statistically significant correlation between subjects carrying at least one copy of the "short" serotonin transporter promoter mechanism and elevated activity in their right amygdalas following exposure to anxiety-producing pictures. Control groups made up of "long–long" individuals recorded significantly lower levels of response (the Hariri et al. [2002] study). Acting instinctively in reaction to messages received from the thalamus, the amygdala sets up the first line of defense against perceived dangers. The linkages with the serotonin carriage system show that when these subjects are particularly fearful, often for genetic reasons, the right amygdala overreacts.

An interesting contrast is provided in the second of these investigations, this time the gene under analysis being the MAOA on the X chromosome. Its job is to break down neurotransmitter deposits to help smooth communication among neurons. The MAOA promoter is a polymorphism of thirty base pairs repeatable from two to five times. The shorter versions, standing alone, may quite possibly

TABLE 2

GAME THEORETIC OR OTHER NEUROPHYSIOLOGICAL MODELS OF POLITICAL BEHAVIORS

Format (Game)	Players	Object or Result	Winners	Losers	Primary Literature Source	Political Science Literature Source
Working memory tasks (MRI)	*met* vs. *val* COMT allele cohorts	Prefrontal cortical efficiency	*met* allele	*val* allele	Egan et al. (2001)	Current study
Anxiety-producing pictures (MRI)	Long vs. short; 5-HTT cohorts	Right amygdala overreaction	Long allelic regime	One/two short allelic sequences	Hariri et al. (2002)	Carmen (2004)
Prisoner's Dilemma (MRI)	Female bargainers	Reward system regions (nucleus accumbens, caudate nucleus, etc.) are activated	Mutual cooperators	Defectors	Rilling et al. (2002)	Current study
Ultimatum game (MRI)	Unfair offerers vs. buyers	Bilateral anterior insula reaction vs. dorsolateral prefrontal cortex reaction in buyers	Passion rules: offer rejected	Reason rules: punishment temporized	Sanfey et al. (2003)	Carmen (2004)
Anger and fear face gaze (MRI)	Human subject responses to anger/fear, direct/averted 4-fold table	Anger/averted and fear/direct gazes differentially more threatening as measured by amygdala response	Left amygdala involvement in threat-related activity	Right amygdala noninvolvement in threat-related activity	Adams et al. (2003)	Ibid.
Amygdalar response to novel vs. familiar faces (MRI)	Adults coded as inhibited or uninhibited as kids	Inhibited subjects exhibited stronger amygdalar responses to novel faces than uninhibited subjects	Uninhibited kids/adults	Inhibited kids/adults	Schwartz et al. (2003)	Ibid.
Sequential Prisoner's Dilemma plus facial assessment (MRI)	Bargainers	Recognizing cooperators activates left amygdala, striatum and other reward centers	Cooperators	Defectors	Singer et al. (2004)	Current study
Monetary payoffs among males (PET)	Givers vs. recipient cheaters	Subcortical striatum activation (revenge centers) same as Rilling (2002): anticipation of a preferred social outcome	Giver's passion	Giver's reason	de Quervain et al. (2004)	Ibid.

Partisan images (MRI)	Dems. and Reps.	VPC: affinity (limbic); DPC: alienation (reason); ACC: conflict (mediation)	Admiration	Antipathy	Freedman (2005)	Ibid.
10-round trust game (MRI)	Investors vs. trustees	Caudate nucleus activation linked to benevolent reciprocity in trustees	Altruists	Cheaters	King-Casas et al. (2005)	Ibid.
Playing card selection from two decks with known and unknown properties (MRI)	(1) Normal subjects; (2) normals vs. OFC defectives	Amygdala and OFC modulate striatum	Risk probabilities	Ambiguity probabilities	Hsu et al. (2005)	Ibid.
Cheaters and noncheaters	Male and female observers	Reduction in empathy-related cortices among men when cheaters are punished	N/A	N/A	Singer et al. (2006)	Ibid.
Anger and fear face gaze (MRI)	MAOA (low) vs. MAOA (high) healthy subjects	Differential activation of amygdala, ACC, and OFC	MAOA (highs)	MAOA (lows): increased left amygdala activation; decreased ACC and OFC	Meyer-Lindenberg et al. (2006)	Ibid.
Anger and fear face gaze (MRI)	MAOA (low) male vs. female; healthy subjects	Differential connectivity: amygdala and OFC; other cranial disparities	Females	Males: connectivity, cognitive impairments; heightened emotion (left amygdalar, hippocampal overreaction)	Ibid.	Ibid.
Ultimatum game	Compromised right DLPFC subjects vs. normal subjects	DLPFC deficiency undermines ability to reject unfair offers	Normals	Impaireds	Knoch et al. (2006)	Ibid.

precipitate impulsivity, even aggression (see Table 1; the Caspi et al. [2002] study). For certain, the shorter versions slow enzymatic expression thus causing neuro-transmitter inefficiency and "cleanup" deficits as regards serotonin. Utilizing samples of MAOA "long" version and "short" version healthy subjects, researchers presented each cluster with a battery of angry and fearful pictorial face gazes. For respondents with genetically compromised expression rates, func-tional MRI tests revealed that left amygdalar activation was enhanced while ante-rior cingulate cortical (ACC) and orbitofrontal cortical (OFC) routines were attenuated. Furthermore, overall connectivity between the amygdala and the OFC was clearly reduced in males. The most robust structural changes were in the ACC, the brain region with the highest density of serotonin receptors and a key regulatory mechanism in amygdalar response (Table 2; the Meyer-Lindenberg et al. [2006] studies).

Table 1 also reported a high correlation between participants bearing the *met* version of the COMT gene, dopamine catabolism, and high executive cognition. When MRI tests were then utilized to measure prefrontal cortical efficiency in *met* versus *val* working memory task performers, the *met* allele individuals scored much higher (the Egan et al. [2001] study). A useful experiment would involve presentation of emotionally arousing pictorial displays to our *mets* and *vals* to assess their impacts on ratiocinative skills.

The amygdala is a complex, socially relevant information processing center, citations to which are just now beginning to appear in the political science liter-ature. When the typical American white sees a picture of the typical American black, the subject's amygdala fires off an emotional response, a loose translation of which might be: here is someone different. We carry around the genomic bag-gage of prehistory when facial recognition developed as a key monitoring device for sorting in-groupers and out-groupers. Environmental conditions can alter the equation. If the typical American white sees a picture of Tiger Woods or Michael Jordan, then chances are that that individual's amygdala will not respond: the sub-ject will have unconsciously coded them as insiders (Carmen 2004, 189–90). Table 2 displays useful findings. We now know through functional MRI amyg-dalar screenings that inhibited infants grow up generally to be "avoidance" adults, while uninhibited infants grow up generally to be novelty-seeking adults (the Schwartz et al. [2003] study). These tests have also detected differential roles played by the left amygdala and the right amygdala in reacting to "anger faces" and "fear faces." The left amygdala shows a high degree of sensitivity as to whether the stimulus gaze is frontal or averted, whereas the right amygdala is unresponsive to such nuances (the Adams et al. [2003] study). And when indi-viduals were well apprised of cooperators, having identified them through the play of Prisoner's Dilemma (PD), a game in which individuals either cooperate with or betray one another in accordance with maximizing their own outcome, subsequent facial assessments triggered the left amygdala reacting in concert with such other reward centers as the striatum (the Singer et al. [2004] study) (cf. the quite different cranial responses to cooperators during the actual playing of PD, at least among women) (the Rilling et al. [2002] study). Finally, the amygdala along with the orbitofrontal cortex becomes much more active when players are challenged to accept ambiguous rather than risky options, that is, individuals much prefer the latter to the former even when the expected payoffs are equal (the Hsu et al. [2005] study). To say that we need to appreciate the genetic main-springs of amygdalar function is a gross understatement, though we have learned recently that the *stathmin* gene is highly expressed in the lateral nucleus of the mouse amygdala, and when this gene is knocked out, subjects do not respond either to learned or innate fear (Shumyatsky et al. 2005).

Applications to more overtly political choice making are inevitable. University of California, Los Angeles, researchers essayed a tentative first step when, during the 2004 presidential election, they used the MRI technology to measure partisan reactions to facial images of President George Bush and Senator John Kerry. They found an intriguing dance between the emotional centers and the cognitive centers, as both Republicans and Democrats fought to convince themselves of their candidates' manifest superiority. That these cranial processes can be captured by the tools of biological science—therefore adding a further layer of richness to our understanding of a key political event—is most informative. From these solid empirical findings, the investigators proceeded to spoil the party by jumping to the conclusion that the red state/blue state divide is a fictional artifact of our own self-deception (the Freedman [2005] study). Equally unwarranted is the assertion that the divide is in fact an expression of genetically driven "gut" affinities (A-F-H). We have a long way to go before we can demonstrate neurophysiological causation for any cultural cleavage among nation-state electoral camps.

From Genetics to Genomics

Thus far, our tale has been a commentary on what might be called "socio-genetics." The theory, methods, and data reflect the good science of twenty years ago brought up to the present moment by recent discoveries. The orientation is wedded to the structure and function of specific genes acting alone to orchestrate social behaviors in sundry species. Even today, sociogenetics comprises, along with the policy implications arising therefrom, the paradigmatic stuff of a viable "genetics and politics" subfield for our discipline. And yet, as we speak, the term sociogenetics is yielding to the term "sociogenomics." What is its genesis and what does it mean?

Access to the human genome, taken as a whole, provides parsimonious entrée to the investigation of complex traits of which human social behavior—human *political* behavior—is a prime example. Complex traits arise from a battery of genes acting together. According to Gene Robinson (2002), a leading entomologist who coined the term and nurtured its growth into full-fledged paradigmatic status among biologists, "sociogenomics" refers to the social behavior of life forms as an outgrowth of global determinants (that is, genomic patterns) employing a comparative species perspective. Sociogenomicists avail themselves of DNA data culled from the fruitfly, the yeast, the mouse, and the rat, among many other species, all of whose genomes have now been sequenced (Robinson 2002). This cross-species approach adds a key evolutionary component to sociogenomics. Genes are no longer treated as static entities, frozen in time. Genes evolve as they negotiate the interspecies journey, and they evolve in humans as our species, forever seeking to maximize reproductive and survival opportunities, copes with exogenous stimuli. Lumsden and Wilson (1981) had argued that culture itself placed certain genes under selective pressure, thus spawning new alleles. There is evidence that the D4DR dopamine receptor has come under selective pressure, enhancing *Homo sapiens'* wanderlust (Olson 2002). There is not much genetics, much less genomics, in Lumsden and Wilson. Sociogenomics provides a corollary article to their canon of truths.

Until very recently, before the dawn of sociogenomics, behavioral traits could be traced down (not without difficulty) by utilizing four categories of inquiry: linkage analysis, allele-sharing technologies, association studies in humans, and model organism comparisons (Lander and Schork 1994). An in-depth treatment of each is beyond the scope of this article. In candor, political scientists cannot hope to perform sociogenetic—not to mention sociogenomic—experiments without forming collaborations with scholars well versed in molecular biology. They still have a responsibility to appreciate the underlying logics and larger theoretical dimensions of the several procedures mentioned here. Suppose one had wanted, ten years ago, to investigate the genetic antecedents of the conservatism–liberalism attitudinal complex. It would first have been necessary to establish objectively the phenotypic characteristics for which to test and then develop family tree blueprints which would serve as transmission models. After a putative gene such as those cited in Table 1 had been mapped, the next step would evidently have been to show that allelic concordance occurred more often than what was expected to occur by chance. One would also construct experimental and control groups to compare unrelated affected individuals with unrelated, unaffected individuals. The question would be whether specific alleles crop up in those displaying a certain personality characteristic at a significantly higher frequency. Finally, as we have seen, some genes can be slipped into or out of animal models to pin down precise behavioral manifestations. Now that researchers can clone mice, sheep, cats, and pigs, we have at our disposal uniform physiological environments for assessing the role of human DNA in a wide variety of animal contexts.

All of this should sound sufficiently daunting to explain why an empirically grounded subfield titled "genetics and politics" has been considered pie in the sky. Capturing the human genome changes everything. At the lowest level of magnitude, the conventional linkage and association procedures mentioned above have generated impressive new insights. With the former, researchers, who have at their disposal genetic markers highly correlated with certain behavioral tendencies, scan the genome in search of precursor DNA chromosomal locations. The short arm of chromosome 6, the short arm of chromosome 8, and the long arms of chromosomes 13 and 22 seem to be prime locations for mutations implicated in various disorders. With the latter, comparing the presence of candidate genes in those displaying sundry antisocial patterns against those immune from these stresses in the context of genomic investigation has yielded virtually all of the probative data found in Table 1 (Bouchard and McGue 2003, 36).

At a higher level of magnitude, new theory also inspires new methods, and, in this case, the breakthrough procedure of choice is called the microarray gene expression technology. In an array experiment, genetic material from two sources of interest, for example species A and species B, or perhaps a human experimental and a human control group, are laid on a glass substrate, and scientists measure the levels of expression occurring simultaneously. Subject clusters provide DNA samples, and putative genes of interest contained in these samples trigger expression responses from their counterparts in the microarray universe. Researchers can place billions of DNA sections on the chip, each one about twenty-five bases in length. In a notable study, honeybee specialists tested fifty-five hundred genes employing seventy-two microarray runs to demonstrate that age-related shifts by adults from hive tasks to foraging tasks could be linked to expression change in 39 percent of the sample; this finding eventually led to nearly perfect predictions of species behavior based on genetic expression profiles (Whitfield et al. 2003). After "competitive hybridization," in which single-stranded complementary DNA from the two discrete samples interdigitate, a greater number of Gene X copies in sample A will lead to one color-coding (say, red) and a greater number of Gene X copies in sample B will inspire a different color-coding (say, green). Put more precisely, the expressed genes are detected by the presence of messenger RNA, which is converted back to complementary DNA (genes without introns or "junk").

Microarrays have led to startling new genetic discoveries in nonhuman subjects. To repeat, all these genes have human counterparts; assessing their functions, however, requires the use of animal models. If we could apply the microarray procedure to humans as we do to honeybees, we could test directly for personality and ideological antecedents in the straightforward manner described above. As we cannot kill human subjects and rescue the messenger RNA expressed in their brains following, say, the play of some game, we must be content now with the rich harvest of behavioral genetic precursors emerging from the laboratories of entomology and related disciplines.

Microarrays become a truly robust vehicle for sociogenomics investigation when the experimental data take the form of human single nucleotide polymorphisms (SNPs). All of us share 99.9 percent of our DNA sequence. Polymorphisms are stretches of DNA we do not share, thus ensuring that we are not all clones. Genes that exhibit different alleles in different people hold the secret to phenotypic variation. That is, they hold the secret to political attitude and behavior heritabilities. Each one of these is called an SNP. By convention, more than 1 percent of the population must share the solitary letter substitution. The human genome, it is now estimated, contains 9 million SNPs; four hundred thousand of them reside in exons; SNPs responsible for amino acid composition shifts could number two hundred thousand. Also to be accounted for are promoter region SNPs, which, as we have seen, can have a marked influence in gene expression levels. To repeat: each SNP variation yields a unique allele. The Holy Grail in the now well-underway SNP race is the identification of all functional SNPs. This article takes the position that the Holy Grail of human sociogenomics is the totality of functional SNPs coding for behavioral propensities. One of the keys to SNP discovery is the microarray procedure. That is to say, microarrays ferret out disparate gene expression levels in nonhuman subjects, the genes implicated in the sundry behavioral repertoires then provide clues to the identities of SNPs in human subjects, following which individual variations are correlated with behavioral/attitudinal differences. Eventually, political scientists working with biological scientists can commence to control for the role of each gene one by one, folding in as well interspecies and pedigree data. The sociogenetic tasks referred to earlier as daunting will become manageable, though exceedingly challenging, sociogenomic tasks.

Genes that exhibit different alleles in different people hold the secret to phenotypic variation. That is, they hold the secret to political attitude and behavior heritabilities.

An alternative vision (Alford and Hibbing 2006, 15) suggests a procedure in which individuals provide saliva specimens for genetic information, after which statistical evaluation of correlations between candidate alleles and behavioral responses can be undertaken. The procedure certainly would permit us to compare SNP composition with phenotypic reaction; a drawback is that gene expression cannot be demonstrated in saliva (or blood for that matter) unless salivary genes were involved, because messenger RNA implicated in the tests of interest to political science would be tissue specific to the brain. It is hard to believe that the DNA relevant to ideology encodes proteins known to be present in saliva. And note, it is proteins, not genes, that would show up in saliva following, say, the play of game theoretic exercises. Even for microbiologists, getting from proteins to DNA is exceedingly difficult.

Working with molecularists to ascertain politically relevant messenger RNA in the brain and working with molecularists to track politically relevant proteins backward in time to DNA is the new world of political science as a science.

The Longer View

In 1999, E. O. Wilson endeavored to sketch a coming worldview of scholarly and intellectual inquiry. The term he used to describe the inevitable fusion of all human knowledge is "consilience." He envisioned social science achieving a heightened maturity as its practitioners labored cheek to jowl with natural scientists. Already, his ideas have mobilized enlightened souls working in the trenches of other fields to rethink their paradigmatic premises. So we see economists, psychologists, and neuroscientists converging into a single, unified discipline called neuroeconomics (Glimcher and Rustichini 2004). These scholars have not even bothered to consider political scientists as allies. We are coded as either irrelevant or hopeless. Perhaps they are right. However, they have already committed a fatal oversight. Yet to be included in their paradigm is a sociogenomic component. Those few of us toiling in "genetics and politics" terrain can, this early in the game, claim a leg up on them. The question is whether our discipline as a whole can achieve a leg up on them. Should we choose to do so, we will make for ourselves a unique contribution in the drive toward consilience. Aristotle, a political science disciplinary founder extraordinaire and the "discoverer" of the DNA principle (Carmen 2004, 16), saw the end of the tunnel but no ways to reach it. He would enjoy, one fervently hopes, a burgeoning consilience of scientific inquiry in which the various tasks find practitioners in a laboratory of discovery faithful to the grand empirical enterprise.

References

Abrahams, B. S., et al. 2005. Pathological aggression in "fierce" mice corrected by human nuclear receptor 2E1. *Journal of Neuroscience* 25 (27): 6263.

Adams, R. B., Jr., et al. 2003. Effects of gaze on amygdala sensitivity to anger and fear faces. *Science* 300:1536.

Alford, J. R., C. L. Funk, and J. R. Hibbing. 2005. Are political orientations genetically transmitted? *American Political Science Review* 99:153.

Alford, J. R., and J. R. Hibbing. 2004. The origin of politics: An evolutionary theory of political behavior. *Perspectives on Politics* 2:707.

———. 2006. How are political orientations genetically transmitted? A research agenda? Paper presented at the Midwest Political Science Association Annual Meeting, Chicago.

Barber, J. D. 1972. *The presidential character*. Englewood Cliffs, NJ: Prentice Hall.

Barrett, T. B., et al. 2003. Evidence that a single nucleotide polymorphism in the promoter of the G protein receptor kinase 3 gene is associated with bipolar disorder. *Molecular Psychiatry* 8:546.

Ben-Shahar, Y., et al. 2002. Influence of gene action across different time scales on behavior. *Science* 296:741.

Bouchard, T. J., Jr., and M. McGue. 2003. Genetic and environmental influences on human psychological differences. *Journal of Neurobiology* 54:4.

Campbell, A., P. E. Converse, W. E. Miller, and D. E. Stokes. 1964. *The American voter*. New York: Wiley.

Carmen, I. H. 2004. *Politics in the laboratory: The constitution of human genomics*. Madison: University of Wisconsin Press.

———. 2007. From genes, to mind, to politics: Finding the yellow brick empirical road. Paper presented at the Midwest Political Science Association Annual Meeting, Chicago.

Caspi, A., et al. 2002. Role of genotype in the cycle of violence in maltreated children. *Science* 297:851.

———. 2003. Influence of life stress on depression: Moderation by a polymorphism in the 5-HTT gene. *Science* 301:386.

de Quervain, D., et al. 2004. The neural basis of altruistic punishment. *Science* 305:1254.

Eaves, L., et al. 1999. Comparing the biological and cultural inheritance of personality and social attitudes in the Virginia 30,000 study of twins and their relatives. *Twin Research* 2:62.

Eaves, L. J., and H. J. Eysenck. 1974. Genetics and the development of social attitudes. *Nature* 249:288.

Egan, M. F., et al. 2001. Effect of COMT val 108/158 met genotype on frontal lobe function and risk for schizophrenia. *Proceedings of the National Academy of Sciences* 98:6917.

Francis, D., et al. 1999. Nanogenomic transmission across generations of maternal behavior and stress responses in the rat. *Science* 286:1155.

Freedman, J. 2005. This is your brain on politics. *New York Times*, January 18, p. A21.

Gibbons, A. 2004. Tracking the evolutionary history of a "warrior" gene. *Science* 304:818.

Glimcher, P. W., and A. Rustichini. 2004. Neuroeconomics: The consilience of brain and decision. *Science* 306:447.

Greenberg, J., and E. Jonas. 2003. Psychological motives and political orientation—The left, the right, and the rigid: Comment on Jost et al. (2003). *Psychological Bulletin* 129:376.

Hamer, D. 2004. *The God gene*. New York: Doubleday.

Hamer, D., et al. 1993. A linkage between DNA markers on the X chromosome and male sexual orientation. *Science* 261:321.

Hamer, D., and P. Copeland. 1998. *Living with our genes*. New York: Anchor.

Hammock, E. A. D., and L. J. Young. 2005. Microsatellite instability generates diversity in brain and sociobehavioral traits. *Science* 308:1630.

Hariri, A. R., et al. 2002. Serotonin transporter genetic variation and the response of the human amygdala. *Science* 297:400.

Hsu, M., et al. 2005. Neural systems responding to degrees of uncertainty in human decision-making. *Science* 310:1680.

Hughes, C., et al. 2005. Origins of individual differences in theory of mind: From nature to nurture? *Child Development* 76:356.

Jacobsen, L. K., et al. 2000. Prediction of dopamine transporter binding availability by genotype: A preliminary report. *American Journal of Psychiatry* 157:1700.

Jost, J. T., et al. 2003. Political conservatism as motivated social cognition. *Psychological Bulletin* 129:339.

King-Casas, B., et al. 2005. Getting to know you: Reputation and trust in a two-person economic exchange. *Science* 308:78.

Knoch, D., et al. 2006. Diminishing reciprocal fairness by disrupting the right prefrontal cortex. *Science* 314:829.

Lander, E. S., and N. J. Schork. 1994. Genetic dissection of complex traits. *Science* 265:2037.

Lee, H.-J., et al. 2003. Allelic variants interaction of dopamine receptor D4 polymorphism correlate with personality traits in young Korean female population. *American Journal of Medical Genetics* Part B, 118B:76.

Lemery, K. S., and L. Doelger. 2005. Genetic vulnerabilities to the development of psychopathology. In *Development of psychopathology*, ed. B. L. Hankin and J. R. Z. Abela. Thousand Oaks, CA: Sage.

Lesch, K.-P., et al. 1996. Association of anxiety-related traits with a polymorphism in the serotonin transporter gene regulatory system. *Science* 274:1527.

Loomis, W. F., and P. W. Sternberg. 1995. Genetic networks. *Science* 269:649.

Lumsden, C. J., and E. O. Wilson. 1981. *Genes, mind, and culture*. Cambridge, MA: Harvard University Press.

Lykken, D., and A. Tellegen. 1996. Happiness is a stochastic phenomenon. *Psychological Science* 7:186.

Martin, N. G., et al. 1986. Transmission of social attitudes. *Proceedings of the National Academy of Sciences* 83:4364.

McCourt, K., et al. 1999. Authoritarianism revisited: Genetic and environmental influence examined in twins reared apart and together. *Personality of Individual Differences* 27:985.

McDermott, R. 2004. The feeling of rationality: The meaning of neuroscientific advances for political science. *Perspectives on Politics* 2:691.

Meng, H., et al. 2005. DCDC2 is associated with reading disability and modulates neuronal development in the brain. *Proceedings of the National Academy of Sciences* 102:17053.

Meyer-Lindenberg, A., et al. 2006. Neural mechanisms of genetic risk for impulsivity and violence in humans. *Proceedings of the National Academy of Sciences* 103:6269.

Millet, B., et al. 2003. Association between the dopamine receptor D4 (DRD4) gene and obsessive-compulsive disorder. *American Journal of Medical Genetics* 116B:55.

Olson, S. 2002. Seeking the signs of selection. *Science* 298:1324.

Plomin, R., et al. 1994. The genetic basis of complex human behaviors. *Science* 264:1733.

Ridley, M. 2000. *Genome*. New York: Perennial.

Rilling, J. K., et al. 2002. A neural basis for social cooperation. *Neuron* 35:395.

Robins, R. W. 2005. The nature of personality: Genes, culture, and national character. *Science* 310:62.

Robinson, G. 2002. Sociogenomics takes flight. *Science* 297:204.

Rossiter, C. 1962. *Conservatism in America*. 2nd ed. New York: Vintage.

Rowe, D. C., et al. 1998. The relation of the dopamine transporter gene (DAT1) to symptoms of internalizing disorders in children. *Behavior Genetics* 28:215.

Rushton, J. P., C. H. Littlefield, and C. J. Lumsden. 1986. Gene-culture coevolution of complex social behavior: Human altruism and mate choice. *Proceedings of the National Academy of Sciences* 83:7340.

Sanfey, A. G., et al. 2003. The neural basis of economic decision-making in the ultimate game. *Science* 300:1755.

Schubert, G. 1965. *The judicial mind*. Evanston, IL: Northwestern University Press.

Schwartz, C. E., et al. 2003. Inhibited and uninhibited infants "grown up": Adult amygdalar response to novelty. *Science* 300:1952.

Segal, J. A., and H. J. Spaeth. 1993. *The Supreme Court and the attitudinal model*. Cambridge: Cambridge University Press.

Shumyatsky, G. P., et al. 2005. *Stathmin*, a gene enriched in the amygdala, controls both learned and innate fear. *Cell* 123:697.

Singer, T., et al. 2004. Brain responses to the acquired moral status of faces. *Neuron* 41:653.

———. 2006. Empathetic neural responses are modulated by the perceived fairness of others. *Nature* 439:466.

Smoller, J. W., et al. 2003. Association of a genetic marker at the corticotropin-releasing hormone locus with behavioral inhibition. *Biological Psychiatry* 54:1376.

Sokolowski, M. B. 2002. Social eating for stress. *Nature* 419:893.

Tellegen, A., et al. 1988. Personality similarity in twins reared apart and together. *Journal of Personality and Social Psychology* 54:1031.

Tetlock, P. E. 1983. Cognitive style and political ideology. *Journal of Personality and Social Psychology* 45:118.

———. 1984. Cognitive style and political belief systems in the British House of Commons. *Journal of Personality and Social Psychology* 46:365.

Whitfield, C. W., et al. 2003. Gene expression profiles in the brain predict behavior in individual honey bees. *Science* 302:296.

Wilson, E. O. 1999. *Consilience*. New York: Vintage.

Zhang, X., et al. 2005. Loss-of-function mutation in tryptophan hydroxylase-2 identified in unipolar major depression. *Neuron* 45:11.

Balancing Ambition and Gender Among Decision Makers

In this article, we use an original laboratory experiment to test how people react to ambitious decision makers, allowing for interactions with gender. In the experiment, participants are told two decision makers will be dividing some valuable resource on their behalf. One decision maker (either high or low in ambition) is "appointed." Participants vote from a slate of candidates, about whom they have information on gender and ambition, for the second decision maker. We find that people tend to associate high ambition with male and self-interested behavior and that the selection of the second decision maker depends on the level of ambition of the first decision maker as well as perceptions of gender of that decision maker. We conclude by suggesting important implications for research on vote choice and representation.

Keywords: ambition; gender; big man; representation

By
CHRISTOPHER W. LARIMER,
REBECCA J. HANNAGAN,
and
KEVIN B. SMITH

Political theorists have long recognized a paradox underlying the exercise of political power: citizens do not trust leaders perceived as desiring power, but those who do not desire power are, by definition, unlikely to become political leaders. Thus, Machiavelli (1515/2004; see chap. VII) advised his prince to avoid publicly revealing a desire for power because to do so

Christopher W. Larimer is an assistant professor of political science at the University of Northern Iowa. He teaches and researches in the areas of public administration, state politics, and political behavior.

Rebecca J. Hannagan is an assistant professor of political science at Northern Illinois University. She researches and teaches in the areas of politics and the life sciences, political psychology, gender politics, and political behavior.

Kevin B. Smith is a professor of political science at the University of Nebraska–Lincoln. His research focuses on the application of evolutionary and biological models to political behavior.

NOTE: This article was originally prepared for presentation at the Hendricks Symposium on Biology and Political Behavior, University of Nebraska–Lincoln, October 13-14, 2006. This research was reviewed and approved by the University of Nebraska–Lincoln Institutional Review Board.

DOI: 10.1177/0002716207305272

ANNALS, *AAPSS*, 614, November 2007

was to invite "hatred and contempt," and James Madison (1788/2003) decried desire for power as poison to republican government. Machiavelli and Madison both recognized that political leaders who take up office as a burden of public service are viewed as more legitimate and trustworthy than those who are perceived to pursue power as an individual prize to be won. The latter are seen as self-interested, untrustworthy, and a threat to the greater good.

This notion that those who crave power invite mistrust rings intuitively true. Alexander Haig's infamous quote, "As for now, I'm in control here," made in response to the shooting of President Ronald Reagan in 1981, was meant to provide a reassurance of effective and competent government in a time of crisis. Instead, Haig was seen as making an unseemly grasp for power—as secretary of state, he constitutionally was not in control. The vice president was, and the resulting negative public outcry forced Haig to resign. More systematically, congressional scholars find negative assessments of Congress have less to do with policy than the perception that the institution is populated by power seekers who use their office as a way to further their own self-interest (Hibbing and Theiss-Morse 2002, 1995).

Overt ambition for power is clearly a political liability; a claim recognized by political thinkers such as Machiavelli and Madison, supported by public opinion studies, and reflected in everything from the popularity of term limit laws to an intuitively understandable preference for political leaders such as, say, George Washington and Colin Powell over, say, Richard Nixon and Alexander Haig. The problem, of course, is that virtually all political leaders *are* ambitious for power. Even Washington stood for election, which is, by definition, an open declaration of a desire to wield political influence. What is it about ambition for authority that creates negative perceptions for some but not for others? Do people really prefer policy makers who exhibit a distinct lack of enthusiasm for the offices they actually hold? If so, why? After all, we presumably do not invest greater confidence in physicians or mechanics who assure us they really are not interested in medical careers or cars.

In this article, we build a conceptual framework to explain why a universal predisposition to mistrust certain types of leaders might exist, what traits would trigger this mistrust, and how people would behaviorally respond to these leaders. We distinguish between *positive ambition* (associated with competence and a desire to carry out multiple responsibilities and serve communal goals, i.e., other-regarding) and *negative ambition* (an individualistic craving for power, i.e., self-regarding). Negative ambition, we argue, triggers mistrust and a loss of legitimacy and predicts behavioral responses to authoritative decisions. A series of original laboratory experiments supports our argument, which have interesting implications for how people are likely to react to political leaders, especially in supporting female versus male political leaders.

Negative Ambition and the "Big Man"

Certain traits are known to be valued in political leaders.[1] Charisma, enthusiasm (Ammeter et al. 2002), being decisive and strong (Miller, Wattenberg, and

Malanchuk 1986), commanding respect, and possessing an ability to "provide strong leadership" (Kinder 1986; Kinder et al. 1980) are positive personal traits that play into voting decisions and evaluations of political candidates (e.g., Campbell et al. 1960; Kinder 1986; Lau 1986; Rahn et al. 1990; Stokes 1966). Some traits, however, are seen as serious drawbacks in political leaders. Specifically, being "power hungry" is the most negative personality attribute that people can assign to a candidate (Kinder et al. 1980, 319). Being power hungry is a strong negative predictor of trustworthiness and clearly shapes dispositional judgments. No wonder candidates take pains to avoid seeming overly ambitious for the office they are running for; everyone wants to be perceived as a Washington outsider reluctantly answering a call to public service (Cornog 2004, 61).

Why should desire to hold a position of influence be such a powerful influence in driving negative evaluations of political leaders? Perhaps citizens perceive they are less likely to get what they want from government from self-interested, power-hungry politicians. This makes intuitive sense, but the empirical case is weak. For example, people generally view members of Congress as self-interested and craving power, yet policy outcomes seem to have little to do with shaping such attitudes (Hibbing and Theiss-Morse 2002). Rather than situational or instrumental outcomes, deep-rooted behavioral predispositions related to process seem to have a better case for being the underlying explanatory cause of such attitudes (see also Tyler 2000; Tyler and Lind 1992).

Citizens perceive they are less likely to get what they want from government from self-interested, power-hungry politicians.

Indeed, there is experimental evidence supporting the claim that humans have an innate aversion to power-hungry or dominant leaders. For example, Hibbing and Alford (2004, 72) found that people respond immediately and negatively to decisions made by decision makers perceived to be "craving" power. Importantly, people are willing to act on these negative assessments even if doing so exacts individual costs. For example, Van Vugt et al. (2004) found people are significantly more likely to exit a group given an autocratic leader (i.e., one in which the leader uses individual discretion in deciding who will contribute), compared to a group with a democratic leader (i.e., one in which contribution to the public good is voluntary) in a public goods game, even though exit can lower individual payoffs.

Anthropologists confirm that aversion to power seeking in leaders is an innate, universal human behavioral predisposition. "Upstartism" or "big man" behavior describes people who act like they deserve special treatment, elevated status, and the freedom to put their individual interests above the group (Boehm 1999). Upstartism routinely prompts a "leveling" response; attitudes and behaviors designed to ridicule, or even harm, the big man, to remove him from power or at least cut him down to size. This predisposition is independent of culture, social complexity, sophistication of political system, and particular policy outcomes. The basic pattern is seen in hunter gatherer groups and in the reaction to Alexander Haig's claim to be in control: political leaders perceived to desire power to serve self-interested ends invite a backlash.

Boehm (1997) argued "anti-big-man" predispositions do not mean leaders are not wanted, just particular types of leaders. Leaders can help coordinate effective collective action, meaning competent leadership confers consider- able benefits to social and political collectives (Erdal and Whiten 1996, 1994). The trick is finding leaders who will use their post to pursue such collective benefits rather than use their authority to pursue their own self-interests. Innate anti-big-man predispositions thus make evolutionary sense; they serve the purpose of promoting "good" leaders (those who are competent, can pro- vide solutions to a range of collective action problems, and are committed to group interests) and discouraging "bad" leaders (those who put their own interests above those of the group). This is what separates *positive ambition* (associated with competence and a desire to carry out multiple responsibilities and serve communal goals) and *negative ambition* (an individualistic craving for power).

Thus, it is not ambition per se that shapes perceptions of political leaders, but the motivations that underlie that ambition. People want strong leaders and are not particularly worried about whether they crave power; instead, they are intensely concerned about *why* they crave power. Basically, people want "neutral, non-self-serving decision makers" to be making the big political decisions (Hibbing and Theiss-Morse 2002, 199).

Negative Ambition and Gender Stereotypes

Aversion to "big-man" behavior is universal in the sense that it elicits negative responses from both genders, but the description itself is deliberately not gender- neutral. Generally speaking, big men are exactly that: males who engage in "upstart" behavior. This is almost certainly because males are more oriented toward and more likely to dominate social hierarchies (Pratto 1996, 179). We forward two potential reasons to explain such gender differences. One is socialization, that is, that a system of gender-specific behavioral expectations or roles are institutional- ized (invariably to the advantage of men and the disadvantage of women; see Ferree, Lorber, and Hess 1999; Ridgeway and Smith-Lovin 1999). The other is that there are innate psychological differences between males and females, products of evolved responses to differing adaptive problems (notably, though not exclusively, reproduction. See Eagly 1995; Buss 1995; Campbell 2002). These are not mutually exclusive explanations—nature *and* nurture can share the explanatory role—and both suggest males are more competitive, physically aggressive, risk-tolerant, status-oriented, and oriented toward dominance hierarchies (for surveys of the relevant literature, see Eagly 1995; Boehm 1993; Buss 1996; Pinker 1997; Ridley 2003). Given this, there is a high probability that a big man—a leader with negative ambition—is indeed going to be a male.

That negative ambition might have gender implications has been acknowledged but rarely empirically explored. Boehm (1999) acknowledged that males tend to be more likely to exhibit upstart behavior, but he did not address this formally as part of his theory. Knauft (1994, 182) wrote that we do not yet know "what role . . . females play in dominance or counterdominance" (see also Erdal and Whiten 1994). Knauft agreed that "dominance and counterdominance in human evolution reflects a strong male bias." Yet while women tend to be less concerned with rivalry and status seeking, they are equally as likely as men to check male upstart behavior (Boehm 1999, 8-9). This suggests counterdominant tendencies exist in females—like males, they will respond negatively to big men. What remains an open question is how people respond to "big women," that is, female leaders who display negative ambition. This is an interesting question because negative ambition is clearly a male behavioral stereotype, and gender stereotypes are undoubtedly used to evaluate the traits of political decision makers (Alexander and Anderson 1993; Huddy and Terkildsen 1993; Sanbonmatsu 2002; see also Shapiro 2003). There is evidence of gender differences in behavior as leaders, responses to styles of leadership, and in various other aspects of authoritative decision making (Kennedy 2003; Rosenthal 1998). Yet we are aware of no empirical studies that directly assess gender differences in the context of ambition or that test the behavioral implications of such differences.

If negative ambition is a particularly male trait, reactions to ambition may be mediated by gender. All else equal, ambition in female decision makers may not prompt such severe leveling mechanism responses as those in males. Female policy makers could conceivably even benefit from ambition if it is seen as a type of leveling mechanism itself, that is, as a way to counter ambition in males. Given a choice between two candidates, one of each gender and both displaying strong negative ambition, the female candidate may actually have an advantage because this particular trait is so stereotypically male. Women tend to be stereotyped according to more prosocial behaviors such as compassion, honesty, and empathy (Alexander and Anderson 1993; Huddy and Terkildsen 1993). Furthermore, women who are successful in gaining office and keeping it are often those who present themselves as having a clear and deliberate message and represent themselves as "independent a decision maker as any man, but more caring and trustworthy" (Witt, Paget, and Matthews 1995, 214). Such empirical results support our expectation that people may be more sensitive to negative ambition in a male decision maker.

Hypotheses

Despite the clear implications for understanding political behavior, there have been surprisingly few empirical attempts to directly assess the behavioral implications of negative ambition.[2] While it is fairly well established that negative ambition will prompt a leveling mechanism response, it is less clear what form that response will take under given circumstances. Will people seek to balance ambitious policy makers with nonambitious policy makers? Is negative ambition really a male trait, and if so, what are the implications for support of female policy makers? Are people so averse to ambition that the behavioral response occurs independent of outcomes?

We are interested in testing three types of hypotheses. The first concerns inferences about ambitious decision makers. We expect negative ambition to be perceived as a distinctly male decision-maker trait and that a negatively ambitious decision maker will be viewed as more self-interested and less fair than unambitious decision makers.

The second type of hypothesis concerns the choices people will make in selecting a decision maker for a group. Absent any information about a decision maker other than his or her desire for power, we believe people will assume the worst: that the decision maker is ambitious for self-interested ends. However, given additional information regarding the gender of the decision maker, we expect people to evaluate decision makers based on both characteristics. People want leaders who are enthusiastic about leading (i.e., ambitious leaders); however, they want positively ambitious leaders. Based on research from anthropology and work on gender stereotypes, we argue the leader that best embodies these characteristics is an ambitious female. Female decision makers, in certain situations, may benefit from a high level of ambition (specifically as a counter to a male with high levels of ambition).

People want leaders who are enthusiastic about leading (i.e., ambitious leaders); however, they want positively ambitious leaders.

Our third type of hypothesis concerns the reaction to unfair allocations. We expect people to think the cause of the unfair outcome was due to the self-interestedness of an ambitious decision maker rather than an unambitious decision maker. If people associate ambition with self-serving behavior, then people are likely to perceive the decision-making process as unfair, given one highly ambitious decision maker.

Methods

We test our hypotheses using an experimental research design. By using experimental methodology we are able to eliminate external influences as well as control for the number of considerations people might use in evaluating political decision makers. For gathering experimental data, we use MediaLab Research Software. Undergraduates from two "Introduction to American Politics" courses at a large Midwestern university make up the sample population.

In the experiment, participants are told that fifteen extra credit points will be divided between three people. Participants are told that two of the three people will decide how the points are divided. The person not selected to be a decision maker will get a chance to "vote" on at least one decision maker. Participants are told that through a random process they have been selected to be a voter rather than a decision maker (in actuality, all participants are voters—the "decision makers" are a computer program). Participants are informed that one decision maker—a highly ambitious decision maker or low ambitious decision maker—has already been selected to the decision-making group. We then asked the participants to vote for the second decision maker who will become part of a group of two people who will divide the fifteen extra credit points among the three of them—the two decision makers and the voter (participant).

Participants are randomly assigned to one of two conditions, a high-ambition condition and a low-ambition condition. In the high-ambition condition, participants are told the first decision maker already selected responded with a strong desire to be the decision maker. In the low-ambition condition, participants are told the first decision maker already selected responded with a weak desire to be the decision maker.

The role of the participants is to vote from a group of candidates, about whom they have information on gender and ambition, for the second decision maker. The list of candidates contains two males (one of high ambition and one of low ambition) and two females (one of high ambition and one of low ambition). Following their vote, participants are then asked to wait a moment while the group makes its decision regarding the division of the extra credit points. All participants receive the same unfair outcome (three out of fifteen extra credit points). Following this division, subjects are asked a series of questions about their impressions of the decision, the decision-making group as a whole, and individuals within the decision-making group. Following these questions, participants are asked a series of demographic questions, including age, year in school, education level, college major, political ideology, political party affiliation, income, religiosity, race, gender, and trust in others.

Upon completion of the experiment, participants are taken to another room and given complete information about the nature of the game. All participants are given the full fifteen extra credit points; thus, each participant's final grade is not dependent on decisions made during the experiment. Informal questioning during the debriefing sessions led us to believe that subjects did indeed believe they were playing the game with two other human decision makers and that the decision makers had treated them unfairly. In other words, subjects expressed a strong indication that they perceived the scenario as real and that their selection for the second decision maker would have a significant impact on the number of points they would receive. This research design was approved by the institutional review board (IRB) at the institution from which participants were recruited.

Results

In presenting the experimental results, we first test whether people tend to associate ambition with male and self-serving behavior. We then analyze the results regarding the selection of the second decision maker. By presenting the results in this manner, we are able test the hypotheses that people associate ambition with male and self-interested behavior and that people will seek to offset ambitious decision makers with decision makers they perceive to be less ambitious and less likely to be self-serving.[3]

Figure 1 provides an analysis of perceptions of the gender of the first decision maker in each experimental condition. We expect people will be significantly more likely to predict that an ambitious first decision maker is male rather than female.

As the top portion of Figure 1 shows, in the high-ambition condition people are significantly more likely to predict the first decision maker is male as compared to female. That is, absent any information about the decision maker other than their strong desire for decision-making authority, people are significantly more likely to assume the decision maker is male compared to the condition in which the decision maker is presented as having a weak desire to be the decision maker. People thus tend to associate a desire for power with males.

If there is an innate tendency to associate high levels of ambition with males, we expect that subjects will respond more quickly to the "gender" item in the high-ambition condition compared to the low ambition condition. In the bottom portion of Figure 1, we present the response time of subjects to the "gender" item for both the high-ambition and low-ambition conditions.

The bottom portion of Figure 1 shows that subjects in the high-ambition condition are quicker to respond to the question about their perceptions of the gender of the first decision maker. The average response time for subjects in the high ambition condition was 2.7 seconds faster than the average response time for subjects in the low ambition condition, a difference that is statistically significant ($t = -1.72$; $p < .10$). We also analyzed the mean response time for subjects in the high-ambition condition only. Although not shown in Figure 1, within the high-ambition condition, the average response time for subjects who thought the first decision maker was male was 6.2 seconds faster than for subjects who thought the

FIGURE 1
THE EFFECTS OF AMBITION ON PERCEPTIONS OF GENDER

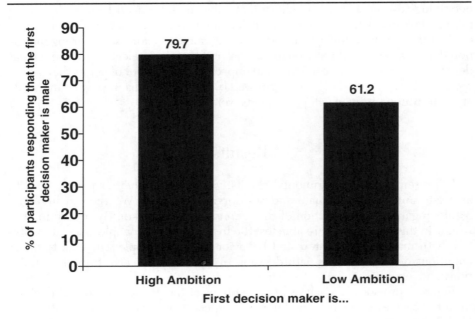

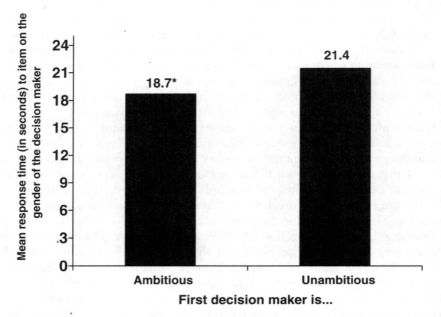

first decision maker was female ($t = -3.07$; $p < .01$), suggesting people are quick to assume ambitious decision makers are male; the association between ambition and male behavior appears to be more intuitive than the association between ambition and female behavior.

Figure 2 shows the effects of ambition on perceptions of self-interestedness and fairness. As Figure 2 demonstrates, people tend to equate ambition with self-serving behavior; in other words, they immediately associate a strong desire for power with negative ambition. Highly ambitious decision makers are perceived as significantly more likely to be self-interested and to be considerably less fair than decision makers who are low in ambition.

If you recall, in the experimental treatment, participants were asked to select a second decision maker from a list of candidates. After their selection, participants were told that the two decision makers had decided to keep twelve points for themselves and give the participant just three points. It is important to note that all participants received this highly unfavorable outcome. What Figure 2 illustrates is that people tend to associate the unfair outcome with the motivations of the first (negatively ambitious) decision maker. Highly ambitious decision makers are seen as being more responsible for the unfavorable outcome than less ambitious decision makers. This is demonstrated by evidence that highly ambitious decision makers are perceived as being more self-interested and less fair than the decision makers the participants chose.[4] This is further supported by our null findings regarding the perceptions of the decision makers as a group. Because people tend to associate the unfavorable outcome with the first decision maker, questions regarding the fairness of the two decision makers as a group do not differ statistically between experimental conditions. Taken with the results presented in Figure 1, this suggests high levels of ambition tend to be associated with unfair, self-interested, and male behavior.

Highly ambitious decision makers are seen as being more responsible for the unfavorable outcome than less ambitious decision makers.

In Figure 3, we examine whether expectations of the gender of the decision maker affect perceptions of fairness and self-interestedness. The top portion of Figure 3 shows that in the high-ambition condition, regardless of whether subjects think the first decision maker is male or female, both are equally as likely to identify this decision maker as the one most likely to be self-interested. However, in the low-ambition condition, there is a significant difference. Subjects who

FIGURE 2
THE EFFECTS OF AMBITION ON PERCEPTIONS
OF SELF-INTERESTEDNESS AND FAIRNESS

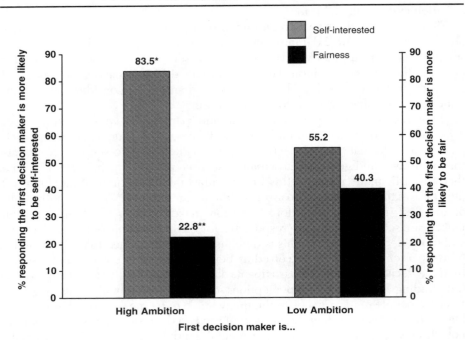

think the first decision maker is female are significantly less likely to identify this decision maker as the one most likely to be self-interested ($p < .10$). In other words, gender and ambition both affect perceptions of self-interestedness. While both ambitious and unambitious males are viewed as highly likely to engage in self-serving behavior, unambitious females are considered less likely to do so when compared to unambitious males.

The bottom portion of Figure 3 switches the focus from perceptions of self-interestedness to perceptions of fairness. In the high-ambition condition, subjects who think the first decision maker is male are significantly less likely to identify this decision maker as the one most likely to be fair compared to subjects who believe this decision maker is female ($p < .05$). In the low-ambition condition, subjects who believe the first decision maker is female are, again, more likely to identify this decision maker as the one most likely to be fair compared to subjects who believe the first decision maker is male. While substantively different, this result does not reach statistical significance ($p = .20$).

If you recall, Figure 2 suggests people tend to believe ambitious decision makers are less likely to be fair and more likely to be self-interested. However, the

FIGURE 3
THE EFFECTS OF PERCEPTIONS OF GENDER
AND AMBITION ON SELF-INTERESTEDNESS AND FAIRNESS

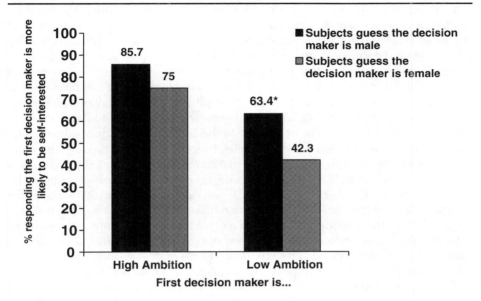

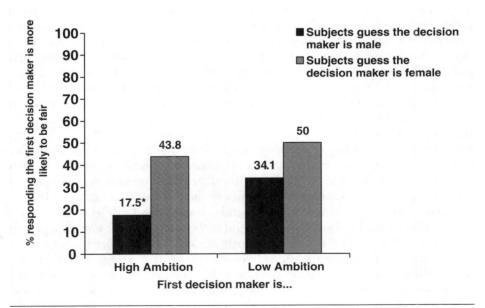

bottom portion of Figure 3 indicates an important interaction with gender. Ambitious females are viewed as significantly more likely to engage in fair behavior compared to ambitious males. In fact, Figure 3 also shows that *ambitious* females are identified as more likely to be fair by 43 percent of the subjects, while *unambitious* males are identified as more likely to be fair by only 34 percent of the subjects. While not a significant difference, it does suggest ambitious females do not evoke the same amount of skepticism associated with ambitious males.

Figure 3 demonstrates that people tend to assume ambitious decision makers are male and that the nature of this response is mediated by perceptions of gender. If ambition is associated with male and self-interested behavior as indicated by Figures 1 and 2, then we expect subjects who think an ambitious decision maker is male will respond more quickly to the "fairness" item than subjects who guess an ambitious decision maker is female. Indeed, subjects in the high-ambition condition who thought the first decision maker was male responded more quickly to the "fairness" item. The mean response time for subjects who thought the ambitious decision maker was male is 7.0 seconds compared to 9.7 seconds for subjects who thought the ambitious decision maker was female ($t = -1.93; p < .06$). Remember, in this experiment, subjects receive an unfair outcome (three out of fifteen points) from two decision makers, one of whom is either ambitious or unambitious. If there is an inherent tendency to associate "big-man" behavior with males, then people should respond more quickly to items regarding the gender and fairness of "big men." Our results indicate people do just that.

The next step is to examine who participants are choosing to be the second decision maker in the experiment. Recall that we are interested in people's reactions to ambitious leaders, specifically what type of leaders people see as appropriate "leveling mechanisms" for ambitious leaders. A descriptive analysis regarding the selection of the second decision maker in each experimental condition indicates that participants overwhelmingly selected high-ambition females to be the second decision maker in the experiment. Moreover, there is no statistical difference between the experimental conditions. In both conditions, participants are more likely to select high-ambition females as the second decision maker (58.2 percent in the high-ambition condition, 53.7 percent in the low-ambition condition).[5] This suggests that females, unlike males, may benefit from being highly ambitious under certain conditions. But do perceptions of gender of ambitious decision makers affect votes for other decision makers? To explore this question, we examine the relationship between perceptions of gender of the first decision maker and selection of a high-ambition female as the second decision maker in Figure 4.

Focusing on the high-ambition condition in the top portion of Figure 4, people who assume the first decision maker is male are significantly more likely to select a high-ambition female as the second decision maker than people who think the first decision maker is female. In the low-ambition condition, we do not find any difference between perceptions of the gender of the first decision maker and selection of a high-ambition female as the second decision maker. In other words, it appears that gender interacts with ambition in the selection of decision makers. Female decision makers with high levels of ambition are a preferred leveling

FIGURE 4
THE EFFECTS OF GENDER AND AMBITION
ON DECISION-MAKER SELECTION

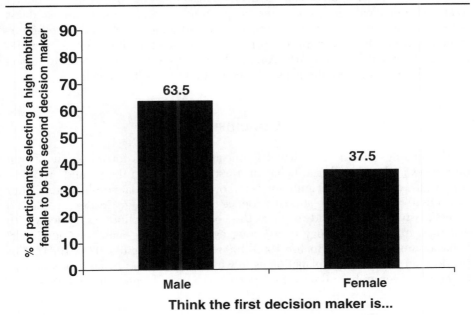

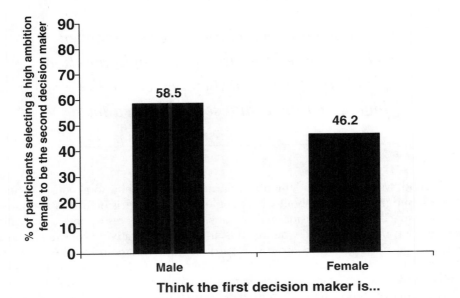

mechanism—they are seen as a way to rein in ambitious male decision makers. Because women are perceived as more compassionate than men (Huddy and Terkildsen 1993), an ambitious female decision maker may be an appropriate counter to an ambitious male decision maker. People tend to associate self-interestedness with males and therefore prefer a female to offset a high likelihood of self-interested behavior. They do not prefer just any female, however, but a female as ambitious as their male counterparts. And, as Figure 3 shows, people tend to expect fairer behavior from ambitious females compared to ambitious males.

Conclusion

The findings of our study have significant implications for the study of trait inferences and mass political behavior. First, we provide a theory and empirical support for why the trait of ambition is important for candidate evaluation. Kinder et al. (1980) provided correlational evidence that power-hungry leaders are viewed as less trustworthy. Our study explains this correlation. Our findings fit nicely with evidence from anthropology of a strong aversion to "big-man" or "dominant" behavior among leaders (Boehm 1999, 1993; Erdal and Whiten 1996, 1994). This provides an interesting explanation as to why the public has reacted vociferously to public power grabs and what they perceive to be self-aggrandizing behavior.

Given one highly ambitious decision maker, people are more likely to select a high-ambition female to offset what they perceive to be a highly ambitious and self-interested male.

Second, we show that judgments of fairness and the behavioral consequences of those judgments is less about what people get from a decision maker and more about a specific set of decision maker traits. Ambition serves as both a cue as to the gender of a person and whether this ambition is negative or positive. These cues shape perceptions of fairness, regardless of the outcome of the decision. Furthermore, we find an important effect for the interaction between gender and ambition on decision-maker selection. Regardless of the ambition of the first decision maker, people tend to prefer highly ambitious females as the second decision maker. Even more revealing, in the high-ambition condition, if participants believe the first decision maker is a male, there is a significant increase in the number of high-ambition females selected to be the second decision maker. In other words, given one highly ambitious decision maker, people are more likely to select a high-ambition female to offset what they perceive to be a highly ambitious and self-interested male. This suggests female ambition is perceived as something different from male ambition.

Third, our argument has important implications for research on gender stereotypes and representation. Scholars of candidate traits consistently find that women tend to be at a trait disadvantage to men in terms of being perceived as "competent" for electoral office (see Huddy and Terkildsen 1993). However, the empirical results presented here suggest women have a trait advantage over men. Specifically, people tend to associate high levels of ambition with male behavior. Decision makers who crave power are perceived as less fair, more self-interested, and most likely male. Moreover, people are quicker to respond to questions about the gender of ambitious decision makers, suggesting people are quick to assume ambitious decision makers are male. Because people tend to view ambition negatively, independent of outcomes, ambitious women are at an advantage to ambitious men. In fact, ambitious decision makers believed to be female are viewed as more likely to be fair than *unambitious* decision makers believed to be male (see Figure 3). High-ambition females were also the most selected candidate in both conditions of the experiment. More pointedly, however, what fueled the selection of a high-ambition female was the belief in the presence of a high-ambition male.

Decision makers who crave power are perceived as less fair, more self-interested, and most likely male.

Notes

1. For discussion and treatment of the various trait dimensions, see Bartels (2002); Funk (1996, 1999); Kinder et al. (1980); Kinder (1986); King (2002); Miller and Shanks (1996); Miller, Wattenberg, and Malanchuk (1986).

2. Ambition is a strong trait of political leaders, but studies of ambition in political science focus on self-reported levels of ambition, not the behavioral responses ambition might trigger in others (e.g., Maestas 2003; Ehrenhalt 1992; Schlesinger 1966).

3. Due to random assignment, there were seventy-nine participants in the high-ambition condition and sixty-seven participants in the low-ambition condition. The gender composition of the high-ambition and low-ambition condition was 59 percent male and 49 percent male, respectively, and the mean age in each condition was 19.97 and 20.03 years, respectively.

4. Although not presented in this article, the results of figures 1 and 2 are further corroborated by logistic models. Controlling for additional covariates such as perceptions of trust, gender of the participant, year

in school, major, ideology, party, income, religiosity, and race, the only significant predictor is the experimental condition.

5. In the high-ambition condition, high-ambition males were selected by 21.5 percent of the subjects, low-ambition males by 3.8 percent of the subjects, and low-ambition females by 16.5 percent of the subjects. In the low-ambition condition, high-ambition males were selected by 19.4 percent of the subjects, low-ambition males by 6 percent of the subjects, and low-ambition females by 20.9 percent of the subjects.

References

Alexander, Deborah, and Kristi Anderson. 1993. Gender as a factor in the attribution of leadership traits. *Political Research Quarterly* 46:527-45.

Ammeter, Anthony P., Ceasar Douglas, William L. Gardner, Wayne A. Hochwarter, and Gerald R. Ferris. 2002. Toward a political theory of leadership. *The Leadership Quarterly* 13:751-96.

Bartels, Larry M. 2002. The impact of candidate traits in American presidential elections. In *Leaders' personalities and the outcomes of democratic elections*, ed. Anthony King. New York: Oxford University Press.

Boehm, Christopher. 1993. Egalitarian behavior and reverse dominance hierarchy. *Current Anthropology* 34:227-54.

———. 1997. Egalitarianism and political intelligence. In *Machiavellian intelligence II: Extensions and evaluations*, ed. Andrew Whiten and Richard W. Byrne. Cambridge: Cambridge University Press.

———. 1999. *Hierarchy in the forest: The evolution of egalitarian behavior*. Cambridge, MA: Harvard University Press.

Buss, David M. 1996. Sexual conflict: Evolutionary insights into feminism and the "battle of the sexes." In *Sex, power, conflict*, ed. David M. Buss and Neil M. Malamuth. New York: Oxford University Press.

Campbell, Anne. 2002. *A mind of her own: The evolutionary psychology of women*. New York: Oxford University Press.

Campbell, Angus, Philip E. Converse, Warren E. Miller, and Donald E. Stokes. 1960. *The American voter*. New York: Wiley.

Cornog, Evan. 2004. *The power and the story: How the crafted presidential narrative has determined political success from George Washington to George W. Bush*. New York: Penguin.

Eagly, Alice H. 1995. The science and politics of comparing women and men. *American Psychologist* 50:145-58.

Ehrenhalt, Alan. 1992. *The United States of ambition: Politicians, power, and the pursuit of office*. New York: Times Books.

Erdal, David, and Andrew Whiten. 1994. On human egalitarianism: An evolutionary product of Machiavellian status escalation? *Current Anthropology* 35:175-83.

———. 1996. Egalitarianism and Machiavellian intelligence in human evolution. In *Modeling the early human mind*, ed. Paul Mellars and Kathleen Gibson. McDonald Institute Monograph. Cambridge, UK: McDonald Institute for Archaeological Research.

Ferree, Myra, Judith Lorber, and Beth Hess. 1999. Introduction. In *Revisioning gender*, ed. Myra Ferree, Judith Lorber, and Beth Hess. Thousand Oaks, CA: Sage.

Funk, Carolyn L. 1996. Understanding trait inferences in candidate images. In *Research in micropolitics*, ed. Michael X. Delli Carpini, Leonie Huddy, and Robert Y. Shapiro. Greenwich, CT: JAI.

———. 1999. Bringing the candidate into models of candidate evaluation. *Journal of Politics* 61:700-720.

Hibbing, John R., and John R. Alford. 2004. Accepting authoritative decisions: Humans as wary cooperators. *American Journal of Political Science* 48:62-76.

Hibbing, John R., and Elizabeth Theiss-Morse. 1995. *Congress as public enemy: Public attitudes toward American political institutions*. Cambridge: Cambridge University Press.

———. 2002. *Stealth democracy: Americans' belief about how government should work*. New York: Cambridge University Press.

Huddy, Leonie, and Nayda Terkildsen. 1993. Gender stereotypes and the perception of male and female candidates. *American Journal of Political Science* 37:119-47.

Kennedy, Carole. 2003. Gender difference in committee decision-making: Process and outputs in an experimental setting. *Women and Politics* 25: 27-45.

Kinder, Donald R. 1986. Presidential character revisited. In *Political cognition: The 19th Annual Carnegie Symposium on Cognition*, ed. Richard R. Lau and David O. Sears. Hillsdale, NJ: Lawrence Erlbaum.

Kinder, Donald R., Mark D. Peters, Robert P. Abelson, and Susan T. Fiske. 1980. Presidential prototypes. *Political Behavior* 2:315-37.

King, Anthony. 2002. Do leaders' personalities really matter? In *Leaders' personalities and the outcomes of democratic elections*, ed. Anthony King. New York: Oxford University Press.

Knauft, Bruce. 1994. Reply to Erdal and Whiten. *Current Anthropology* 35:181-82.

Lau, Richard R. 1986. Political schemata, candidate evaluations, and voting behavior. In *Political cognition: The 19th Annual Carnegie Symposium on Cognition*, ed. Richard R. Lau and David O. Sears. Hillsdale, NJ: Lawrence Erlbaum.

Machiavelli, Niccolo. 1515/2004. *The prince.* Edited by Quentin Skinner, and Russell Price. Cambridge: Cambridge University Press.

Madison, James. 1788/2003. Federalist no. 51: The structure of the government must furnish the proper checks and balances between the different departments. In *The federalist papers*, ed. Clinton Rossiter. New York: Signet Classics.

Maestas, Cherie. 2003. The incentive to listen: Progressive ambition, resources, and opinion monitoring among state legislators. *Journal of Politics* 65:439-56.

Miller, Arthur H., Martin P. Wattenberg, and Oksana Malanchuk. 1986. Schematic assessments of presidential candidates. *American Political Science Review* 80:521-40.

Miller, Warren E., and J. Merrill Shanks. 1996. *The new American voter.* Cambridge, MA: Harvard University Press.

Pinker, Steven. 1997. *How the mind works.* New York: Norton.

Pratto, Felicia. 1996. Sexual politics: The gender gap in the bedroom, the cupboard, and the cabinet. In *Sex, power, and conflict: Evolutionary and feminist perspectives*, ed. David M. Buss and Neil M. Malamuth. New York: Oxford University Press.

Rahn, Wendy M., John H. Aldrich, Eugene Borgida, and John L. Sullivan. 1990. A social-cognitive model of candidate appraisal. In *Information and democratic processes*, ed. John A. Ferejohn and James H. Kuklinski. Urbana: University of Illinois Press.

Ridgeway, Cecilia, and Lynn Smith-Lovin, 1999. The gender system and interaction. *Annual Review of Sociology* 25:191-216.

Ridley, Matt. 2003. *Nature via nurture: Genes, experience, and what makes us human.* New York: HarperCollins.

Rosenthal, Cindy Simon. 1998. *When women lead: Integrative leadership in state legislatures.* New York: Oxford University Press.

Sanbonmatsu, Kira. 2002. Gender stereotypes and vote choice. *American Journal of Political Science* 46:20-34.

Schlesinger, Joseph A. 1966. *Ambition and politics: Political careers in the United States Senate.* Chicago: Rand NcNally.

Shapiro, Virginia. 2003. Theorizing gender in political psychology research. In *The Oxford handbook of political psychology*, ed. David O. Sears, Leonie Huddy, and Robert Jervis. New York: Oxford University Press.

Stokes, Donald E. 1966. Some dynamic elements of contests for the presidency. *American Political Science Review* 60:19-28.

Tyler, Tom R. 2000. Social justice: Outcome and procedure. *International Journal of Psychology* 35:117-25.

Tyler, Tom R., and E. A. Lind 1992. A relational model of authority in groups. *Advances in Experimental Social Psychology* 25:115-91.

Van Vugt, Mark, Sarah F. Jepson, Claire M. Hart, and David De Cremer. 2004. Autocratic leadership in social dilemmas: A threat to group stability. *Journal of Experimental Social Psychology* 40:1-13.

Witt, Linda, Karen Paget, and Glenna Matthews. 1995. *Running as a woman: Gender and power in American politics.* New York: Free Press.

An Evolutionary Model of Racial Attitude Formation: Socially Shared and Idiosyncratic Racial Attitudes

By
THOMAS CRAEMER

A growing body of research in political science has uncovered evidence of a "split personality" among Americans when it comes to racial attitudes—people express different attitudes in public than they personally hold. At present *no* theoretical model can account for the emergence of this discrepancy. This article proposes a simple neural model of racial attitude formation that makes an important distinction between *socially shared* and *idiosyncratic* racial attitudes. A computational model based on Kimura's (1983) Neutral Theory of Evolution predicts that *socially shared* racist attitudes may be able to coexist with, and eventually be replaced by, more favorable *idiosyncratic* racial attitudes. Results of a laboratory-based study ($N = 555$) involving reaction-time-based implicit measures of *socially shared* and *idiosyncratic* attitudes are consistent with the predictions derived from the computational model. The implications of the theoretical model and the empirical findings are discussed.

Keywords: implicit racial attitudes; explicit racial attitudes; affirmative action; cognitive overlap; computational modeling; Hebbian learning; neutral theory of evolution; random drift

1. Introduction

A growing body of research in political science and social psychology has uncovered evidence of a "split personality" among Americans when it comes to racial attitudes (e.g., Devine 1989; Terkildsen 1993; Fazio et al. 1995; Greenwald, McGhee, and Schwarz 1995; Kuklinski, Cobb, and Gilens 1997; Berinsky 2004; Feldman and Huddy 2005). People appear to voice different attitudes publicly than privately when given the

Thomas Craemer received his PhD from Stony Brook University (2005) and a doctorate from the University of Tuebingen. Currently he is an assistant professor at the University of Connecticut's Department of Public Policy. He recently received a faculty grant to investigate implicit and explicit racial attitudes and their impact on public opinion regarding slavery reparations and other current issues.

DOI: 10.1177/0002716207305979

opportunity to express their personal views anonymously (e.g., Kuklinski, Cobb, and Gilens 1997). This discrepancy is often interpreted as a social desirability effect among White[1] Americans who engage in self-monitoring. According to this interpretation, self-monitoring White respondents may adjust their old-fashioned, unfavorable views of African Americans to a new, pro-Black norm of political correctness. To control for this social desirability effect, some researchers use Snyder and Gangestad's (1986) self-monitoring scale (e.g., Terkildsen 1993; Berinsky 2004; Feldman and Huddy 2005). Other researchers attempt to measure unfavorable attitudes directly outside the respondents' awareness using reaction time measures (Devine 1989; Fazio et al. 1995; Greenwald, McGhee, and Schwarz 1995). They generally find a powerful pro-White and anti-Black bias among their White respondents on the nonconscious (implicit) level even among respondents who express favorable views on the conscious (explicit) level. Reviewing a large volume of evidence from the Implicit Association Test (IAT) in different domains of explicit and implicit attitudes, ranging from race and ethnicity to gender and age stereotypes, Greenwald et al. (2002, 18) detect a general "empirical dissociation between the two types of measures." Social desirability explanations of this dissociation seem to imply that explicit attitudes are more susceptible to social norms than implicit ones. This may lead to the interpretation that implicit attitudes more faithfully represent an individual's "personal" attitudes. A radically different interpretation is implied by the model of dual attitudes proposed by Wilson, Lindsey, and Schooler (2000). According to this model, implicit and explicit attitude measures tap different aspects of an individual's attitudes, both of which may be influenced by personal feelings or social norms. The main difference is that implicit attitudes tend to reflect attitudes that have been rehearsed for a longer period of time and have become automatic. Such automatic responses require no conscious thought, while newer attitudes require conscious effort. According to their interpretation, explicit attitudes may be just as genuine as implicit ones, and they compare the rehearsal process to motor skills such as playing the piano or playing tennis. The conscious attempt to rehearse a new musical piece or a new serve cannot be interpreted as a disingenuous attempt at yielding to social norms, but as a genuine desire to play well. Similarly, favorable attitudes toward African Americans on the explicit level may represent a genuine desire to adopt a positive attitude, rather than a superficial attempt to satisfy social norms.

Whether social norms lead individuals to publicly misstate their personally held attitudes, or whether they infuse individuals with a genuine desire to adopt and rehearse new attitudes, neither interpretation offers a scenario that could explain how these social norms may emerge. This article provides a simple theoretical model of racial norms evolution that is based on a few simple assumptions about neural organization and social communication. This model will be explained in the following section. A number of hypotheses are derived from the model and empirically tested based on a sample of 555 college students in section 3. Finally, section 4 presents simulation results based on a computational version of the racial norms evolution model and compares the patterns observed in the simulations to the patterns observed in the student experiment.

2. A Simple Model of Racial Norms Evolution

The model of racial norms evolution proposed in this article combines intrapersonal properties of neural brain organization with interpersonal properties of social communication processes. On the intrapersonal level, it assumes that sensory perceptions of *internal* body states and sensory perceptions of *external* stimuli are processed in different brain regions (see section 2.1). The model further assumes that both types of sensory perception, internal as well as external, are subjected to a process of Hebbian learning (Hebb 1949), whereby repeated rehearsal leads to automaticity. This process is equivalent to the rehearsal process described in Wilson, Lindsey, and Schooler's (2000) dual attitude model. Its neural basis will be described in greater detail in section 2.2. Finally, on the interpersonal level, the model of racial norms evolution is inspired by Motoo Kimura's (1983) Neutral Theory of Evolution. It predicts the emergence of dominant norms by random drift even in the absence of selective advantages. This aspect of the model will be described in section 2.3.

2.1. Idiosyncratic and socially shared attitudes

The *idiosyncratic versus socially shared* distinction is based on the assumption that sensory perceptions of internal body states (internal stimuli) are processed in different brain regions than sensory perceptions of environmental events (external stimuli). While the latter can be observed by a number of individuals at the same time, the former is perceived only by the individual. When people communicate, it is easier to reach agreement about external stimuli than about internal ones. In addition, communications by others (whether in verbal form, in body language, or other symbols) enter the individual's brain as external stimuli and may be easier to communicate to others simply because they are received in an already communicable format. In contrast, internal body states enter the brain as diffuse sensations that are more difficult to translate into a communicable format. Due to high levels of interconnectivity within the brain, these two regions are not assumed to be isolated but rather to be interconnected in a peculiar form: idiosyncratic perceptions of internal body states can be expressed in a communicable format with probability p(idiosyncratic) reflecting the level of difficulty expressing internal sensations. It may be easier, for example, to express the internal body state of "feeling hungry" than the complex sensation of feeling a "sense of chemistry" with a complete stranger.[2]

It is important to note that the expression of idiosyncratically perceived internal body states is a one-way street. External perceptions of environmental stimuli, including communications from others, are assumed to be unable to systematically influence internal body states. This is not an arbitrary assumption; it is rooted in the consideration that the same external stimulus may elicit very different body reactions in two different individuals. For example, a seafood connoisseur and an individual who is allergic to seafood may be able to talk about "seafood" based on a socially shared understanding of language.

However, it will be associated with pleasant internal body states in the connoisseur and highly unpleasant ones in the allergic individual. No amount of emphasis on the part of the connoisseur of how delicious seafood is will be able to eliminate the unpleasant body state in the allergic individual. Figure 1 represents the spatial distinction between idiosyncratic attitudes (*i*) based on the perception of internal body states and socially shared attitudes (*s*) based on external stimulation. It is important to note that *no anatomical accuracy is implied*; the spatial *separation*, not the exact location, is of importance for the model proposed here.

It may be easier . . . to express the internal body state of "feeling hungry" than the complex sensation of feeling a "sense of chemistry" with a complete stranger.

2.2. Implicit and explicit attitudes

In line with Wilson, Lindsey, and Schooler's (2000) dual attitude model, the model of racial norms evolution assumes that frequently repeated (well-rehearsed) thoughts, feelings, or motor functions are processed significantly faster than not so frequently repeated ones. This rehearsal effect is based on the principle of Hebbian learning. Donald O. Hebb (1949) formulated this principle based on the observation that the synaptic gap between two connected neurons tends to grow narrower with repeated simultaneous activation of the two neurons. The narrower the gap, the faster the signal transmission between the two neurons. Thus, frequently repeated thoughts, feelings, or motor functions are executed significantly faster than new thoughts, feelings, or motor functions. The principle of Hebbian learning leads to associative learning in artificial neural nets and may provide a neural basis to Wilson, Lindsey, and Schooler's dual attitudes model as well as to the implicit-explicit attitude distinction made in the racial norms evolution model proposed here. The principle of Hebbian learning suggests that both types of racial attitudes discussed in section 2.1—*idiosyncratic* as well as *socially shared*—should become automatic after frequent activation (rehearsal). Thus, both types of racial attitudes should be detectable on the implicit level, outside of an individual's conscious control. This leads to a two-by-two classification scheme of racial attitudes distinguishing (1) *implicit idiosyncratic attitudes*, (2) *implicit socially shared attitudes*, (3) *explicit idiosyncratic attitudes*, and (4) *explicit socially shared attitudes*. Possible measurement methods for these four types of racial attitudes are discussed in section 3.

FIGURE 1
DISTINCTION BETWEEN IDIOSYNCRATIC (*i*) VERSUS SOCIALLY
SHARED ATTITUDES (*s*)

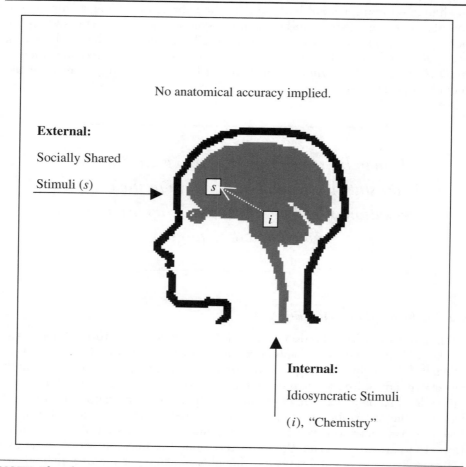

NOTE: The white arrow indicates the probability that an idiosyncratic attitude will be translated into an externally communicable format, *p*(idiosyncratic).

2.3. Random norms evolution

In addition to the two intrapersonal processes described in sections 2.1 and 2.2, the model of racial norms evolution contains an interpersonal element that links various individual neural networks in a social network. Within this network, neighbors communicate with one another and exchange their socially shared attitudes (denoted *s* in Figure 1). The fact that they exchange socially shared attitudes rather than idiosyncratic ones is based on the fact that these attitudes are already stored in a communicable format while idiosyncratic attitudes require translation into such a format (see section 2.1). When two neighbors communicate, one neighbor is randomly designated as "persuader" and the other as "persuadee." The persuadee is assumed to adopt the socially shared attitude of the persuader. Since each individual has exactly the same probability of being designated persuader or persuadee, no selection mechanism for a particular attitude is built into the model that could explain why a given attitude becomes socially dominant. Nonetheless, a process invariably occurs by which one out of any number of equal alternatives eventually emerges as a socially dominant majority attitude. This process, referred to in biological theory as "random drift," has been mathematically analyzed by Motoo Kimura (1983) in his Neutral Theory of Evolution.

A process invariably occurs by which one out of any number of equal alternatives eventually emerges as a socially dominant majority attitude. This process [is] referred to in biological theory as "random drift."

Since this evolutionary model is new to the social sciences, a brief description of its biological origin is in place. It was developed by Kimura (1983) to explain evolutionary phenomena that cannot be explained by the Darwinian principle of natural selection. It became necessary when molecular geneticists in the late 1960s, to their own surprise, encountered unequal distributions of selectively neutral synonymous alleles. Synonymous alleles are different DNA sequences that code for the same protein. Since an organism's selective advantage relies on the proteins it is composed of, these synonymous DNA sequences are indistinguishable from one another by natural selection. This puzzle was solved by the strange dynamic of the Neutral Theory of Evolution (Kimura 1983) that demonstrates how a purely random process will inevitably lead to distinct patterns in which one neutral alternative will dominate and eventually replace other equal alternatives. Kimura stated, "The neutral theory asserts that the great majority of evolutionary changes at the molecular level . . . are caused not by Darwinian selection but by random drift of selectively neutral . . . mutagens" (Kimura 1983, S. xi). By virtue of the fact that Kimura's theory emphasizes the formative power of random mutational processes, it has become the dominant theory of evolution on the molecular level. Interestingly, the use of random evolution models in political science precedes Kimura's neutral theory. In 1963, William N. McPhee proposed a "Campaign Simulator" (1963, 169) based on similar ideas, and together with his colleagues Jack Ferguson and Robert B. Smith, he applied a related model to voting behavior (McPhee, Ferguson, and Smith 1963). Due to the popularity of Darwinian models in social science applications, however, the power of Kimura's neutral evolution remains largely unexplored in contemporary political science. The main advantage of Kimura's neutral evolution model is its maximal parsimony, which makes it attractive as a null model against which more restrictive theories can be tested.

When all three elements of the racial norms evolution model are taken together—the distinction between idiosyncratic versus socially shared attitudes described in section 2.1, the distinction between implicit and explicit attitudes described in section 2.2 (see also Wilson, Lindsey, and Schooler 2000), and the phenomenon of "random drift" based on Kimura's (1983) Theory of Neutral Evolution—a number of predictions can be derived. First, due to the dynamic of Kimura's Neutral Theory of Evolution, we should observe a single attitude become a dominant social norm even in an otherwise random communication process. Based on the idea that socially shared and idiosyncratic attitudes may be processed in different brain regions (see section 2.1), the expectation naturally follows that over time idiosyncratic attitudes and socially shared ones should diverge for most individuals on topics that are widely discussed in the population. Furthermore, attitudes (whether idiosyncratic or socially shared) that have been held by the individual for a longer period of time should tend to become automatic due to the process of Hebbian attitude rehearsal described in section 2.2 (compare also Wilson, Lindsey, and Schooler 2000). Section 3 will discuss possible measures of implicit idiosyncratic and implicit socially shared attitudes, and it will present empirical findings based on a college student study ($N = 555$). Section 4 will compare the patterns observed in the student study to simulation results based on a computational version of the racial norms evolution model described in this section.

3. Empirical Measures and Empirical Results ($N = 555$)

For the purpose of empirical study, a number of measurement methods exist that may be able to tap into the different types of attitudes distinguished here. Aron et al. (1991) developed a trait-based reaction time task to measure implicit feelings of closeness among individual partners in close relationships (implicit idiosyncratic attitudes). This method has been successfully applied to measure implicit feelings of closeness toward social groups (Coats et al. 2000; Smith and Henry 1996) and will be described in greater detail in section 3.1. Explicit idiosyncratic attitudes are more difficult to measure in an empirical setting, especially if they deviate from social norms. Due to their private nature, people may be reluctant to express them to a stranger in a survey inter-view. To measure implicit aspects of socially shared attitudes, racial priming measures are applied in this study (implicit socially shared attitudes). These measures rely on association of word meaning (positive or negative) and are likely to be socially shared by virtue of the fact that language, by its very nature, is socially shared. The implicit racial priming measure applied in this study will be described in section 3.2. Finally, to measure socially shared explicit atti-tudes, traditional survey measures are used—questions like "How close do you feel towards African Americans?" and "How close do you feel towards White Americans?" as well as standard Feeling Thermometer ratings. Survey responses allow participants sufficient time to consciously monitor their responses, and, in a politically sensitive area such as race, it is likely that some respondents will adjust their responses to conform to dominant social norms. In the following two sections, the two main implicit measurement procedures that were obtained for this study will be explained: implicit closeness toward African Americans and White Americans (section 3.1) and implicit racial priming (section 3.2).

3.1. Measuring idiosyncratic racial attitudes implicitly

Idiosyncratic measures of closeness toward African Americans and White Americans were obtained utilizing a timed trait self-rating procedure developed by Arthur Aron and his collaborators (1991). This measure operationalizes the idea that feelings of closeness may originate from an overlap of representations for the self and others in an individual's mind. Their reaction-time-based implicit measure was originally developed to measure feelings of closeness between part-ners in individual relationships. It has been successfully applied to the group level by Eliot R. Smith and Susan Henry (1996), as well as Susan Coats and her col-laborators (2000). In both studies, the timed trait rating procedure was used to measure subjective closeness between the self and a non-political group (a soror-ity or fraternity). Coats et al. also investigated whether the implicit closeness measure would correlate with explicit paper-and-pencil measures of closeness. They found a strong correspondence between explicit and implicit closeness measures, a finding that does not seem surprising since the in-groups and out-groups they used (sororities and fraternities) appear innocuous from a social desirability point of view. Coats et al. wrote, "The advantages of implicit measures are obvious. They are not subject to self presentational or social desirability con-cerns. In addition, because implicit measures tap nonconscious, uncontrolled cognitive elements, they are less subject to demand characteristics" (313). This makes the application of the implicit closeness measure particularly attractive to the sensitive area of race and politics.

The timed trait self-rating task proceeds in two steps, an initial trait survey, and, after a distracter task, the actual timed self-rating procedure (see Figure 2). The first step is required for classification purposes (a detailed description is

FIGURE 2
SCHEMATIC REPRESENTATION OF IMPLICIT CLOSENESS
MEASUREMENT PROCEDURE

Implicit Closeness Measure

Based on Aron et al. (1991)

- **Step (1) Trait Survey:** Rating Self, African Americans, and Whites on 90 Traits:

  ```
  "ALERT" Is this trait descriptive of (you as an individual /
  African Americans as a group / white Americans as a group)?
  1 = "Not at all"; 4="Moderately" 7 = "Extremely"
  ```

- **Step (2) Timed Trait Rating Task:** (after a distracter task and a break) Rating Self Only:

  ```
  Ask yourself this question:
  'Does this trait describe ME as an individual?'
  "ALERT"
  Yes, No.
  ```

provided in Appendix A; see also Craemer 2006) while the actual implicit closeness measure is obtained in the second step. In the following paragraphs, both steps of the procedure will be described in detail.

In the first step of the procedure (see Figure 2), each individual participant is asked to rate each of the ninety personality trait words listed in Table A1 in Appendix A as descriptive of the self, of "White Americans as a group," and of "African Americans as a group."[3] Responses are given on a 7-point scale ranging from (1) *not at all* to (7) *extremely* descriptive with option (4) labeled as *neutral*. Based on these ratings, each trait is classified as either matching between the individual and a given group, or as mismatching. Note, although the meaning of the trait words themselves is likely to be socially shared, the question whether any given trait is descriptive of the respondent is highly idiosyncratic. Furthermore, the self-ratings and group ratings in this first step of the procedure are *not* used to measure closeness, they serve for classification purposes only and allow the researcher to identify "matching" and "mismatching" traits. A matching trait is one that the individual respondent uses to describe both, the self, *and* a given group; and a mismatching trait is one that the individual uses to describe only the self and not the group or vice versa. The actual measure of closeness occurs in the second step of the procedure in the timed self-rating task.

The timed self-rating task is the most crucial component of the implicit closeness measure. Each of the ninety trait words appears on the computer screen, and the participant is asked to indicate as quickly as possible whether each word

TABLE 1
COMPUTING IMPLICIT CLOSENESS TO A GROUP (EXAMPLE)

Trait	Trait Survey		Timed Self-Description	
	Descriptive of . . .			
	. . . Self?	. . . Group?	Classification	Reaction Time (t)
"Alert"	Yes	Yes	Matching Trait	Facilitation (faster t)
"Neat"	No	Yes	Mismatching Trait	Inhibition (slower t)

Example: A participant who describes herself as "alert" but not "neat" feels close to a group that she describes as both "alert" and "neat": Implicit Closeness Score = mean(t_{Mismatch}) − mean(t_{Match}) > 0.

is self-descriptive. The instructions read, "Ask yourself this question: 'Does this trait describe ME as an individual?'" followed by a trait word, for example, "ALERT" (see Figure 2). The participant then presses a button labeled as "yes" or "no" as quickly as possible to record the response. What renders the timed trait rating measure implicit is the fact that the timed trait description only refers to the self. No reference is made to groups at this point. The psychological phenomenon that makes this procedure viable as an implicit measure of closeness is the curious fact that distinct facilitation and inhibition patterns occur for groups the individual feels close to, while no such patterns occur for groups with whom the individual does *not* feel close. If, in the mind of a respondent, he or she shares a trait with a close group, the trait is significantly more quickly identified as self-descriptive (facilitation). If the self differs from a close group on a trait, the trait is identified significantly more slowly as self-descriptive (inhibition). No such facilitation or inhibition effects occur for groups with whom the individual does not feel close. Table 1 shows an example for a participant who describes herself as "alert" but not "neat" and who feels close to a group that she describes as both "alert" *and* "neat." Since she rates both herself *and* the group as "alert," the researcher classifies this trait as a self-group "match"; and since the participant rates the group but not herself as "neat," the researcher classifies that trait as a self-group "mismatch." If the participant feels close to the group, her reaction time will be faster in describing herself as "alert" (the "matching" trait), while her reaction time in describing herself as "neat" (the "mismatching" trait) will be slowed down. The resulting difference between the respondent's average responses to mismatching and to matching traits can be converted into an implicit closeness score according to the formula given in Table 1. This score will be greater than zero (0) if the participant feels close to the group, and it will be indistinguishable from zero if the participant does *not* feel close to the group. For details on how the measures were obtained and converted into implicit closeness scores, see Table A2 in Appendix A (see also Craemer 2006).

These characteristic facilitation and inhibition effects that occur for close others and groups are interpreted by Aron et al. (1991) as indicating an overlap between the self-representation and the representation of others in the mind of an individual, "an actual overlap or confusion of cognitive structures" (249). They wrote, "A possible explanation of the . . . effect is that the cognitive structure of the self overlaps with the cognitive structure about the other. . . . Thus when a trait is descriptive of self but not other, there is a bit of confusion in deciding whether it actually represents the self" (248).

3.2. Measuring socially shared racial attitudes implicitly

To measure socially shared implicit racial attitudes, an implicit priming procedure was employed. The methodology of implicit priming was originally developed by James H. Neely (1977) and adapted for the purpose of measuring racial attitudes by Greenwald, McGhee, and Schwarz (1995), as well as Fazio et al. (1995). The Implicit Association Test (IAT) developed by Greenwald, McGhee, and Schwarz (1995) and Fazio's et al. (1995) racial priming method differ in a number of respects, but they share the idea that the positive or negative meaning of a prime word that flashes up on the participant's computer screen is associated with the meaning of an otherwise unrelated target word. The participant is asked to indicate as quickly as possible whether the target word has a positive or negative meaning by pressing a button. Table 2 lists the prime and target words used for this study. To exclude conscious control on the part of the participant, prime words were displayed for a mere 20 ms, too fast for conscious recognition. Thus, for participants, only the target words were consciously visible on the computer screen, appearing after a brief flash. The target words were selected from M. M. Bradley and P. J. Lang's (1999) List of Affective Norms for English Words (ANEW) and are listed in Table 2 along with their mean valence ratings.[4] A participant who associates negative meaning with Black racial primes will be able to recognize the target word "joy" as positive more quickly when it follows the prime word "White" than when it follows the prime word "Black." Similarly, the participant will recognize the target word "funeral" as negative more quickly when it follows the word "African American" than when it follows the word "White American." For details on how the measures were obtained and converted into racial priming scores, see Craemer (2005).

3.3. Results based on 555 college students

A sample of 555 undergraduate students participated in this study for credit at the Department of Political Science at Stony Brook University during the fall semester of 2003 and during the spring term of 2004. The demographic profile of the sample is not representative of the United States, but it closely reflects the racial and ethnic composition of the undergraduate student body at Stony Brook. Fifteen percent of the sample consisted of international students (non-U.S. citizens of any race) while 85 percent consisted of U.S. citizens. Of these, 47 percent

TABLE 2
RACIAL PRIMING: PRIME AND TARGET WORDS

Prime Words	Target Words	Mean Valence	Standard Deviation
	Love	8.72	0.70
	Joy	8.60	0.71
"Black"	Friendly	8.43	1.08
	Win	8.38	0.92
"African American"	Success	8.29	0.93
	Funeral	1.39	0.87
"White"	Cancer	1.50	0.85
	Rejected	1.50	1.09
"White American"	Sad	1.61	0.95
	Death	1.61	1.40

NOTE: Target words and mean valence ratings for target words from Bradley and Lang (1999).

self-identified as White non-Hispanic, 10 percent as Black non-Hispanic, 11 percent as Hispanic of any race, 24 percent Asian non-Hispanic, and 8 percent chose the residual "other" category.

Each participant filled in a self-administered computer questionnaire in the Behavioral Labs of Stony Brook University's Political Science Department. The computer questionnaire was programmed using Inquisit, a software package that allows precise reaction time measurements by controlling the computer's task-prioritizing functions. This prevents programs running in the background from distorting reaction time measures. The study consisted of a political survey including questions about feelings towards social groups (closeness questions and Feeling Thermometer ratings) and a number of standard survey items on policy issues and demographic questions (including ideology, party identification, ethnicity, and race). The study contained the two sets of implicit reaction time measures described in sections 3.1 and 3.2. A racial policy score was computed from four standard racial policy items (see Appendix B). This summary score was coded so that greater numbers represent more liberal views and smaller numbers more conservative views on issues such as affirmative action and government aid to African Americans.

To investigate the construct validity of the implicit and explicit racial attitude measures, they are entered as predictors into a maximum-likelihood model of Pro-Black Policy Support in Table 3. The variable "Motivation to Control Prejudice" represents a control for social desirability consisting of a three-item scale by Fazio et al. (1995). This scale contains questions that gauge how important it is to an individual to appear unprejudiced. The last column lists the impact of each independent variable, from the smallest to the largest observed value and allows for comparison among predictor variables. The explicit survey question "How close do you feel towards African Americans/White Americans" (Explicit Black/White Closeness in Table 3) emerges as the most powerful predictor of racial policy preferences, whereby explicit closeness toward African Americans

TABLE 3
RACIAL POLICY LIBERALISM BY IMPLICIT AND EXPLICIT ATTITUDES

Racial Policy Liberalism[a]	Coefficient	SE	$p(z)$	Impact[b]
Implicit Black closeness	**0.004**	**0.002**	**.009**	**2.489**
Implicit White closeness	−0.002	0.002	.220	−1.139
Implicit Black priming	0.397	1.560	.799	0.647
Implicit White priming	−0.320	1.704	.851	−0.401
Explicit Black closeness	**1.105**	**0.164**	**.000**	**3.315**
Explicit White closeness	**−0.441**	**0.180**	**.014**	**−1.323**
Ideology (liberal to conservative)	**−0.413**	**0.110**	**.000**	**−2.478**
Republican Party identification	**−0.757**	**0.358**	**.034**	**−0.757**
Prejudice monitoring	**0.098**	**0.031**	**.002**	**1.760**
White non-Hispanic	−0.610	0.515	.236	−0.610
Black non-Hispanic	0.339	0.646	.599	0.339
Hispanic (any race)	0.668	0.607	.271	0.668
Asian non-Hispanic	0.512	0.543	.346	0.512
Constant	10.779	1.017	.000	—

Log-likelihood = −608.613
Wald χ^2 (13 df) = 209.870
Prob > χ^2 = .000
N = 416

NOTE: Estimation method: maximum likelihood; significant coefficients in bold to facilitate interpretation.
a. Four-item summary scale; for wording, see Appendix B.
b. Impact of each independent variable going from the smallest observed value to the largest one.

predicts more liberal and explicit closeness towards Whites more conservative opinions (both reaching or approaching significance at $p = .01$). Even after controlling for explicit closeness, implicit feelings of closeness toward African Americans predict liberal opinions on race-related policies at the $p < .01$ level of significance. While this idiosyncratic implicit measure exerts a powerful and significant effect of roughly the same magnitude as the standard 7-point ideology scale, the effect of the socially shared implicit racial priming measures are statistically indistinguishable from zero.

Republican partisanship is predictive of racially conservative opinions ($p < .05$) and the "Motivation to Control Prejudice" is predictive of racially liberal opinions ($p < .01$). The latter coefficient suggests that participants who state that it is important to them to appear unprejudiced may exaggerate their support for race-targeted policies such as affirmative action. Interestingly, once implicit and explicit feelings of closeness toward racial groups are controlled for, racial and ethnic group membership ceases to exert any significant influence. The fact that implicit idiosyncratic feelings of closeness toward African Americans appear to be large and significant predictors of racial policy liberalism supports the construct validity of this implicit idiosyncratic measure. The fact, however, that racial priming measures appear to be unrelated to racial policy liberalism at first blush casts doubt on their validity as measures of implicit socially shared racial attitudes. At closer inspection, however, their lack of predictive power and their lack of correlation with explicit measures of socially shared racial attitudes may not be so surprising. This lack of correlation is consistent with a large body of literature on the IAT, and it follows from the prediction of the racial norms evolution model presented in section 2. Thoroughly rehearsed, socially shared attitudes should be universally shared due to the process of "random drift" described by Kimura (1983; see section 2.3). As a universally shared attitude, it should take on a near constant value, resulting in zero correlations.

[P]articipants who state that it is important to them to appear unprejudiced may exaggerate their support for race-targeted policies such as affirmative action. Interestingly, once implicit and explicit feelings of closeness toward racial groups are controlled for, racial and ethnic group membership ceases to exert any significant influence.

This lack of correlation between implicit priming measures has been described in the literature on the IAT (Greenwald, McGhee, and Schwarz 1995) in the areas of race, ethnicity, gender, and age (Greenwald, et al. 2002, 18). Interestingly, it has been confirmed not only in socially sensitive domains, but also in purely linguistic comparisons of flowers versus insects and musical instruments versus weapons (Greenwald, McGhee, and Schwarz 1995, experiment 1). The lack of correlation in the latter domains is consistent with an interpretation of the measure as tapping socially shared aspects of word meaning and is inconsistent with a social desirability interpretation of the results. The same is true for a number of studies that suggest that a pro-White and anti-Black bias of the IAT occurs not only among White participants (e.g., Greenwald, McGhee, and Schwarz 1995) but also among non-Whites (Dasgupta et al. 2000),[5] and even among African American participants (e.g., Nosek, Banaji, and Greenwald 2002; Ashburn-Nardo, Knowles, and Monteith 2003; Jost, Banaji, and Nosek 2004).

Ashburn-Nardo, Knowles, and Monteith (2003), for example, obtained IAT measures of 80 African Americans and found "the IAT effect was significantly different from zero and in a negative direction . . . underscoring the degree to which many black participants in our sample exhibited relatively negative ingroup associations" (73).

To compare the results of this study to the studies cited above, all racial attitude variables obtained in this study were converted into scores ranging from a pro-White extreme to a pro-Black one with zero representing the neutral midpoint (where attitudes toward African Americans and Whites are equal). To make the measures comparable, they were converted to z-scores, and midpoint was preserved by adding the z-score for the neutral zero point to each original z-score. This z-score with neutral midpoint is denoted as $z' = z + (0 - \text{mean})/\text{standard deviation}$. Figure 3 displays the z'-scores for the three racial attitude measures under consideration in this study. Bars flagged with two asterisks represent z'-scores that are significantly different from the neutral zero-point, whereby positive numbers represent comparatively more pro-Black attitudes and negative numbers comparatively more pro-White ones. The results suggest that implicit idiosyncratic attitudes (Implicit Closeness represented by black bars), despite their powerful predictiveness of racial policy preferences, do not significantly deviate from zero in any racial group under consideration. This is consistent with the idea of an idiosyncratic measure that should display meaningful variance between individuals, not between groups.

In contrast, explicit socially shared attitudes measured by Explicit Closeness questions (grey bars) display systematic and large differences between groups. White and Asian American participants express significantly more pro-White than pro-Black attitudes, while African Americans express overwhelmingly pro-Black attitudes (all deviations from the neutral zero-point are significant at $p <$ .01). When the results of implicit socially shared measures are considered (Racial Priming represented by white bars), no group differences are visible, instead all groups display a highly significant ($p < .01$) pro-White and anti-Black bias. This is consistent with the findings from the IAT literature cited above and supports the interpretation that reaction time procedures based on word associations may tap socially shared, not necessarily individually endorsed, aspects of racial attitudes. Consistent with this interpretation, Greenwald, McGhee, and Schwarz (1995, 1469) stated, "IAT measures were highly sensitive to evaluative discriminations that are well established in the connotative meaning structure of the English language." To test for the existence of a universal norm, a t-test was conducted for the deviation of the grand mean from the neutral midpoint of the scale. As would be expected for an implicit idiosyncratic measure (Implicit Closeness), no group differences emerge (see black bars in Figure 3) and no systematic racial bias can be detected based on the t-test ($t = 0.821$; $p[t] = .413$). In contrast, for the explicit measure of socially shared attitudes (Explicit Closeness), significant group differences emerge (grey bars in Figure 3), and despite these group differences, the grand mean of the sample is significantly and

FIGURE 3
COLLEGE STUDENT DATA BY RACIAL GROUPS

FIGURE 3
COLLEGE STUDENT DATA BY RACIAL GROUPS

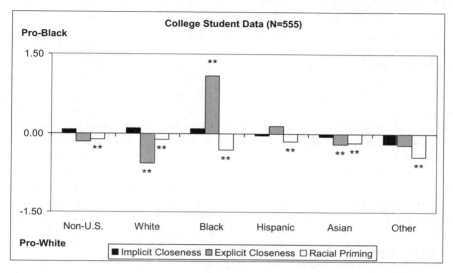

NOTE: Difference from neutral midpoint: $^{\circ\circ}p < .01$.

systematically biased in a pro-White and anti-Black direction ($t = -4.468$; $p[t] =$ .000). Finally, for implicit socially shared attitudes (Racial Priming), all groups are biased in the same direction (see white bars in Figure 3), resulting in a significant and systematic universal pro-White and anti-Black bias ($t = -3.915$; $p[t] = .000$). The latter finding is consistent with the universal IAT effect observed in extant literature (Greenwald, McGhee, and Schwarz 1995; Greenwald et al. 2002; Dasgupta et al. 2000; Jost, Banaji, and Nosek 2004; Nosek, Banaji, and Greenwald 2002; Ashburn-Nardo, Knowles, and Monteith 2003). To investigate the theoretical consistency of these empirical findings with the model of racial norms evolution presented in section 2, a computational version of the model is presented in the following section, and simulated results are compared to the patterns observed in Figure 3.

4. A Computational Model of Racial Norms Evolution

The computational model of racial norms evolution simulates a population of the same size as the sample of college students in section 3 ($N = 555$). Individuals are arranged on a two-dimensional grid of 15 × 37 cells. The racial composition of the simulated population reflects that of the college student sample in section 3, and group members are clustered to mimic racially segregated living arrangements frequently encountered in the contemporary United States. Each individual is assumed to have two racial attitudes, one idiosyncratic and one socially shared. Attitudes are represented by random numbers between zero and one, whereby zero represents extremely pro-White and one extremely pro-Black attitudes. The midpoint of the scale represents neutrality where attitudes towards Whites and Blacks are equal. At the beginning of the simulation process, attitudes are randomly initialized from a uniform distribution between zero and one, and idiosyncratic as well as socially shared attitudes are identical. Throughout the simulation process, idiosyncratic attitudes are kept constant, while socially shared attitudes are subject to change through random persuasion. In each simulation round t, one individual is selected at random to be the "persuader" I_t and one of the direct neighbors in the grid is randomly selected as the "persuadee" J_t. The persuadee takes on the socially shared attitude of the persuader, so that $J_t = I_t$. There is a probability of translating one's own idiosyncratic attitude into one's socially shared attitude instead of taking on the persuader's attitude and this probability is denoted by p(idiosyncratic). This probability is set at different values during five simulations ranging from p(idiosyncratic) = .00, .25, .50, .75, to 1.00. At one extreme, p(idiosyncratic) = .00, individuals never express their idiosyncratic racial attitudes and are maximally susceptible to persuasion by others. At the other extreme, where p(idiosyncratic) = 1.00, they express only their idiosyncratic attitudes and are entirely immune to persuasion by others. The implicit-explicit dimension is represented by time (the number of persuasion rounds). Applying the Hebbian interpretation of attitude rehearsal, attitudes that have been rehearsed for longer periods of time should become automatic (implicit). Thus, simulated attitudes after 50,000 persuasion rounds might represent explicit socially shared attitudes, while simulated attitudes after 300,000 rounds might represent implicit socially shared attitudes.

Figure 4 presents the results of the five simulations described above. Each square in the matrices represents the socially shared racial attitude of one individual, shaded to represent the most pro–African American attitudes as black, and the most pro-White American attitudes as white. For each simulation, the initial distribution at round 1 is displayed on the left, the results after 50,000 persuasion rounds in the middle, and after 300,000 persuasion rounds on the right. Idiosyncratic attitudes are omitted from Figure 4 since they are equal to the initial distributions on the left-hand side and remain constant throughout the simulation process. This does not imply that idiosyncratic attitudes are viewed as immutable in reality; they are simply held constant for purposes of simulation to investigate the dynamics of persuasion on the socially shared level. In all simulations in Figure 4 in which p(idiosyncratic) is less than 1.00, clustering of socially shared attitudes is evident. That is, as long as social communication is permitted to have any influence at all, norms of varying strength emerge. This process is most pronounced in simulations 1 and 2 where the influence of idiosyncratic attitudes is relatively low (simulations 1 and 2 with p[idiosyncratic] = .00 and p[idiosyncratic] = .25, respectively). While a relatively pro-White and anti-Black

FIGURE 4
FIVE SIMULATIONS OF RACIAL NORMS EVOLUTION WITH
DIFFERENT SETTINGS OF p(idiosyncratic)

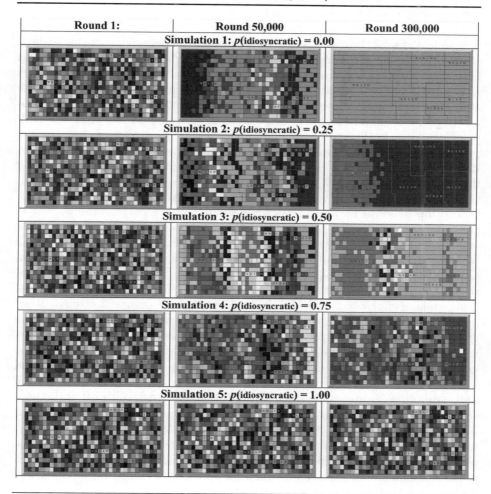

NOTE: p(idiosyncratic) represents the probability of an individual's idiosyncratic attitude being expressed. Each square in this 15×37 matrix represents a single individual ($N = 555$); the number of individuals in clusters represent the number of individuals of the indicated racial or ethnic category in the college student experiment described in section 3. Attitudes are shaded from most pro–African American (black) to most pro-White American (white).

norm emerges as dominant in simulation 1 (light grey to white coloring), a relatively pro-Black and anti-White one emerges in simulation 2 (dark grey to black coloring). This process of random norms evolution emerges according to the dynamics of Kimura's (1983) Neutral Theory of Evolution and is only absent in simulation 5 in which the social influences are precluded by virtue of setting p(idiosyncratic) to 1.00. In simulations 3 and 4, with p(idiosyncratic) ≥ .50, the norms formation is less pronounced and statistical analysis is required to detect the degree to which social norms emerge.

Figure 5 presents bar graphs similar to the bar graphs for the college student sample in Figure 3. For each of the racial groups, the bars represent mean deviations from the neutral midpoint of the simulated racial attitude scale, deviations in a positive direction representing more pro-Black attitudes (dark grey to black in Figure 4) and deviations in a negative direction representing more pro-White attitudes (light grey to white in Figure 4). Each simulation starts with random values (see black bars in Figure 5) that do not significantly deviate from the midpoint of the scale. The t-test provided underneath each bar graph tests for the presence of a universal norm after 300,000 rounds (see white bars in Figure 5). If the universal norm is pro-Black, the t-value is positive and significant, and if the universal norm is pro-White, the t-value is negative and significant. If no universal norm evolves, the t-value fails to reach significance at conventional levels.

The top panel in Figure 5 represents simulation 1 for which the p(idiosyncratic) was set at zero (0). Invariably, under this setting a single attitude survives and the simulation comes to an end once no further changes are possible. The bar chart shows initial (idiosyncratic) attitudes (black bars) not differing significantly from the neutral midpoint of the racial attitude scale. After 50,000 persuasion rounds (see grey bars), significant group differences emerge, with some groups taking on norms that deviate from the neutral midpoint in a positive direction, and others in a negative direction. After 300,000 persuasion rounds, all groups share a universally pro-White and anti-Black norm. The t-test for universal norms evolution in the top row of Figure 5 confirms this conclusion. The graph on the right hand side of the top panel in Figure 5 plots the mean (bold black line) and the standard deviation (thin black line) of racial attitudes for the entire duration of simulation 1. It illustrates how the mean starts off at the neutral midpoint initially and veers from the neutral midpoint for a while until it reaches an equilibrium state far from the neutral midpoint. As the norm crystallizes, the standard deviation gradually decreases over the first third of the evolution (about 300,000 rounds) and remains just above zero for the remainder of the simulation until the last individual adopts the social norm in round 950,000 and the standard deviation goes to zero.

This is the process of random drift described in Kimura's (1983) Theory of Neutral Evolution. The only prediction that can be made with certainty in this random model is the fact that a norm will inevitably evolve (see significant t-test)—the direction of the norm (i.e., the sign of t), however, is entirely unpredictable, as is the question of how far away from the neutral midpoint the norm will fall. The process becomes indefinite once idiosyncratic attitudes supply a constant supply of new minority attitudes.

A large number of simulations were run apart from the simulations displayed in Figure 5 to ensure that the results are not simply peculiar patterns, but predictably reoccurring patterns. When the bar graphs for the four simulations are

FIGURE 5
SIMULATIONS OF RACIAL ATTITUDES IN ROUND 1 (IMPLICIT IDIOSYNCRATIC), ROUND 50,000 (EXPLICIT SOCIALLY SHARED), AND ROUND 300,000 (IMPLICIT SOCIALLY SHARED)

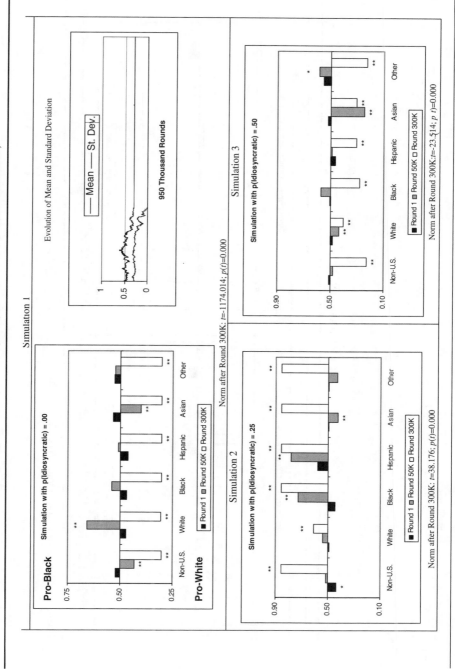

(continued)

FIGURE 5 (CONTINUED)

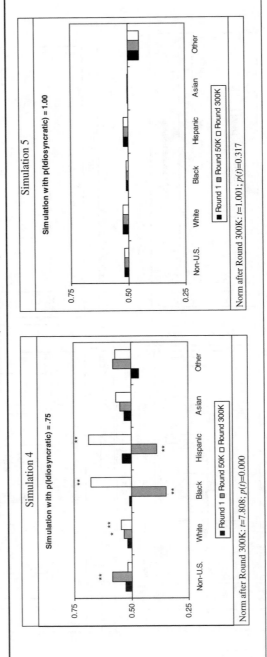

NOTE: Difference from neutral midpoint: °$p < .05$; °°$p < .01$.

compared for which p(idiosyncratic) < 1.00, the results are surprisingly similar. In each case, initial idiosyncratic attitudes (black bars) are, on average, close to the neutral midpoint without significant group differences. After 50,000 persuasion rounds (grey bars), socially shared attitudes display significant group differences and bars point in different directions. Finally, after 300,000 persuasion rounds, white bars generally point in the same direction (universal norm) and are significantly different from the neutral midpoint for most groups. In all simulations, the t-test for the existence of a universal norm is significant after 300,000 rounds. The only exception is simulation 5 for which p(idiosyncratic) = 1.00 and social influences are ruled out by definition. In this case the initial idiosyncratic distribution remains constant, no group differences occur, and no universal norm emerges that is significantly different from the neutral midpoint.

The patterns for simulations 1 through 4 mirror those of the student data in Figure 3 in many important respects—no significant universal norm exists in round 1 (idiosyncratic attitudes), while significant deviations from the neutral midpoint emerge after social communication has taken place (explicit and implicit socially shared attitudes). The only simulation in which no norm evolves is simulation 5, for which social communication has been excluded by definition (p[idiosyncratic] = 1.00). This simulation experiment suggests that the random norms evolution process is a robust phenomenon that emerges as long as any persuasion is possible at all. Although the simulated process has been a highly simplified and parsimonious version of a real-world process, the complex patterns that emerge display some surprising similarities to the observed data in section 3.

5. Conclusions

The theoretical model of racial norms evolution presented here combines two assumptions of neural organization with one assumption about social communication processes. The first of these assumptions holds that perceptions of internal body states ("chemistry" or idiosyncratic attitudes), and perceptions of external stimuli (socially shared attitudes) are processed in different (yet interconnected) areas of the brain. The second assumption holds that attitudes rehearsed for a longer period of time become automatic by a process of Hebbian learning (Hebb 1949; see also Wilson, Lindsey, and Schooler 2000). This leads to a two-by-two classification of attitudes: (1) implicit idiosyncratic, (2) explicit idiosyncratic, (3) implicit socially shared, and (4) explicit socially shared, three of which were considered in this study (1, 3, and 4). The third assumption of the model holds that social communication can produce social norms by virtue of a process that has been described by Kimura (1983) as "random drift." The tendency for computational models of social communication processes to produce unanimity as a function of random rather than systematic processes has been noted with puzzlement by some social scientists. Nowak, Szamrej, and Latané (1990, 363), for example, criticized "the implicit null hypothesis seemingly held by most social psychologists is that group processes, if allowed to work themselves through to their conclusion, would lead to a final distribution of opinion . . . with zero variance." Due to the fact that public opinion research generally focuses on divisive issues rather than unanimous ones, this general tendency of random norms evolution has been dismissed by political scientists as an anomaly and several computational modelers have sought to limit this tendency by including restrictive elements in their models. Nowak, Szamrej, and Latané, for example, proposed a computer model in which stable local "pockets" of dissent remain due to the fact that some members of the society have zero persuasiveness. Similarly, Robert Axelrod (1997, 211) proposed a model for the dissemination of culture in which communication is a function of "similarity" between two individuals and stable pockets of dissent remain if similarity between some individuals is set to zero. In practice, however, it is hard to imagine what "zero similarity" between two people could mean, since they will at least share their common humanity. Similarly, it is hard to imagine what "zero persuasiveness" means as long as a human being is able to communicate at all. Despite these rather strong and restrictive assumptions, these models do not produce stable opinion splits close to the 50 percent mark typical for the ones identified in many public opinion surveys, but produce rather small pockets of dissenting views and sometimes none at all. This article takes a different approach and allows for the possibility that this general tendency of random norms evolution may have a parallel in real-world communication processes. It may help us explain the otherwise puzzling observation that people adjust their views to powerful social norms (e.g., Devine 1989; Terkildsen 1993; Fazio et al. 1995; Greenwald, McGhee, and Schwarz 1995; Kuklinski, Cobb, and Gilens 1997; Berinsky 2004; Feldman and Huddy 2005). If we assume that social norms are simply an additive function of individual attitudes, no systematic differences should occur between average idiosyncratic and average socially shared attitudes.

If we assume that social norms are simply an additive function of individual attitudes, no systematic differences should occur between average idiosyncratic and average socially shared attitudes.

According to the college student experiment described in section 3, no systematic racial bias is observable at the level of implicit idiosyncratic measures

(Implicit Closeness), while a significant anti-Black bias is observable at the level of both explicit and implicit socially shared attitudes (Explicit Closeness and Racial Priming, respectively). The simulation results presented in section 4 faithfully replicate these patterns as long as social communication is possible at all, that is, as long as p(idiosyncratic) < 1.00. The model is maximally parsimonious, holding idiosyncratic attitudes constant and allowing changes in socially shared attitudes due to random persuasion among neighbors. More sophisticated versions of the computational model could allow for random change in idiosyncratic attitudes, and it could allow for individual differences in p(idiosyncratic). While these changes might lead to more realistic results, it is noteworthy that a maximally parsimonious baseline model suffices to produce considerable similarity between observed and simulated racial attitude data. Due to its parsimony, the model of racial norms evolution presented here may serve as a null model against which more complex models can be tested in the future.

Appendix A
Computing Implicit Closeness Scores

TABLE A1
NINETY TRAIT ADJECTIVES FOR THE TIMED SELF-TRAIT-RATING TASK
(ARON ET AL. 1991)

DOMINEERING	UNPREDICTABLE	AMBITIOUS	SUSPICIOUS	MATERIALISTIC
SHREWD	ANTISOCIAL	CORDIAL	TOLERANT	MATURE
SYMPATHETIC	NEAT	TIMID	SUBMISSIVE	PERSUASIVE
CHEERFUL	SHOWY	FORWARD	NAIVE	IRRITABLE
COWARDLY	CHOOSY	INDEPENDENT	SELF-RIGHTEOUS	APPRECIATIVE
SYSTEMATIC	LAZY	DECEPTIVE	WORRIER	SHY
TACTFUL	PROMPT	AGGRESSIVE	SOPHISTICATED	JEALOUS
GOOD-TEMPERED	IRRATIONAL	ILL-MANNERED	TENDER	FOOLISH
ARGUMENTATIVE	WEAK	RESPONSIBLE	AMUSING	ATTENTIVE
TACTLESS	WORDY	SUPERFICIAL	COLD	SPITEFUL
VAIN	SELF-RELIANT	FOOLHARDY	OBJECTIVE	ENVIOUS
FRANK	UNRELIABLE	METHODICAL	TRUSTING	SENSIBLE
EMOTIONAL	BLUNT	UNFAIR	VERSATILE	HOT-HEADED
NOSEY	ACTIVE	RESTLESS	CONGENIAL	SKEPTICAL
CONSIDERATE	GENEROUS	OBSERVANT	SPENDTHRIFT	OPPORTUNIST
SERIOUS	PROUD	SELF-CENTERED	DULL	ALERT
SCORNFUL	CRUDE	CREATIVE	INVENTIVE	PRODUCTIVE
NONCHALANT	PERSISTENT	PREJUDICED	BOASTFUL	SARCASTIC

NOTE: Trait adjectives selected from N. H. Anderson's (1968) norms by Aron et al. (1991).

To classify matching and mismatching traits, questionnaire responses are dichotomized with responses from (1) through (3) coded as "not descriptive" and (5) through (7) as "descriptive."[a] The top panel of Table A2 gives an overview of the classification of matching (M) and mismatching ($\mathcal{M}$) traits based on the responses to the initial trait survey. The number of matching traits ($A + B$ in Table A2) and mismatching ones $(C + D)$ varies from one individual to the next. Thus, if an individual rates a given trait as descriptive of the self and a given group, a self-group match is recorded (T_a in the top panel of Table A2). The same is true if the individual rates a given trait as nondescriptive of the self and nondescriptive of the group (T_b in the top panel of Table A2). If the individual rates a given trait as descriptive of the self but not of the group or nondescriptive of the self but descriptive of the group a self-group mismatch is recorded (see entries for traits T_c and T_d in the top panel of Table A2). This procedure is applied to establish match and mismatch patterns for both groups under investigation, African Americans and White Americans. Thus, each trait is classified as a self-Black match, a self-Black mismatch, a self-White match, or a self-White mismatch. The center panel in Table A2 shows how the distinction of matches (M) and mismatches $(M̶)$ allows comparing average reaction times for matching and mismatching trait words in the subsequent timed self-rating task.

TABLE A2
COMPUTING IMPLICIT CLOSENESS SCORES FROM TIMED SELF-TRAIT RATING RESPONSES

Step 1: Trait Survey—Classifying Matching (M) and Mismatching $(M̶)$ Traits (T)

Trait	Descriptive of Self?	Descriptive of Group?	Pattern
Trait T_a of A Traits	Yes	Yes	Match M_x
Trait T_b of B Traits	No	No	Match M_y
Trait T_c of C Traits	Yes	No	Mismatch $M̶_x$
Trait T_d of D Traits	No	Yes	Mismatch $M̶_y$
Trait T_e of E Traits	Undecided	Undecided	Neutral (excluded)

Whereby $A + B + C + D + E = 90$ traits from Aron et al. (1991); see Table A1.

Step 2: Timed Trait Rating Task—Reaction Time (t) to Correctly Recognize Trait (T)

Reaction Time Score t	"Does This Trait Describe *Me* as an Individual?"	Mean Reaction Time
$t_{M_x} = \sum_{a=1}^{A} t_a$	t_a: reaction time to recognize[a] T_a as self-descriptive	$\overline{M} = \dfrac{t_{M_x} + t_{M_y}}{A + B}$
$t_{M_y} = \sum_{b=1}^{B} t_b$	t_b: reaction time to recognize[a] T_b as non-self-descriptive	
$t_{M̶_x} = \sum_{c=1}^{C} t_c$	t_c: reaction time to recognize[a] T_c as self-descriptive	$\overline{t_{M̶}} = \dfrac{t_{M̶_x} + t_{M̶_y}}{C + D}$
$t_{M̶_y} = \sum_{d=1}^{D} t_d$	t_d: reaction time to recognize[a] T_d as non-self-descriptive	

Step 3: Implicit Closeness Score toward Either African Americans or White Americans

---

Implicit Closeness Score i_G toward group G:

$$i_G = \overline{t_{\cancel{M}}} - \overline{t_M}$$

If the participant feels close to group G, the average reaction time for mismatching traits should be greater than that for matching traits ($\overline{t_{\cancel{M}}} > \overline{t_M}$) and the implicit closeness score i_G should be positive, else it should be close to zero or negative if the participant feels neutral or distant.

---

a. Only reaction times of correctly recognized traits are used to compute implicit closeness scores, totals A, B, C, and D are adjusted accordingly.

To compute implicit closeness scores toward each group (see center and bottom panels in Table A2), reaction times (t) for all traits that are matching for the self and a given group are averaged ($\overline{t_M}$) and subtracted from the average reaction times for all traits that are mismatching between the self and that group ($\overline{t_{\cancel{M}}}$). If the individual feels neutral towards the group (neither close nor distant) there should be no observable reaction time difference between matching and mismatching traits and the implicit closeness score should be close to zero. If the individual feels close to the group, matching traits should be recognized as self-descriptive significantly faster than mismatching traits and the implicit closeness score should be positive. The implicit closeness score should take on negative values if the individual feels distant to the group on the non-conscious level.[b]

---

a. Following Coats et al. (2000), neutral responses (4) are treated as missing information. No significant difference in missing information occurred between racial groups in the sample (see section 3).
b. To reduce the inevitable skewness of reaction time measures, response times shorter than 300 ms or longer than 2,000 ms are excluded from this computation (Coats et al. 2000, 308-9).

Appendix B
Components of the Racial Policy (RP) Dependent Variable

RP 1   Because of past discrimination, minorities should be given special consideration when decisions are made about hiring applicants for jobs—do you *strongly agree, somewhat agree, somewhat disagree*, or *strongly disagree*?

RP 2   The government in Washington should make every possible effort to improve the socioeconomic position of Blacks and minority groups—do you *strongly agree, somewhat agree, somewhat disagree*, or *strongly disagree*?

RP 3   Where would you place the government in Washington's efforts to improve the social and economic position of Blacks and other minority groups on a scale . . . where 1= *the government should not make any special effort* and 7 = *the government should make every possible effort*?

RP 4:   The government should not make any special effort to help Blacks and other minorities because they should help themselves—do you *strongly agree, somewhat agree, somewhat disagree*, or *strongly disagree*?

SOURCE: Source for question wording: NES, NBES; see Tate (1993).
NOTE: The responses are summed up and recoded so that greater numbers represent greater racial policy liberalism and smaller numbers greater racial policy conservatism.

Notes

1. To emphasize the socially constructed character of the race concept, names of racial and ethnic groups are capitalized in this article, even if they refer to colors (e.g., Black, White, Black Americans, and White Americans).

2. Section 4 provides simulation results based on the model of racial norms evolution in which p(idiosyncratic) takes on various values.

3. Thirty of the trait words have a negative connotation, thirty are neutral, and thirty positive, based on ratings provided by Anderson (1968); see Aron et al. (1991).

4. Five positive and 5 negative words were chosen from this list of 1,036 normed words. Race-unrelated words were chosen with a frequency of at least $F = 25$ and valence ratings greater than 8 for positive words and less than 2 for negative ones.

5. Dasgupta et al. (2000) found pro-White and anti-Black reaction time patterns despite the fact that more than half (53 percent) of their sample was composed of non-White respondents.

References

Anderson, N. H. 1968. Likableness ratings of 555 personality-trait words. *Journal of Personality and Social Psychology* 9:272-79.

Aron, Arthur, Elaine N. Aron, Michael Tudor, and Greg Nelson. 1991. Close relationships as including other in the self. *Journal of Personality and Social Psychology* 60 (2): 241-253.

Ashburn-Nardo, Leslie, Megan L. Knowles, and Margo J. Monteith. 2003. Black Americans' implicit racial associations and their implications for intergroup judgment. *Social Cognition* 21 (1): 61-87.

Axelrod, Robert. 1997. The dissemination of culture: A model with local convergence and global polarization. *Journal of Conflict Resolution* 41 (2): 203-26.

Berinsky, Adam J. 2004. Can we talk? Self-presentation and the survey response. *Political Psychology* 25 (4): 643-59.

Bradley, M. M. and P. J. Lang. 1999. *Affective Norms for English Words (ANEW)*. Gainesville: The NIMH Center for the Study of Emotion and Attention, University of Florida.

Coats, Susan, Eliot R. Smith, Heather M. Claypool, and Michele J. Banner. 2000. Overlapping mental representations of self and in-group: Reaction time evidence and its relationship with explicit measures of group identification. *Journal of Experimental Social Psychology* 36:304-15.

Craemer, Thomas. 2005. Ingroup derogation and the norm of racial pride. Divergence of implicit and explicit racial attitudes. Paper prepared for poster presentation at the annual meeting of the American Political Science Association, Washington, DC, September.

———. 2006. Forming pro-black policy preferences by "including outgroups in the self"? Paper prepared for presentation at the annual meeting of the International Society of Political Psychology in Barcelona, Spain, July.

Dasgupta, Nilanjana, Debbie E. McGee, Anthony G. Greenwald, and Mahzarin R. Banaji. 2000. Automatic preference for white Americans: Eliminating the familiarity explanation. *Journal of Experimental Social Psychology* 36:316-28.

Devine, Patricia G. 1989. Stereotypes and prejudice: Their automatic and controlled components. *Journal of Personality and Social Psychology* 56:5-18.

Fazio, Russell H., Joni R. Jackson, Bridget C. Dunton, and Carol J. Williams. 1995. Variability in automatic activation as unobtrusive measure of racial attitudes: A bona fide pipeline? *Journal of Personality and Social Psychology* 69 (6): 1013-27.

Feldman, Stanely, and Leonie Huddy. 2005. Racial resentment and white opposition to race-conscious programs: Principles or prejudice? *American Journal of Political Science* 49 (1): 168-83.

Greenwald, Anthony G., Mahzarin R. Banaji, Laurie A. Rudman, Shelly D. Farnham, Brian A. Nosek, and Deborah S. Mellott. 2002. A unified theory of implicit attitudes, stereotypes, self-esteem, and self-concept. *Psychological Review* 109 (1): 3-25.

Greenwald, Anthony G., Debbie E. McGhee, and Jordan L. K. Schwarz. 1995. Measuring individual differences in implicit cognition: The Implicit Association Test. *Journal of Personality and Social Psychology* 74 (6): 1464-80.

Hebb, Donald O. 1949. The organization of behavior. A neuropsychological theory. New York: John Wiley.

Jost, John T., Mahzarin R. Banaji, and Brian A. Nosek. 2004. A decade of system justification theory: Accumulated evidence of conscious and unconscious bolstering of the status quo. *Political Psychology* 25 (6): 881-919.

Kimura, Motoo. 1983. *The neutral theory of molecular evolution*. Cambridge: Cambridge University Press.

Kuklinski, James H., Michael D. Cobb, and Martin Gilens. 1997. Racial attitudes and the "New South." *Journal of Politics* 59 (2): 323-49.

McPhee, William N. 1963. *Formal theories of mass behavior*. New York: The Free Press of Glencoe.

McPhee, William N., Jack Ferguson, and Robert B. Smith. 1963. A theory of informal social influence. In *Formal theories of mass behavior*, by William N. McPhee. New York: The Free Press of Glencoe.

Neely, James H. 1977. Semantic priming and retrieval from lexical memory. *Journal of Experimental Psychology: General* 106 (3): 226-54.

Nosek, Brian A., Mahzarin R. Banaji, and Anthony Greenwald. 2002. Harvesting implicit group attitudes and beliefs from a demonstration Web site. *Group Dynamics: Theory Research, and Practice* 6 (1): 101-15.

Nowak, A., J. Szamrej, and B. Latané. 1990. From private attitude to public opinion: A dynamic theory of social impact. *Psychological Review* 97 (3): 362-76.

Smith, Eliot R., and Susan Henry. 1996. An in-group becomes part of the self: Response time evidence. *Personality and Social Psychology Bulletin* 22 (6): 635-42.

Snyder, Mark, and Steven W. Gangestad. 1986. On the nature of self-monitoring. *Journal for Personality and Social Psychology* 51 (1): 125-39.

Tate, Katherine. 1993. From protest to politics: The new black voters in American elections. New York: Russell Sage Foundation.

Terkildsen, Nayda. 1993. When white voters evaluate black candidates: The processing implications of candidate skin color, prejudice, and self-monitoring. *American Journal of Political Science* 37 (4): 1032-53.

Wilson, T. D., S. Lindsey, and T. Y. Schooler. 2000. A model of dual attitudes. *Psychological Review* 107:101-26.

Neuroendocrine Mechanisms, Stress Coping Strategies, and Social Dominance: Comparative Lessons about Leadership Potential

By
WILLIAM D. ANDERSON
and
CLIFF H. SUMMERS

The authors examine dominance and subordination in the social psychology, political science, and biology literatures. Using Summers and Winberg (2006) as a guide, the authors suggest that extreme dominance or subordination phenotypes—including social dominance orientation and right-wing authoritarianism—are determined by an organism's genetic predispositions, motivations, stress responses, and long-term hormone release and uptake states. The authors offer hypotheses about the likely neurochemical profiles for each of these extreme dominance and subordination phenotypes and suggest two designs that begin to test these hypotheses.

Keywords: social dominance; authoritarian; Five Factor Model; neurochemistry; neurotransmitters; leadership

Leadership demands followership. Understanding leadership and subordination, however, is no simple task, and scholarship splits along two analytic fronts: leadership *emergence* and leadership *effectiveness* (Lord, De Vader, and Allinger 1986). Leadership emergence research focuses on the psychological preconditions that best predict leadership emergence (Hogan, Curphy, and Hogan 1994). In this tradition, leaders are thought to have personalities or personality traits—Hogan's (1991, 875) "recurring regularities or trends in a person's behavior"—that inspire one individual to begin or continue following another. Leadership effectiveness, however, addresses an individual's ability to affect the behavior of his or her subordinates via his or her own behaviors. Judge et al. (2002, 767) suggested that analyses of leadership emergence and effectiveness differ according to the unit of analysis—intergroup

William D. Anderson is an assistant professor of political science and director of the Government Research Bureau at the University of South Dakota. His work on legislative and presidential behavior has been published in Legislative Studies Quarterly.

Cliff H. Summers is a professor of biology and neuroscience at the University of South Dakota.

DOI: 10.1177/0002716207305585

versus intragroup—such that discussions about leadership effectiveness must naturally be preceded by assessments about how one came to be a leader.

The study of human leadership has an analogue among animals that exhibit social interaction. Complex social hierarchies in some animal species devolve ontogenetically from simple dominant–subordinate relationships developing between two individuals in social groups, close proximity, or territorial relationships (Korzan and Summers forthcoming). Similarly, simple dominant–subordinate relationships or hierarchies found in relatively less complex organisms (including invertebrates like crayfish and lobsters, or vertebrates like fish and lizards) have developed over evolutionary time into more complex hierarchical relationships in nonhuman primates that we may recognize as having similar leadership qualities as human social relationships.

[S]imple dominant–subordinate relationships or hierarchies found in relatively less complex organisms . . . have developed over evolutionary time into more complex hierarchical relationships in nonhuman primates that we may recognize as having similar leadership qualities as human social relationships.

Among animals, social relationships are stressful (Summers and Winberg 2006, 4581). The neurochemistry of these responses to stressful social conditions is evolutionarily conserved. That is, experimental scientists measure responses to stress in similar brain areas in vertebrate species from fish to humans. In addition, these ubiquitous stress responses use the same neurotransmitters (such as serotonin = 5-hydroxytryptamine or 5-HT) and hormones (like the glucocorticoids cortisol = F or corticosterone = B) in all species (including humans). Not surprisingly, the same neuroendocrine systems mediate such uniquely human maladies as depression, addiction, aggression, anorexia, and obsessive compulsive disorder (Korte et al. 2005, 3).

What is more, the specific neuroanatomy and neurochemistry appears to be particularly important for creating the personality traits that result in dominant (α individual) or leadership roles (Larson and Summers 2001, 95; Øverli et al. 2007, 396; Summers, Korzan, et al. 2005, 679; Summers, Watt, et al. 2005, 21). The same could be said for subordinate animals or non-α humans. Among animals, the behaviors associated with dominant/leadership or subordinate social rank are heritable (Pottinger and Carrick 1999, 122; Veenema, Meijer, de Kloet, Koolhaas, et al. 2003, 197), with two specific behavioral phenotypes emerging from natural populations. Specifically, that means that the protein framework of the underlying neuroanatomical and neuroendocrine profile of these behavioral phenotypes can be artificially or naturally selected. Koolhaas and colleagues (1999, 925) have begun to define the two most obvious, naturally occurring behavioral phenotypes (i.e., occurring in natural populations as well as genetically selected lines) and aptly named them "proactive" and "reactive."

Proactive animals have very specific physiological as well as behavioral characteristics. With respect to stress hormones, proactive traits include lower glucocorticoid (from the adrenal cortex: cortisol in humans, sheep, and fish; corticosterone in most other vertebrates) response to stress, but a higher release of adrenaline (or epinephrine, Epi; from the adrenal medulla) and noradrenaline (norepinephrine, NE; from the sympathetic nervous system). Recent work also suggests that baseline levels (prior to behavioral action) of the neurotransmitter serotonin (5-HT) are also lower in proactive animals (Summers, Korzan, et al. 2005, 679). Reactive animals have higher blood glucocorticoid concentrations, but lower Epi and NE, induced by stress, and higher baseline 5-HT. The behavioral result is that proactive animals are more likely to initiate social interaction, and tenaciously adhere to a course of action during the interaction, once it has begun. Proactive animals are therefore invariably socially dominant, at least initially (Korzan, Øverli, and Summers 2006, 48; Øverli et al. 2004, 235; Pottinger and Carrick 2001, 419). These neural, endocrine, and social characteristics, being evolutionarily conserved, are likely to be informative regarding human leadership potential.

In this article, we first broadly focus on the traits and social and psychological foundations for leadership and subordination. Our concern is with leaders, followers, the creation of social dominance hierarchies, plus traits and behaviors that drive individuals to leadership (dominance) or followership (subordination). Later, we address two extreme but useful cases of leadership and followership—social dominance orientation (SDO) and right-wing authoritarianism (RWA)—as areas ripe for additional scholarly investigation. We next concern ourselves with the specific biological precursors of those personality traits that prompt behaviors inspiring dominance and subordination and use a series of existing animal models studies (Summers and Winberg 2006, 4581) to structure how one might best pursue research in this nexus between neuroscience/neurobiology and leadership. In doing so, we use animal models to aid us in constructing neurobiological profiles for extreme dominance and subordination phenotypes in humans. In the final section of our article, we suggest two potentially fruitful directions for research. First, we present a brief design for understanding the neurobiological correlates of personality phenotypes such as SDO, RWA, and more typical Big Five personality traits that drive ordinary dominance and subordination. We next propose a research direction that will elucidate the neurobiological and neurochemical reactions individuals have to politically related threat or stress periods.

Our suggested research approach fits into recent scholarship in the leadership and human resources (Ilies, Gerhardt, and Le 2004) and the biological psychiatry and neurobiology literatures (Koolhaas et al. forthcoming, among others) that address how genetics, neurobiology, and animal models explain human behaviors such as leadership, social dominance, and stress coping (Koolhaas et al. forthcoming; McCann 1997; Mitman 1990; Fiedler 1995; Sarason 1986). Furthermore, our suggested research directions provide a strong foundation for more fully addressing how personality factors (Hogan, Hogan, and Roberts 1996) and behaviors combine with fundamental life processes to produce "Great Men" (Stogdill 1974) and successful leaders.

Leadership Emergence and Effectiveness

Leadership emergence is the first step in the leadership process (Ilies, Gerhardt, and Le 2004, 208) and thus requires at least a cursory mention in our discussion of leadership effectiveness. The emergence of leadership traits such as intelligence, perseverance, and self-confidence is irregular and prompted only by idiosyncratic or unique situation conditions (Stogdill 1948, 1974), a finding confirmed in animal models of aggression and stress-adaptive behavior (Summers and Winberg 2006, 4581; Wingfield et al. 1990, 829; Koolhaas et al. 1999). Furthermore, unique individual leadership characteristics—those that are hardwired and more difficult to change—are partly heritable (Ilies, Gerhardt, and Le 2004, 215) and these characteristics are highly correlated with individual behaviors across weak (ambiguous) but not strong social situations (Hughes, Ginnett, and Curphy 2005, 160-61; Hogan and Holland 2003; Tett and Burnett 2003).

Three blocks of individual characteristics—intelligence; personality traits; and values, interests, motives, and goals—seem to provide the strongest foundation for leadership emergence and, ultimately, success (Sternberg 2002, 2003).[1] Individuals who are selected and prove to be effective leaders are more likely than followers to be intelligent, or have an "all-around effectiveness in things directed by thought" (Hughes, Ginnett, and Curphy 2005, 175; Arvey et al. 1994). Leaders are more effective learners, critical thinkers, and problem-solvers and are better able to forecast potential problems two or three steps following a decision (Savin-Williams 1979; Lord, DeVader, and Allinger 1986; Sternberg 2002, 2003; Salgado 2003). Furthermore, intelligence is fairly difficult to change[2] and, consistent with its importance in leadership emergence, it only can be most accurately determined through a potential follower's observations rather than through paper-and-pencil intelligence tests (Judge, Colbert, and Ilies 2004; Hughes, Ginnett, and Curphy 2005, 175).

More important for our purposes are personality traits, which bear directly on leadership emergence and effectiveness (Ozer and Benet-Martinez 2006, 409-10). While few scholars agree on a uniform list of personality traits that correlate with leadership, the Five Factor Model, or FFM (Tupes and Christal 1961), has become one steady framework for understanding the personality traits most closely related to leadership emergence and effectiveness (Azar 1995; Hogan 1991; Hogan, Hogan, and Roberts 1996). The FFM arrays individuals along five major dimensions, including extraversion; agreeableness or empathy (Hughes, Ginnett, and Curphy 2005, 162; Hogan and Holland 2003); openness to new experiences; conscientiousness or dependability (Judge et al. 2002; Hogan and Holland 2003); and adjustment, self-control, or narcissistic tendencies (Hughes, Ginnett, and Curphy 2005, 163).

Leaders have scores on these Big Five dimensions that are distinctive from the average follower. Those likely to emerge and be effective as leaders have higher dominance or surgency (Judge et al. 2002; Hogan and Holland 2003; Salgado 2003), agreeableness (Hogan and Holland 2003; Salgado 2003), and dependability scores (Salgado 2003); adjust better to ambiguous or stressful situations; and are more open to new experiences than are nonleaders (Judge et al. 2002; Hogan and Holland 2003; Salgado 2003). These commonalities persist across cultures but not necessarily situations and "the strength of the personality-leadership performance relationships will depend on the particular demands of the situation and the job" (Hughes, Ginnett, and Curphy 2005, 179). In general, however, some individuals are equipped with personality traits that engender more affiliative or subordinate support.

The connection between leadership selection and personality traits—such as those enumerated in the FFM—emerges early among human peer groups and finds ready support in the child and adolescent dominance literature. Social leaders are regarded by others as having a great deal of social control (Lease, Musgrove, and Axelrod 2002, 526), are more socially aggressive, and are regarded by peers as being more extraverted (Anderson et al. 2001), intelligent, athletic, and playful. Leaders are viewed as being adept at effectively carrying out coercive strategies, but doing so in a subtle manner. In general, such leaders employ a balanced mix of prosocial and coercive strategies to build and maintain their dominance over their subordinates (Lease, Musgrove, and Axelrod 2002; Hawley 1999).[3] Leadership emergence is unrelated to an individual's agreeableness, conscientiousness, or openness (Ozer and Benet-Martinez 2006, 410; Anderson et al. 2001) but "may play a role in more formal organizations and professional groups, where task performance and achievement play a central role" (Ozer and Benet-Martinez 2006, 410).

The early emergence of dominance-related personality traits in peer groups is unsurprising and supports that dominance and submission have biological—genetic, hormone, and neuroendocrine—origins. Hughes, Ginnett, and Curphy (2005, 179) noted that the Big Five are "hard-wired," heritable (Bouchard 1997; Loehlin 1992; Loehlin et al. 1998), and "stronger predictors of leadership emergence than intelligence" (Ilies, Gerhardt, and Le 2004, 215). Consequent behaviors and decisions such as political party and ideology preferences also appear to be heritable (Alford, Funk, and Hibbing 2005). Even so, these heritability effects are limited and nongenetic sources of variance also are important "because genetic variance rarely accounts for as much as half of the variance of behavioral traits" (Plomin 1990, 187; but see also Hibbing et al. [2007] for a more robust conclusion). The size of Ilies, Gerhardt, and Le's (2004) partial correlations between intelligence, personality type, and leadership behavior ($R^2 = .23$) are suggestive, then: leadership emerges from a genetic foundation but also of non-genetic necessity (Summers and Winberg 2006, 4581).

The human personality traits most closely related with dominance and leadership—confidence, initiative, and extraversion—also have heritable hormonal antecedents (Booth et al. 2006, 168). Among the potential hormones or neurotransmitters that might be studied, testosterone has received the most attention. High testosterone predicts social dominance, but not aggression, among peers (Tremblay et al. 1998) and peer-identified leaders have higher basal testosterone levels than do nonleaders (Rowe et al. 2004, 549), leading to the conclusion that "high testosterone might be associated with socially valued characteristics in prosocial environments" (Rowe et al. 2004, 550). The testosterone–leadership correlation appears to persist across genders: higher testosterone levels are correlated with helpfulness, extraversion, and appropriate aggression in social situations (Dabbs et al. 2001) and also associated with testosterone-associated dominance behaviors (Grant and France 2001; Udry, Morris, and Kovenock 1995; Cashdan 1995), regardless of the research subject's sex.

The mechanisms causing elevated testosterone concentrations in the blood appear to have two independent stimuli: environmental and social (Goymann, Landys, and Wingfield forthcoming). While seasonal environmental regulation of androgens[4] may set the stage and timing of more aggressive human social interaction, the more important factor for human leadership is androgenic responsiveness to challenge (Archer 2006, 319). The "Challenge Hypothesis" posits that increased androgen secretion is stimulated by aggressive social interaction in a way that is specifically context-dependent (Wingfield et al. 1990, 829).[5] This hypothesis suggests that any political forum with a socially aggressive atmosphere should produce androgen responses that are distinguishable, based on the FFM qualities of leadership, and revealing about leadership potential.

It may also suggest, however, that while inherent leadership potential may be unmasked, it may also be flexible, and that future leaders may emerge based on context-dependent experience. For example, the challenge of aggressive social interaction has been demonstrated to provoke elevated plasma[6] testosterone concentrations in a variety of different animal models (Greenberg and Crews 1990, 246; Oliveira et al. 2002, 203; Wingfield 1985, 174). This change in androgen secretion is amenable to influence by simple observation of others in aggressive social interaction (Oliveira, Almada, and Canario 1996, 2; Oliveira, McGregor, and Latruffe 1998, 1045; Oliveira et al. 2001, 475; Oliveira, Carneiro, and Canario 2005, 207). Increased androgen only accrues to dominant individuals, and no effect on plasma androgen is seen when social interactions end in a tie (Oliveira, Carneiro, and Canario 2005, 207). The contexts to which this challenge stimulated androgen secretion is dependent include stressful conditions. Plasma testosterone concentrations are influenced by hormones secreted during stress[7] and by the neurotransmitter systems that regulate hormonal and behavioral stress responsiveness.

Chronic elevation of glucocorticoid hormones, often associated with subordinate social status, inhibits androgen secretion, and also inhibits aggression (Blanchard et al. 1993, 113; DeNardo and Licht 1993, 184). However, acutely activated corticosteroid secretion stimulates aggression (Kruk et al. 2004, 1062), or at least permits it (Summers, Watt, et al. 2005, 21). Very low glucocorticoid concentrations have been demonstrated to promote abnormal aggression (Haller et al. 2004, 550).

Another kind of abnormal aggression, important for this story because of recently increased illicit anabolic steroid use in teens and adults, is the effect that these artificial androgenic steroids have stimulating an aggressive phenotype in animals (DeLeon, Grimes, and Melloni 2002, 182; Melloni et al. 1997, 359; Melloni and Ferris 1996, 372). At the same time that androgens and glucocorticoids are reciprocally influenced and affecting aggression, they also affect brain neurotransmitters like 5-HT (Summers et al. 2000, 151; Summers, Matter, et al. 2003, 245). In addition, it appears that the effect of androgens and glucocorticoids on aggression and social dominance, and therefore perhaps on leadership potential, is affected by the brain's serotonergic system (Bonson et al. 1994, 313; Cologer-Clifford, Smoluk, and Simon 1996, 339; Cologer-Clifford et al. 1999, 823; Simon et al. 1998, 325).[8]

The serotonergic system has broadly projecting axons emanating from a relatively small number of cells in the brain stem, particularly from the raphé nuclei, terminating in virtually all regions of the brain (Jacobs and Azmitia 1992, 165). Serotonin influences a variety of human maladies or disorders including stress, anxiety, panic, depression, anorexia, obsessive compulsive disorder, schizophrenia, suicide, and aggression (Dinan 1996a, 1683; Dinan 1996b, 19; Graeff et al. 1996, 129; Graeff 1997, 723; Nemeroff 1998b, 517). Far from being a transmitter that is only activated by the advent of pathology, 5-HT is involved in regulating important normal functions like feeding, mood, temperature, and biological rhythms as well as behavioral arousal and motor activity (Challet, Pevet, and Malan 1997, 235; Jacobs and Fornal 1999, 9S), and it only is pirated by pathological processes.

Two of the normal functions regulated primarily by 5-HT and important for determining the distinction between leaders and followers are aggression and mood (Nelson and Chiavegatto 2001, 713). However widely 5-HT is distributed in the brain, its functions are regulated specifically for each brain region by seventeen different receptor subtypes and topographical stimulation (Lowry 2002, 911; Summers, Kampshoff, et al. 2003, 1122; Valentino, Liouterman, and Van Bockstaele 2001, 450). This means that serotonergic activity modulating aggressive behavior is limited to specific brain regions linked into a neurocircuit to control aggression (Summers, Korzan, et al. 2005, 679). While other areas are involved, the anterior hypothalamus appears to be the focal point for initiation and regulation of aggression. It is in the anterior hypothalamus that 5-HT and testosterone actively influence aggression, by acting on vasopressinergic cells[9] (DeLeon, Grimes, and

Melloni 2002, 182; Delville, Mansour, and Ferris 1996, 813; Ferris et al. 1997, 4331). Interestingly, the neurocircuitries and neurochemistry controlling aggression, mood, and stress overlap and interact (Summers and Winberg 2006, 4581).

Evidence in animal systems suggests that stress, aggression, and mood overlap in neurocircuitry and neurochemistry, and it seems plausible that this same evolutionarily conserved convergence in neural function also underlies the establishment and progressive development of leaders and followers. Humans exhibit elevated testosterone in response to a social challenge and aggression (Archer 2006, 319). However, the relationship between androgens and aggression in humans (and animals) is not necessarily direct or causal, as increased androgen secretion during puberty fails to promote increased aggression in young men (Halpern, Udry, Campbell, and Suchindran 1994, 8; Halpern, Udry, Campbell, Suchindran, et al. 1994, 217). Verbal insults and aggression, which may be common during establishment of leadership roles, elevate both plasma testosterone and aggressive, domineering behavior (Cohen et al. 1996, 945). In addition, in competitively aggressive situations, such as judo, testosterone levels prior to the competition predict the level of aggressive behavior (Berman, Gladue, and Taylor 1993, 125; Salvadora et al. 1999, 205). However, the correlation between testosterone and aggression suggest that testosterone accounts for only 20 to 30 percent (attack, r^2 = .29; fighting, r^2 = .20) of the variability in aggressive response (Salvadora et al. 1999, 205). Since we know that testosterone appears to rather indirectly affect the aggression neurocircuitry, an interpretation of the data other than a dose-dependent increase in aggression with testosterone is possible, and that has to do with motivation. In laboratory studies of competition between men, those with high testosterone levels had a greater motivation for the agonistic task than did individuals with lower testosterone (Berman, Gladue, and Taylor 1993, 125). What is more, competitive interactions produce an anticipatory rise of both testosterone and cortisol[10] (Suay et al. 1999, 551). Significantly higher cortisol, but not testosterone, levels were found in winners in comparison to losers. These data suggest that both motivation and anxiety, regulated by neural and endocrine modulators, are elements forming the mechanistic foundations for a dichotomy in behavioral strategies for coping with stressful conditions, aggression and submission, winning and losing, leading and following.

Two findings above are relevant and suggestive for our purposes. First, basal hormone and other neurochemical levels are both heritable and related to prosocial behaviors such as leadership selection/emergence. Second, these findings suggest that deviant dominance or submission behaviors—those that are extreme compared to the prosocial dominance behaviors noted above—may also have a strong relationship with hormone or neurochemical levels. This second assertion is noncontroversial, to be sure, but it also implies that antisocial dominance behaviors likely are related both to an individual's basal hormone and/or neurochemical levels *and* the social context in which that individual finds herself or himself.

[Findings imply] that antisocial dominance behaviors likely are related both to an individual's basal hormone and/or neurochemical levels and the social context in which that individual finds herself or himself.

Extreme Domination and Subordination as Ideal Test Cases: The Social Psychological View

The FFM framework suggests that variations in each of the Big Five personality dimensions—and their accompanying leadership phenotypes—will accompany changes in the probability of leadership emergence and effectiveness (Hughes, Ginnett, and Curphy 2005, 163-65). Few studies, however, have examined how personality predictors shape leadership and status in adulthood (Ozer and Benet-Martinez 2006, 409). Furthermore, the FFM says little about what *combinations* of extraversion, conscientiousness, openness, neuroticism, and agreeableness motivate some to become healthy, well-adjusted leaders and followers while pushing others to destructive or extreme leader–subordinate relationships (Ekehammar et al. 2004, 472; Heaven and Bucci 2001, 54). Rather than focusing exclusively on individual personality characteristics, then, it may be more fruitful to turn to individuals' perceptions of in-groups and out-groups to better understand leader and subordinate emergence or effectiveness.

More useful approaches for understanding dominance relationships and the resulting policy and worldviews come from intergroup and intragroup analyses of extreme phenotypes such as high-SDO (Sidanius and Pratto 1999) and high-RWA (Altemeyer 1996, 1998, 2004). Both are distinct clusters of attitudes (Duriez and Soenens 2006, 409) that provide important perspective on leadership emergence—and eventual effectiveness—and both phenotypes produce and perpetuate destructive, hierarchy-enhancing social attitudes. Individuals with these phenotypes share some similar policy and worldviews (Altemeyer 1998; Lippa and Arad 1999; Thomas and Esses 2004; Van Hiel, Pandelaere, and Duriez 2004) and have scaled scores on tests measuring each phenotype that are mildly and positively related but that are mediated by age, nationality, and group attachment (Ekehammar et al. 2004, 472-75; Duckitt 2001; Roccato and Ricolfi 2005, 197).[11] The two personality profiles also demonstrate statistical independence from many of the personality traits commonly affiliated with the FFM (Pratto et al. 1994, 751; Heaven and Bucci 2001, 49; Altemeyer 1998; Duriez and Soenens 2006, 409),[12] suggesting that high-SDOs and high-RWAs have social and political attitudes that diverge from those of more typical FFM-predicted leaders and followers.

High-SDOs and high-RWAs are distinctive both in their motivation and rationale for building and maintaining hierarchical relationships. High-SDOs wish to dominate, while high-RWAs have a leadership desire or directiveness (Ray 1976); RWAs are dogmatic (Altemeyer 2003, 162), while SDOs rarely have such a doctrine by which their behavior is governed; SDOs are prejudiced and self-aware, but RWAs lack such self-awareness because of a narrowed worldview (Altemeyer 2004, 426). The two are further distinguishable in each one's view of intergroup and intragroup relations. SDOs are concerned with maintaining hierarchical relationships between groups, while RWAs concern themselves mostly with intragroup order (Duckitt 1989; Pratto et al. 1994, 756). These are two sides of the same coin (Altemeyer 1998): high-SDOs wish to seize and maintain control; while high-RWAs prefer to be controlled, do the bidding of the dominant leader, and do so within a moral or religious framework (Sibley, Robertson, and Wilson 2006, 765). High-SDOs, as Altemeyer (2003, 163) noted, are likely to become "authoritarian ('dictatorial') leaders to whom High RWAs would submissively flock."[13]

Perhaps most important for our purposes, RWA and SDO—coupled with perceived threat or stress—have proven to be strong predictors of political attitudes and behaviors. After the 9/11 terrorist attacks, Crowson, Debacker, and Thoma (2006, 746) found that both SDOs and RWAs were more supportive of restrictions on rights and the use of aggression in U.S. foreign policy. Moreover, SDOs and RWAs evince a preference for conservative over liberal political candidates (Kemmelmeier 2004; Sidanius and Pratto 1999; Crowson, Debacker, and Thoma 2006). We expect that these similarities in social policy views and system-justifying ideologies that RWAs and SDOs share might be suggestive about shared neurobiological/neurochemical profiles, something we discuss in the final section of this article.

SDO

Social dominators—those with the high-SDO phenotype—are, by some accounts, "altogether nastier [people] who [are] more difficult to get along with" (Heaven and Bucci 2001, 55). The sixteen-item social dominance scale (Pratto et al. 1994; Sidanius and Pratto 1999) taps a "general attitude orientation toward intergroup relations, reflecting whether one generally prefers relations to be hierarchy-enhancing rather than ambiguous or progressive" (Pratto et al. 1994, 742). High-SDOs prefer interpersonal dominance to normal relationships, are immoral (Altemeyer 1998; Wilson 2003; Georgesen and Harris 2006, 453), tough-minded (Duckitt et al. 2002), lacking in empathy (Duriez 2004; Duckitt 2001; Heaven and Bucci 2001; Lippa and Arad 1999) and benevolence (Cohrs, Moschner, et al. 2005; Duriez, Van Hiel, and Kossowska 2005), and score highly on Machiavellianism and psychoticism measures (Altemeyer 1998; Heaven and Bucci 2001).

High-SDOs emphasize group-based dominance and superiority (Sibley, Robertson, and Wilson 2006, 756). Such individuals seek social, political, and economic status at all costs (Duriez and Van Hiel 2002; Duriez, Van Hiel, and

Kossowska 2005; Pratto et al. 1997; Sidanius and Pratto 1999); strive—indeed, disproportionately self-nominate—for leadership positions (Altemeyer 2003, 165); and are willing to use unethical means such as exploitation to achieve social or political gain (Son-Hing et al. 2007, 79; Wilson 2003, 555). Dominant leaders have more sensitive physiological threat (read: stress) responses and the will to use force and hierarchy-legitimizing myths (Georgesen and Harris 2006, 453) when their social standing is challenged (Scheepers and Ellemers 2005; Georgesen and Harris 2006, 464-65). Social dominance is biological, and the literature on gender differences among SDOs supports this idea: men score more highly on SDO measures than do women, while women have higher idealism scores than do men (McHoskey 1996; Wilson 2003, 555; Altemeyer 2003).

Individuals with higher SDO scale scores hold hostile worldviews and are prejudiced against those in identified out-groups. Individuals with high SDO scores are likely to report high values for measures of prejudice[14] and hostility against other races, sexes, and people with disabilities (Altemeyer 1998; Whitley 1999; Sibley, Robertson, and Wilson 2006, 761-63; Heaven et al. 2006, 605; Ekehammar et al. 2004, 472). In addition, SDOs prefer disharmony and order to egalitarianism: those with higher SDO scale scores demonstrate higher scale scores on preferences for war, national strength and order, and international disharmony and inequality (Heaven et al. 2006, 605). Altemeyer (2003) found high-SDOs to be "the new bullies on the block . . . [who] seem to be power hungry, domineering, mean, Machiavellian, and amoral, and hold 'conservative' economic and political outlooks" (p. 163) and are more likely to "rise to the top of movements thickly sewn with high RWAs" (p. 164).

Taken together, the elements of the high-SDO leadership profile suggests predominately male individuals who lack a moral center and who disproportionately manipulate followers—even to those followers' harm—to achieve political and social ends. These dominant leaders may, as Ludwig (2002, 268-269) noted, evince "much of the grandiosity and ebullience associated with mania and, moreover . . . such rulers are more likely to have poor judgment and be megalomaniacal and impulsive." Among SDOs, then, we might expect a neurobiological profile that mirrors that of highly dominant, aggressive, and male lower-order animals, a point we return to later in our discussion.

RWA

RWAs are "followers who have submissive attitudes toward established authorities, show a general aggressiveness toward persons 'targeted by those authorities' and adhere to social conventions" (Altemeyer 2003, 161; Heaven and Bucci 2001, 55). The RWA designation finds its foundation in historical works on the psychosocial foundations for prejudice (Adorno et al. 1950). Altemeyer's (1981, 1988, 1996, 1998, 2004) thirty-item RWA scale contains items that focus on the respondent's need for a strong leader and his or her commitment to "old fashioned values" (Altemeyer 2004, 426). Although the psychosocial origins of the RWA personality cluster are uncertain, they appear to be experiential (McHoskey 1996; Wilson 2003, 555; Altemeyer 2003) and rely on an individual's personal insecurity and perceptions about the social world as being meaningless and difficult to control (see Roccato and Ricolfi [2005, 188] for an explanation).

RWAs demonstrate a reverence for value, tradition, conformity, and security (Altemeyer 1998; Cohrs, Moschner, et al. 2005; Duriez and Van Hiel 2002; Duriez, Van Hiel, and Kossowska 2005). The RWA personality cluster is cognitively rigid, and individuals evincing it prefer conservatism[15] and closure over the stress or threat of uncertainty (Kossowska and Van Hiel 2003, 513; Jost et al. 2003, 366; Chirumbolo 2002; Van Hiel, Pandelaere, and Duriez 2004). Such individuals have a moral and ethical worldview based in religion (Heaven and Bucci 2001, 55; Altemeyer 2004, 426) that serves as a foundation for narrow and prejudiced social behaviors and beliefs (Altemeyer 2003).

In supporting dominant leaders, RWAs are willing to restrict rights and unfailingly approve the injustices of governing authorities during periods of stress or threat (Crowson, Debacker, and Thoma 2006, 746; Cohrs, Kielmann, et al. 2005, 271; Heaven and Bucci 2001, 55; Altemeyer 1996). RWAs believe that the world is a dangerous place (Altemeyer 1998; Duckitt 2001) and treat out-groups accordingly by demonstrating prejudice against different races, ethnicities, genders, religions, and sexual preferences (Altemeyer 2003, 162; Stones 2006, 1145). Furthermore, when put into positions of power, high-RWA leaders produce destructive social and global outcomes, particularly when those outcomes are compared to the results found among low-RWA leaders and teams (Altemeyer 1996, 130-36; Altemeyer 2003, 163).

As with SDOs, RWAs have rigid worldviews and intolerant or prejudicial policy preferences. Unlike SDOs, RWAs clearly prefer subordination over dominance and, more important, are willing to follow highly dominant leaders without fail. This distinction is an important one, because in the next section, we offer a series of hypotheses about the neurochemical profiles for SDOs and RWAs. We anticipate that the dominance/subordination difference between SDOs and RWAs will be the critical driver shaping differences in the neurochemical profiles among these two personality clusters.

Animal Analogues and Thinking about Comparable Neurochemical Profiles for SDOs and RWAs

Research on animal models suggests that like social support systems for humans, affiliative behaviors can provide a buffer against stressful social conditions that often arise during establishment of social rank relationships (DeVries, Glasper, and Detillion 2003, 399). While these buffering systems suggest alternative strategies for leader-follower or dominant-subordinate relationships than a strictly proactive-reactive dichotomy (Koolhaas et al. forthcoming), they may also help to explain overly aggressive dominance of human social dominators and the special relationship that produces unquestioning submission from RWAs.

The animal model that best fits the strongly dichotomous relationship between SDOs and RWAs has been demonstrated in numerous species from fish (Øverli et al. 2007, 396) to reptiles (Korzan and Summers forthcoming) to mammals (Benus et al. 1991, 1008; Veenema, Meijer, de Kloet, and Koolhaas 2003, 256). While it is never wise to underestimate the social and behavioral complexity of lower vertebrates, an unelaborated dichotomy between dominant leader and submissive subordinates seems the simplest foundation for the evolutionarily ancient strategies for coping with stress between proactive social dominators and reactive individuals. The current model for the proactive–reactive relationship strategies posits that emotionality is independent from coping with stress (Koolhaas et al. forthcoming), which broadens the range of personality types driving the behavior of potential leaders and followers. That is to say, a proactive leader may be either bold or panicky (Koolhaas et al. forthcoming). Reactive followers may be either obedient or shy. In nonhuman primates, such as baboons, dominant males often seek more affiliative relationships with subordinate individuals, stabilizing the social hierarchy, minimizing group aggression and competition, and lowering basal plasma cortisol concentrations (Creel, Creel, and Monfort 1996, 212; Ray and Sapolsky 1992, 231). Unstable social relationships produce elevated aggressiveness and plasma cortisol. In other monkeys,[16] when hierarchy relationships are unstable, active serotonin systems help to engender affiliative relationships and thereby permit males (Raleigh et al. 1991, 181) or females (Higley, King, et al. 1996, 67) to attain high-dominance status. Conversely, low serotonergic activity[17] can produce aggression in male rhesus macaques (Higley et al. 1992, 436; Higley, Mehlman, Poland, et al. 1996, 1067), which usually results in dominant social status. However, low serotonergic activity specifically incites extremely stressful severe unrestrained aggression, not simply increased rates of aggression overall, and also produces behavioral impulsivity, with increased plasma ACTH and cortisol levels. High testosterone is associated with increased general aggressiveness in these macaques, but not impulsively severe aggression (Higley, Mehlman, Poland, et al. 1996, 1067). Low CSF 5-HIAA, which is correlated with severe aggression and low impulse control in monkeys (Mehlman et al. 1994, 1485), also is associated with a high mortality rate in these primates (Higley, Mehlman, Higley, et al. 1996, 537) and suicide in humans (Mann et al. 1996, 576).

    Social dominators fit the profile of impulsive proactive individuals that produce fits of unrestrained severe aggression, but not affiliative or cooperative behavior. While low 5-HIAA in human CSF is measured after a history of suicide, suicide attempts, homicide, and/or impulsive violent aggression (Lidberg et al. 1985, 230; Virkkunen et al. 1995, 271), the evidence from animal (including primate) studies suggests that 5-HT is part of a larger neurotransmitter and hormone mix that depends on timing and magnitude of response to produce a particular result, including leadership or dominant status (Summers and Winberg 2006, 4581). Recent studies suggest that serotonergic activity is only predictive of behavioral outcomes when it is measured before a socially aggressive interaction begins to establish social rank relationships (Summers, Korzan, et al. 2005, 679). Clearly, prior experience and opponent recognition plays a critical role in the neuroendocrine state of the individual prior to social interaction, and therefore the behavioral outcome (Forster et al. 2005, 733; Korzan et al. 2007; Oliveira et al. 2001, 475). It is at the inception of the stressful leadership-defining moments that individual differences in the neural and endocrine mechanisms that produce specific stress coping strategies define distinctions in behavior that results in leaders and followers, or dominant and subordinate animals (Summers and Winberg 2006, 4581). At this initiating moment, low 5-HT (or 5-HIAA) may make a difference (Summers, Korzan, et al. 2005, 679), a fast spike in glucocorticoids may allow or provoke aggression (Summers, Watt, et al. 2005, 21), and an anticipatory pulse of testosterone (Suay et al. 1999, 551) combined with elevated dopamine in reward centers of the brain (Korzan et al. 2006, 93; Korzan and Summers forthcoming) may provide the appropriate motivation and even course for action. Fast response time to social and stressful situations, both in initiating and terminating the response, appears to be the hallmark of leaders and dominant individuals (Korzan, Øverli, and Summers 2006, 48; Summers and Winberg 2006, 4581), and while these traits appear to be somewhat heritable (Benus et al. 1991, 1008; Pottinger and Carrick 1999, 122), they are also to some extent reversible (Korzan and Summers forthcoming; Summers, Forster, et al. 2005, 241). It seems likely that aberrant leadership types, such as social dominators, and their aberrant followers, RWAs, will show variation from the normal stages of stress/aggression response development (Summers and Winberg 2006, 4581) in some significant way.

It seems probable that a special mix of neurochemical events produces particular leadership and follower qualities. The timing and magnitude of dopamine, serotonin, testosterone, and cortisol help define the difference between dominant and subordinate social status in animals (Korzan and Summers forthcoming; Summers and Winberg 2006, 4581). Said simply, dominant proactive animals initiate their stress response quickly and terminate it just as fast when important events are over. Subordinate reactive animals are slower to respond and have a hard time ending stressful events and the neuroendocrine responses that go with them. This slow reactive response timeline also accurately describes depressed humans (Nemeroff 1998a, 42). We hypothesize that human leaders, like dominant animals, show anticipatory and motivational increases in testosterone and dopamine[18] just prior to significant social interaction; they may have lower serotonergic activity during this motivational phase, but it increases rapidly along with plasma cortisol during aggressive or other stressful events. The temporal juxtaposition of these neurochemicals and hormones are likely to change slightly in aberrant leadership styles, such as that displayed by SDOs. Consider that aggression has been demonstrated to be rewarding or addictive, but that the rewarding properties are not robust (Martinez et al. 1995, 323). Normally glucocorticoids, while stimulatory to aggression, also may counteract its aversive effects as a part of a stress-coping strategy (Piazza and Le Moal 1997, 359). However, hypersensitivity to secretion of cortisol exacerbates the rewarding effects of aggression and may produce reward-related pathologies. This is because glucocorticoid receptors in the ventral tegmental area of the hindbrain[19] create a hypersensitivity in the reward circuitry of the brain (Cho and Little 1999, 837). These ideas together suggest a framework for a possible neurochemical profile of the social dominator: (1) Very low serotonergic activity in the anterior hypothalamus or "attack area" of the brain (Summers, Korzan, et al. 2005, 679; Van Praag 1991,

15). This low 5-HT means that no brakes on aggression are present, as they would normally be for most people and animals (Delville, Mansour, and Ferris 1996, 813). The aggressive act usually produces a stress response with a concomitant rise in serotonergic activity, which does not immediately block aggression, but may inhibit future aggressive acts (Summers and Winberg 2006, 4581). Therefore we hypothesize (2) little to no increase in serotonergic activity in response to the stress of aggression. On the other hand, (3) we expect a hyperactive sensitivity to cortisol release. This promotes aggressive response (Kruk et al. 2004, 1062) and may lead to an addiction for aggression. It is important to mention that an unusually low glucocorticoid response may also be an appropriate stimulus for the social dominator style of leadership. That is because extremely low glucocorticoids have been shown to stimulate aberrant aggression (Halasz et al. 2002, 561). Finally, (4) we hypothesize that social dominators do not show a normal anticipatory increase in plasma testosterone. In this case, we believe that social interaction of a more or less aggressive nature is impulsive and addictive in social dominators, driven by low serotonergic activity and rapid cortisol responsiveness. Glucocorticoids have been demonstrated to be a part of a rapid feedback system to the "attack area" to produce almost instant unrestrained aggression (Kruk et al. 2004, 1062). The anticipatory testosterone release is normally a part of a developing motivational progression, perhaps unimportant for impulsive aggression, and likely to be inhibited by cortisol. Our hypothesis posits that the social dominator has a neuroendocrine profile that supports addictive and impulsive behavior.

[D]ominant proactive animals initiate their stress response quickly and terminate it just as fast when important events are over. Subordinate reactive animals are slower to respond and have a hard time ending stressful events and the neuroendocrine responses that go with them.

Social dominators have a socially intricate relationship with RWAs and share some behavioral characteristics. As such, some of the neuroendocrine profile of RWAs may be similar to social dominators. RWAs behave much as animals with conditioned fear responses do. They fear new experiences and (1) may produce rapid cortisol responses like social dominators, but in this case, only to specific conditions that they have learned produce fearful emotions. As RWAs are submissive to authority, so it seems likely that (2) they have high levels of 5-HT in limbic regions like the hippocampus and amygdala and high hypothalamic "attack area" 5-HT, before socially aggressive situations occur, similar to subordinate animals (Summers, Summers, et al. 2003, 553; Summers, Korzan, et al. 2005, 679). (3) Submissive individuals should also show a slower rise in serotonergic activity in the limbic brain during socially antagonistic circumstances. However, this kind of follower can be aggressive, but primarily toward those that are opposed to authority, and this suggests a neurochemical override of the normal serotonergic inhibition of aggression. The motivational push that likely brings the RWA to aggressiveness is (4) an anticipatory elevation of testosterone. Presumably, the increased androgen hypothesized for dominant proactive male animals (de Ruiter et al. 1992, 149), should grow and build motivation more slowly in RWAs, as indignation toward those that opposed authority developed. As opposition to authority also threatens RWAs with new leadership, with new rules, and invariably with new experiences, this kind of opposition is also a harbinger of additional stress for this kind of follower. Cortisol and testosterone levels should therefore rise concomitantly in RWAs during any threat to authority. This neurochemical profile would indicate that social dominators do not emerge from RWAs, however synergistic their neurochemistry and behavior must be.

Next Steps: The Neurochemical Foundations for Human Dominance and Subordination

The preceding sections suggested that dominance and subordination—or leadership and followership—have clear biological foundations. We offered neurochemical profiles that might best describe these personality clusters. More important, we offered a connection between these neurochemical profiles and the behaviors and political attitudes predicted by them. To understand whether our suggested neurochemical profiles map to SDOs, RWAs, or other personality clusters, however, it is necessary to go from hypotheses to tests. In this section, we offer approaches that may permit us to move from the theoretical to the empirical.

Before offering these research approaches, it is important also to detail the challenges that come from this sort of human-based neurochemical research. Much of the literature on neurochemical profiles and responses to threat and stress come from animal models because of the relative simplicity (compared to human models) of doing such research. Human subjects, however, provide challenges for doing this sort of research for two principal reasons. First, human subjects display a wide variability in temporal androgen and neurochemical concentrations. Measures of these androgens or neurochemicals must be neutral with respect to circadian cyclicity. Experiments that examine hormones, for example, most frequently rely on blood or saliva samples that

are drawn from subjects over a wide range of time periods without consideration for when these hormones or neurochemicals are at their peak(s) or
nadir(s). The rigor and persistence required of this approach with human subjects makes it more challenging than a typical animal model experiment might
otherwise be.

Second, human subjects present an ethical challenge that extends beyond subject discomfort to recruitment and retention of those subjects. For example,
gathering optimal measures of both blood hormone and neurochemical concentrations relies on particularly invasive procedures. Measuring androgen and glucocorticoid concentrations is easier: experimental subjects would be best to have
blood drawn continuously or at selected intervals prior to, during, and after any
experiment that is being conducted. Ideally, subjects would have a blood draw
prior to the experiment, following the presentation of a negative stress-inducing
experimental treatment, within minutes following the treatment, after presenting
a eustress, and after the experiment.

Neurochemicals present a bigger challenge: serotonin (5-HT) cannot be measured in a blood draw. Researchers must instead draw cerebrospinal fluid—via a
spinal tap—or otherwise assess 5-HT binding by using probes inserted into the living subject's brain. Absent these techniques, less invasive measures of neurotransmitter binding—such as fMRI or PET or CAT scans—might be used. It should be
clear, however, that such research differs significantly from animal models of neurochemical research where experimental subjects can be dispatched and dissected
immediately following the introduction of a stress-inducing event. Moving to
human subjects presents challenges that demand researcher creativity. Keeping
all of these challenges and limitations in mind, we offer two potential approaches
to understanding the neurochemical profiles of leaders and subordinates.

Basal neurochemical profiles for SDOs and RWAs

The first approach to testing our hypothesized neurochemical profiles for
SDOs and RWAs is to understand the basal neurochemical profiles for highly
dominant, highly submissive, and healthy dominance–submission profiles. It is
clear from our earlier discussion that threat- and stress-prompt behaviors that one
might call dominant or submissive. Furthermore, these behaviors—or even the
personality types that subjects self-identify—will have neurochemical
antecedents and consequents.

It is less clear, however, whether SDOs and RWAs will evince differences in
basal neurochemical profiles if no stress or a eustress is present. We could expect
that high-SDOs and high-RWAs will have neurochemical profiles that significantly
differ from those individuals who gravitate toward healthier leader–follower
relationships. To test these hypotheses, we suggest a simple, three-stage experimental design with minimal unintentional or incidental negative stressors. Our
focus in this experiment will first be on the androgens (testosterone) and glucocorticoids (cortisol) that we anticipate will shape the high-SDO and high-RWA
attitude clusters.

Experimental subjects will be selected from the population of undergraduate, graduate, and professional students at a public Upper Midwestern university and will be volunteers from a university-run human subjects pool. Subjects will receive a gift certificate for a local merchant for completing the entire experimental protocol. Participants will be asked to sign informed consent forms authorizing blood sampling. During the experiment, subjects will first be intravenously cannulated and a first small (1 ml) blood sample will be drawn. A second small sample will be drawn prior to subjects being informed that they will be asked to complete a questionnaire that requests their ideas about "people different than they are: immigrants, racial and ethnic minorities, homosexuals, and the opposite sex." The third 1 ml sample will be drawn just after subjects are informed about the questionnaire. Our hypotheses from above suggest that even this minimal negative stressor—being asked about people different than they are—will prompt a rise in anticipatory testosterone among RWAs but not SDOs, while both should see a rise in aggression-inducing cortisol.

Subjects will then be given a questionnaire consisting of eight separate personality indicators and attitude inventories, replicating the work of Ekehammar et al. (2004, 469-71). Most significant is the inclusion of the sixteen-item Social Dominance Orientation scale (Pratto et al. 1994), the thirty-item Right Wing Authoritarianism scale (Altemeyer 1981), and the forty-four-item Big Five Inventory (John and Srivastava 1999). The remaining scales and items specifically will tap modern racial prejudice (Akrami, Ekehammar, and Araya 2000) and sexism (Swim et al. 1995), among other social and political views (Ekehammar et al. 2004, 470-71). A fourth small sample will be taken following individual subjects completing the questionnaire. Subjects will then receive a distraction task—a simple Sudoku puzzle that should take between ten and fifteen minutes—before we take a final 1 ml blood sample.

Using enzyme-linked analysis (ELISA), we will analyze the testosterone and cortisol concentrations in each of the subjects' samples. Basal cortisol and testosterone concentrations will be assessed from the prequestionnaire sample. The subjects' questionnaires will be scored and grouped into the SDO, RWA, and Big Five clusters, and each subject's scores on these three tests—including each of the Big Five subitems—will be correlated with the subject's basal cortisol and testosterone concentrations.

Our earlier hypotheses suggest what we might expect from this analysis: individuals who score higher on the SDO and RWA measures will be likely to have higher basal cortisol concentrations than will individuals who have low scores on either measure. Following the (theoretically) minimal stress prompted by the idea of taking the questionnaire, we anticipate that high-SDOs will have no rise in anticipatory testosterone, compared with RWAs who will. Both, however, should have rises in cortisol concentrations. Although this experiment will not test the subjects' 5-HT concentrations, we expect that if it did, we would find depressed serotonin concentrations among those scoring highly on the SDO or RWA scales. Such a finding suggests that those self-identifying in either attitude cluster will be more likely to be uninhibited in their aggression toward out-groups.

Neurochemical profiles under stress: SDOs and RWAs

The above design suggests introducing a mild stressor—the questionnaire—and measuring the subjects' androgen and glucocorticoid concentrations. It is reasonable to assume, however, that such a stressor will be sufficiently benign as to render moot any judgments about the relationships between motivation, stress, RWAs, SDOs, and basal, anticipatory, and stress-induced glucocorticoid and androgen concentrations. That weakness, however, can be limited by constructing a similar experimental design that makes the stressor more salient to the experimental subjects.

To do so, we suggest creating an experimental protocol identical to the one noted above. Instead of introducing the questionnaire during the experiment, however, we provide it to the subjects in advance of the experiment. In doing so, we also request that they complete the questionnaire and return it to our research team before they participate in the experiment. This will ensure that the questionnaire avoids becoming a confounding variable in the remainder of our analyses. It also enables us to selectively include high-SDOs, high-RWAs, and control subjects in appropriate proportions.

As in the previous research design, we will ask subjects to come to an experiment session and will cannulate them, drawing a first 1 ml blood sample. Subjects then will be asked to either (1) read a scenario in which an out-group gets the better of an in-group (mildly negative and motivating stress); (2) watch a real-time local television newscast, during which "national news" breaks in to provide details about a potential terrorist plot unfolding in a distant American city (negative and inflammatory stress); (3) read a passage or watch a video about the American Revolution (positive stress or eustress); or (4) participate in a control group in which they simply will be asked to watch an episode of a popular American sitcom (no stress). We will take a second small blood draw, and subjects then will then be asked to fill out a brief questionnaire that assesses their opinions and behaviors about the experimental intervention. This instrument will focus on mapping the subjects' attitude clusters (SDO, RDO, or otherwise) with their sociopolitical beliefs. Subjects next will be asked to provide a blood sample, complete shortened versions of the SDO and RWA scales, complete a distraction task—in this case, an easy Sudoku—and a fourth and final small blood sample.

With this research design, we can augment the findings from our earlier experiment by deliberately provoking SDOs and RWAs with threatening, inflammatory, negative-stress events. Consistent with our hypotheses, we would expect that SDOs will have lower anticipatory androgen and glucocorticoid concentrations than RWAs. Both SDOs and RWAs will have lower preexperimental and postexperiment cortisol concentrations than will low-scoring SDOs and RWAs. Furthermore, high-RWAs will have higher anticipatory testosterone concentrations than will low-RWAs. Finally—and if we were able to test the subjects' 5-HT concentrations—we likely would find depressed preexperiment and postexperiment serotonin concentrations among those scoring highly on the SDO or RWA scales.

The findings from this and the previous analysis could be suggestive: that SDOs and RWAs have basal androgen and glucocorticoid profiles that are significantly different from subjects not sharing these clusters of attitudes. Furthermore, the threat of even a mild stressor—the questionnaire—likely will spur increases in anticipatory testosterone among RWAs but not SDOs, while it is possible that high-SDOs likely will have higher, stress-induced cortisol concentrations than will high-RWAs. Our approach could offer leverage over a question that is implicit throughout our discussion: might we predict social and political attitudes, worldviews, and prejudice based on those individuals' basal and stress-induced androgen and glucocorticoid concentrations?

Conclusion: A New Way of Understanding Political Dominance and Subordination

In this article, we have provided a view of leadership emergence and effectiveness that centers on two extreme phenotypes: individuals having high-SDO or high-RWA profiles. We suggest that these two attitude clusters may provide insights into the broader question of dominance and subordination because they produce policy and political outcomes that encourage intolerance, sexism, racism, prejudice, and aggression toward out-groups. Such insights may help us understand what motivates both healthy and destructive leadership arrangements.

[Social dominance orientation and right-wing authoritarianism] attitude clusters may provide insights into the broader question of dominance and subordination because they produce policy and political outcomes that encourage intolerance, sexism, racism, prejudice, and aggression toward out-groups. Such insights may help us understand what motivates both healthy and destructive leadership arrangements.

We offer a comprehensive assessment of the likely neurochemical profiles for these unusual dominance and subordination phenotypes. In doing so, we forward a series of testable hypotheses that may provide insights into the neurobiological foundations for social and political behavior. We suggest that unique elements in the SDO and RWA personality profiles may provide insights into differences in the temporal frame of reference for neural and endocrine responsivity between these personality phenotypes. Finally, we suggest two potential directions for testing these hypotheses using human, rather than animal, models.

Although the tests we suggest provide some elucidation of the neuroendocrine profiles that differentiate high-SDOs and high-RWAs, a focus only on peripheral chemical messengers—such as androgens and glucocorticoids—is only preliminary. Real understanding of these behavioral phenotypes requires some measure of the subject's brain neurochemistry. It may be possible to do this through similar experiments that add neural imaging and pharmacological indications of neural receptor activity. Such an approach will allow us to make even stronger inferences about the neurochemical foundations for leadership, dominance, subordination, and any resulting political and social behaviors.

Notes

1. Our primary concern is with personality type, and that will be the focus of the remainder of our discussion. We are, however, mindful that intelligence is heritable and that values, morals, and ethics bear perhaps more on an individual's leadership effectiveness and success than his or her selection as a leader. Regardless, a more complete analysis of morals, ethics, and values will have to happen out of the boundaries of this particular discussion.

2. Intelligence is not, however, a fixed commodity; education and experience can alter one's intelligence in meaningful ways (Sternberg 2002, 2003; Rushton 1997, among others).

3. Subordinates, however, are regarded by peers as unsure, clumsy, socially awkward (Savin-Williams 1979, 933), and neurotic (Anderson et al. 2001).

4. Testosterone is one of a variety of steroid hormones known as androgens.

5. See also Schaal et al. (1996, 1329).

6. Plasma is the fluid portion of blood, without the red and white blood cells, in which hormones are found.

7. Stressful conditions stimulate activity in the hypothalamic-pituitary-adrenal (HPA) axis, which secretes a cascade of hormones including (in order) corticotropin releasing factor (CRF), adrenocorticotropic hormone (ACTH), and the adrenal cortex steroid hormones cortisol (F) or corticosterone (B) known as corticosteroids or glucocorticoids.

8. Van Goozen et al. (2007) forwarded a model of childhood antisocial behavior—including controlled and impulsive aggression—that regards such persistent antisocial behavior as a function of genetic factors influencing the development of stress response systems (the HPA axis and the sympathetic nervous system), neurotransmitter systems (chiefly 5-HT), and environmental factors such as early exposure to adversity (i.e., stress).

9. Vasopressinergic cells secrete the neuropeptide arginine vasopressin (AVP) also known as antidiuretic hormone.

10. Cortisol is the glucocorticoid hormone produced by the human adrenal cortex as a part of a stress-induced HPA response.

11. But see also Altemeyer (2004), who found that a rare phenotype—high social dominance orientation (SDO)–high right-wing authoritarianism (RWA)—exists and that these individuals are among the most prejudiced people in society. Such individuals inherit the worst of both extreme personality types: power-hunger, intolerance, amorality from the social dominance personality type, and dogmatism and religious ethnocentrism from the authoritarian personality type (p. 421).

12. Duriez and Soenens (2006, 399) highlighted a series of studies suggesting that SDOs and RWAs have low Openness to Experience scores. SDOs have lower Agreeableness scores, while RWAs have a positive—but not always statistically significant—relationship with Conscientiousness.

13. Duncan (2003) suggested an augmentative typology by which one might examine the relationship between SDO and RWA. She suggested, citing Klatch (1987), that high-SDOs/low-RWAs may most resemble "apolitical 'laissez-faire' conservatives," while "high/highs" (Altemeyer 2003, 2004) may be the most likely to emerge as authoritarian or dictatorial leaders (Duncan 2003, 182). High-RWAs/low-SDOs, however, may most resemble social conservatives and may be the most willing high/high followers. These hypotheses merit further testing using the approaches we highlight later in this article.

14. Although Stones (2006, 1145) found that high-SDOs are less likely than high-RWAs to have negative attitudes or stereotypes about homosexuals. He attributed this difference to the link between RWAs and strong religious beliefs, a link that does not exist with SDOs.

15. See, however, Crowson, Thoma, and Hestevold (2005, 589), who argued that RWA is not synonymous with mainstream conservatism or self-reported political conservatism. They made an argument suggesting that RWAs may present an entirely different type of conservatism and that subsequent studies should attempt to address this question more directly.

16. Male vervet monkeys in one study (Raleigh et al. 1991) and female rhesus macaques (Higley, King, et al. 1996) in another.

17. Measured as the serotonin metabolite 5-HIAA (5-hydroxyindoleacetic acid) in the cerebrospinal fluid (CSF).

18. Especially in the reward centers of the nucleus accumbens and striatum.

19. The ventral tegmental area (VTA) produces dopamine, which is released in reward centers like the nucleus accumbens.

References

Adorno, T. W., E. Frenkel-Brunswick, D. J. Levinson, and R. N. Sanford. 1950. *The authoritarian personality*. New York: Norton.

Akrami, N., B. Ekehammar, and T. Araya. 2000. Classical and modern racial prejudice: A study of attitudes toward immigrants in Sweden. *European Journal of Social Psychology* 30:521-32.

Alford, J. R., C. L. Funk, and J. R. Hibbing. 2005. Are political orientations genetically transmitted? *American Political Science Review* 99 (2): 153-67.

Altemeyer, B. 1981. *Right-wing authoritarianism*. Winnipeg, Canada: University of Manitoba Press.

———. 1988. *Enemies of freedom: Understanding right-wing authoritarianism*. San Francisco: Jossey-Bass.

———. 1996. *The authoritarian specter*. Cambridge, MA: Harvard University Press.

———. 1998. The other "authoritarian personality." *Advances in Experimental Social Psychology* 30:47-92.

———. 2003. What happens when authoritarians inherit the earth? A simulation. *Analyses of Social Issues and Public Policy* 3 (1): 161-69.

———. 2004. Highly dominating, highly authoritarian personalities. *Journal of Social Psychology* 144 (4): 421-47.

Anderson, C., O. P. John, D. Keltner, and A. M. Kring. 2001. Who attains social status? Effects of personality and physical attractiveness in social groups. *Journal of Personality and Social Psychology* 81 (1): 116-32.

Archer, John. 2006. Testosterone and human aggression: An evaluation of the challenge hypothesis. *Neuroscience & Biobehavioral Reviews* 30 (3): 319-45.

Arvey, R. D., et al. 1994. Mainstream science on intelligence. *Wall Street Journal*, December 13.

Azar, B. 1995. Searching for intelligence beyond G. *APA Monitor* 26 (1): 1.

Benus, R. F., B. Bohus, J. M. Koolhaas, and G. A. van Oortmerssen. 1991. Heritable variation for aggression as a reflection of individual coping strategies. *Experientia* 47 (10): 1008-19.

Berman, M., B. Gladue, and S. Taylor. 1993. The effects of hormones, Type A behavior pattern, and provocation on aggression in men. *Motiv.Emot.* 17:125-38.

Blanchard, D. C., R. R. Sakai, B. McEwen, S. M. Weiss, and R. J. Blanchard. 1993. Subordination stress: Behavioral, brain, and neuroendocrine correlates. *Behavioral Brain Research* 58 (1-2): 113-21.

Bonson, K. R., R. G. Johnson, D. Fiorella, R. A. Rabin, and J. C. Winter. 1994. Serotonergic control of androgen-induced dominance. *Pharmacol.Biochem.Behav.* 49 (2): 313-22.

Booth, A., D. A. Granger, A. Mazur, and K. T. Kivlighan. 2006. Testosterone and social behavior. *Social Forces* 85 (1): 167-91.

Bouchard, T. J. 1997. IQ similarity in twins reared apart: Findings and responses to critics. In *Intelligence: Heredity and environment*, ed. R. J. Sternberg and E. L. Grigorenko, 126-60. New York: Cambridge University Press.

Cashdan, E. 1995. Hormones, sex, and status in women. *Hormones and Behavior* 29:354-66.

Challet, E., P. Pevet, and A. Malan. 1997. Lesion of the serotonergic terminals in the suprachiasmatic nuclei limits the phase advance of body temperature rhythm in food-restricted rats fed during daytime. *J.Biol.Rhythms* 12 (3): 235-244.

Chirumbolo, A. 2002. The relationship between need for cognitive closure and political orientation: The mediating role of authoritarianism. *Personality and Individual Differences* 32:603-10.

Cho, K., and H. J. Little. 1999. Effects of corticosterone on excitatory amino acid responses in dopamine-sensitive neurons in the ventral tegmental area. *Neuroscience* 88 (3): 837-45.

Cohen, D., R. E. Nisbett, B. F. Bowdle, and N. Schwarz. 1996. Insult, aggression, and the southern culture of honor: An "experimental ethnography." *J.Pers.Soc.Psychol.* 70 (5): 945-59.

Cohrs, J. C., S. Kielmann, J. Maes, and B. Moschner. 2005. Effects of right-wing authoritarianism and threat from terrorism on restriction of civil liberties. *Analyses of Social Issues and Public Policy* 5 (1): 263-76.

Cohrs, J. C., B. Moschner, J. Maes, and S. Kielmann. 2005. The motivational bases of right-wing authoritarianism and social dominance orientation: Relations to values and attitudes in the aftermath of September 11, 2001. *Personality and Social Psychology Bulletin* 31:1425-34.

Cologer-Clifford, A., N. G. Simon, M. L. Richter, S. A. Smoluk, and S. Lu. 1999. Androgens and estrogens modulate 5-HT$_{1A}$ and 5-HT$_{1B}$ agonist effects on aggression. *Physiol Behav.* 65 (4-5): 823-28.

Cologer-Clifford, A., S. A. Smoluk, and N. G. Simon. 1996. Effects of serotonergic 1A and 1B agonists in androgenic versus estrogenic systems for aggression. *Ann.N.Y.Acad.Sci.* 794:339-42.

Creel, S., N. M. Creel, and S. L. Monfort. 1996. Social stress and dominance. *Nature* 379:212.

Crowson, H. M., T. K. Debacker, and S. J. Thoma. 2006. The role of authoritarianism, perceived threat, and need for closure or structure in predicting post-9/11 attitudes and beliefs. *Journal of Social Psychology* 146 (6): 733-50.

Crowson, H. M., S. J. Thoma, and N. Hestevold. 2005. Is political conservatism synonymous with authoritarianism? *Journal of Social Psychology* 145 (5): 571-92.

Dabbs, J. M., F. J. Bernieri, R. K. Strong, R. Campo, and R. Milun. 2001. Going on stage: Testosterone in greetings and meetings. *Journal of Research in Personality* 35:27-40.

DeLeon, K. R., J. M. Grimes, and R. H. Melloni Jr. 2002. Repeated anabolic-androgenic steroid treatment during adolescence increases vasopressin V$_{1A}$ receptor binding in Syrian hamsters: Correlation with offensive aggression. *Hormones and Behavior* 42 (2): 182-91.

Delville, Y., K. M. Mansour, and C. F. Ferris. 1996. Serotonin blocks vasopressin-facilitated offensive aggression: Interactions within the ventrolateral hypothalamus of golden hamsters. *Physiol Behav.* 59 (4-5): 813-16.

DeNardo, D. F., and P. Licht. 1993. Effects of corticosterone on social behavior of male lizards. *Hormones and Behavior* 27 (2): 184-99.

de Ruiter, A. J., J. M. Koolhaas, J. N. Keijser, G. A. van Oortmerssen, and B. Bohus. 1992. Differential testosterone secretory capacity of the testes of aggressive and non-aggressive house mice during ontogeny. *Aggressive Behav.* 18:149-57.

DeVries, A. C., E. R. Glasper, and C. Detillion. 2003. Social modulation of stress responses. *Physiology and Behavior* 79 (3): 399-407.

Dinan, T. G. 1996a. Serotonin and the regulation of hypothalamic-pituitary-adrenal axis function. *Life Sci.* 58 (20): 1683-94.

———. 1996b. Serotonin: Current understanding and the way forward. *Int.Clin.Psychopharmacol* 11 (Suppl. 1): 19-21.

Duckitt, J. 1989. Authoritarianism and group identification: A new view of an old construct. *Political Psychology* 10:63-84.

———. 2001. A dual-process cognitive-motivational theory of ideology and prejudice. *Advances in Experimental Social Psychology* 33:41-113.

Duckitt, J., C. Wagner, I. du Plessis, and I. Birum. 2002. The psychological bases of ideology and prejudice: Testing a dual process model. *Journal of Personality and Social Psychology* 83:75-93.

Duncan, L. E. 2003. Understanding leaders of repressive social movements. *Analyses of Social Issues and Public Policy* 3 (1): 181-84.

Duriez, B. 2004. A research note on the relation between religiosity and racism: The importance of the way in which religious contents are being processed. *International Journal for the Psychology of Religion* 14:175-89.

Duriez, B., and B. Soenens. 2006. Personality, identity styles, and authoritarianism: An integrative study among late adolescents. *European Journal of Personality* 20:397-417.

Duriez, B., and A. Van Hiel. 2002. The march of modern fascism: A comparison of social dominance orientation and authoritarianism. *Personality and Individual Differences* 32:1199-1213.

Duriez, B., A. Van Hiel, and M. Kossowska. 2005. Authoritarianism and social dominance in Western and Eastern Europe: The importance of sociopolitical context and of political interest and involvement. *Political Psychology* 26:299-320.

Ekehammar, B., N. Alrami, M. Gylje, and I. Zakrisson. 2004. What matters most to prejudice: Big Five personality, social dominance orientation, or right-wing authoritarianism? *European Journal of Personality* 18:463-82.

Ferris, C. F., R. H. Melloni Jr., G. Koppel, K. W. Perry, R. W. Fuller, and Y. Delville. 1997. Vasopressin/serotonin interactions in the anterior hypothalamus control aggressive behavior in golden hamsters. *J.Neurosci* 17 (11): 4331-40.

Fiedler, F. E. 1995. Cognitive resources and leadership performance. *Applied Psychology: An International Review* 44 (1): 5-28.

Forster, G. L., M. J. Watt, W. J. Korzan, K. J. Renner, and C. H. Summers. 2005. Opponent recognition in male green anoles, *Anolis carolinensis*. *Animal Behaviour* 69 (3): 733-40.

Georgesen, J., and M. J. Harris. 2006. Holding onto power: Effects of powerholders' positional instability and expectancies on interactions with subordinates. *European Journal of Social Psychology* 36:451-68.

Goymann, W., M. M. Landys, and J. C. Wingfield. Forthcoming. Distinguishing seasonal androgen responses from male-male androgen responsiveness—Revisiting the challenge hypothesis. *Hormones and Behavior*.

Graeff, F. G. 1997. Serotonergic systems. *Psychiatr.Clin.North Am.* 20 (4): 723-39.

Graeff, F. G., F. S. Guimaraes, T. G. De Andrade, and J. F. Deakin. 1996. Role of 5-HT in stress, anxiety, and depression. *Pharmacol.Biochem.Behav.* 54 (1): 129-41.

Grant, V. J., and J. T. France. 2001. Dominance and testosterone in women. *Biological Psychology* 58 (1): 41-47.

Greenberg, N., and D. Crews. 1990. Endocrine and behavioral responses to aggression and social dominance in the green anole lizard, *Anolis carolinensis*. *General and Comparative Endocrinology* 77 (2): 246-55.

Halasz, J., Z. Liposits, M. R. Kruk, and J. Haller. 2002. Neural background of glucocorticoid dysfunction-induced abnormal aggression in rats: Involvement of. *European Journal of Neuroscience* 15 (3): 561-69.

Haller, J., J. Halasz, E. Mikics, and M. R. Kruk. 2004. Chronic glucocorticoid deficiency-induced abnormal aggression, autonomic hypoarousal, and social deficit in rats. *J Neuroendocrinol* 16 (6): 550-57.

Halpern, C. T., J. R. Udry, B. Campbell, and C. Suchindran. 1994. Relationships between aggression and pubertal increases in testosterone: A panel analysis of adolescent males. *Social Biol.* 40:8-24.

Halpern, C. T., J. R. Udry, B. Campbell, C. Suchindran, and G. A. Mason. 1994. Testosterone and religiosity as predictors of sexual attitudes and activity among adolescent males: A biosocial model. *J.Biosoc.Sci.* 26 (2): 217-34.

Hawley, P. H. 1999. The ontogenesis of social dominance: A strategy-based evolutionary perspective. *Developmental Review* 19:97-132.

Heaven, P. C. L., and S. Bucci. 2001. Right-wing authoritarianism, social dominance orientation, and personality: An analysis using the IPIP measure. *European Journal of Personality* 15:49-56.

Heaven, P. C. L., L. Organ, S. Supvadeeprasit, and P. Leeson. 2006. War and prejudice: A study of social values, right-wing authoritarianism, and social dominance orientation. *Personality and Individual Differences* 40:599-608.

Hibbing, J. R., J. R. Alford, P. Hatemi, N. Martin, and L. Eaves. 2007. Not by twins alone. Paper presented at the annual meeting of the Midwest Political Science Association, April 12-14, Chicago.

Higley, J. D., S. T. King Jr., M. F. Hasert, M. Champoux, S. J. Suomi, and M. Linnoila. 1996. Stability of interindividual differences in serotonin function and its relationship to severe aggression and competent social behavior in rhesus macaque females. *Neuropsychopharmacology* 14 (1): 67-76.

Higley, J. D., P. T. Mehlman, S. B. Higley, B. Fernald, J. Vickers, S. G. Lindell, D. M. Taub, S. J. Suomi, and M. Linnoila. 1996. Excessive mortality in young free-ranging male nonhuman primates with low cerebrospinal fluid 5-hydroxyindoleacetic acid concentrations. *Arch.Gen.Psychiatry* 53 (6): 537-43.

Higley, J. D., P. T. Mehlman, R. E. Poland, D. M. Taub, J. Vickers, S. J. Suomi, and M. Linnoila. 1996. CSF testosterone and 5-HIAA correlate with different types of aggressive behaviors. *Biol.Psychiatry* 40 (11): 1067-82.

Higley, J. D., P. T. Mehlman, D. M. Taub, S. B. Higley, S. J. Suomi, J. H. Vickers, and M. Linnoila. 1992. Cerebrospinal fluid monoamine and adrenal correlates of aggression in free-ranging rhesus monkeys. *Arch.Gen.Psychiatry* 49 (6): 436-41.

Hogan, J., and B. Holland. 2003. Using theory to evaluate personality and job-performance relations: A socio-analytic perspective. *Journal of Applied Psychology* 88 (1): 100-112.

Hogan, R. 1991. Personality and personality measurement. In *Handbook of industrial and organizational psychology*, vol. 2, ed. M. D. Dunnette and L. M. Hough, 873-919. Palo Alto, CA: Consulting Psychologists Press.

Hogan, R., and G. J. Curphy, and J. Hogan. 1994. What do we know about leadership? *American Psychologist* 49 (6): 493-504.

Hogan, R. T., J. Hogan, and B. W. Roberts. 1996. Personality measurement and employment decisions: Questions and answers. *American Psychologist* 51 (5): 469-77.

Hughes, R. L., R. C. Ginnett, and G. J. Curphy. 2005. *Leadership: Enhancing the lessons of experience.* 5th ed. Boston: McGraw-Hill.

Ilies, R., M. W. Gerhardt, and H. Le. 2004. Individual differences in leadership emergence: Integrating meta-analytic findings and behavioral genetics estimates. *International Journal of Selection and Assessment* 12 (3): 207-19.

Jacobs, B. L., and E. C. Azmitia. 1992. Structure and function of the brain serotonin system. *Physiol Rev.* 72 (1): 165-229.

Jacobs, B. L., and C. A. Fornal. 1999. Activity of serotonergic neurons in behaving animals. *Neuropsychopharmacology* 21 (2, Suppl.): 9S-15S.

John, O. P., and S. Srivastava. 1999. The Big Five trait taxonomy: History, measurement, and theoretical perspectives. In *Handbook of personality: Theory and research*, 2nd ed., ed. L. A. Pervin and O. P. John, 102-38. New York: Guilford.

Jost, J. T., J. Glaser, A. W. Kruglanski, and F. J. Sulloway. 2003. Political conservatism and motivated social cognition. *Psychological Bulletin* 129 (3): 339-75.

Judge, T. A., I. E. Bono, R. Ilies, and M. W. Gerhardt. 2002. Leadership and personality: A qualitative and quantitative review. *Journal of Applied Psychology* 87 (4): 765-80.

Judge, T. A., A. Colbert, and R. Ilies. 2004. Intelligence and leadership: A quantitative review and test of theoretical propositions. *Journal of Applied Psychology* 89:542-52.

Kemmelmeier, M. 2004. Authoritarianism and candidate support in the U.S. presidential elections of 1996 and 2000. *Journal of Social Psychology* 144:218-22.

Klatch, R. E. 1987. *Women of the new right.* Philadelphia: Temple University Press.

Koolhaas, J. M., S. F. de Boer, B. Buwalda, and K. van Reenen. Forthcoming. Individual variation in coping with stress: Ultimate and proximate mechanisms. *Brain Behavior and Evolution.*

Koolhaas, J. M., S. M. Korte, S. F. de Boer, B. J. van der Vegt, C. G. van Reenen, H. Hopster, I. C. de Jong, M. A. Ruis, and H. J. Blokhuis. 1999. Coping styles in animals: Current status in behavior and stress-physiology. *Neuroscience and Biobehavioral Reviews* 23 (7): 925-35.

Korte, S. M., J. M. Koolhaas, J. C. Wingfield, and B. S. McEwen. 2005. The Darwinian concept of stress: Benefits of allostasis and costs of allostatic load and the trade-offs in health and disease. *Neurosci.Biobehav.Rev.* 29 (1): 3-38.

Korzan, W. J., G. L. Forster, M. J. Watt, and C. H. Summers. 2006. Dopaminergic activity modulation via aggression, status, and a visual social signal. *Behavioral Neuroscience* 120 (1): 93-102.

Korzan, W. J., E. Höglund, M. J. Watt, G. L. Forster, Ø. Øverli, J. L. Lukkes, and C. H. Summers. 2007. Memory of opponents is more potent than visual sign stimuli after social hierarchy has been established. *Behavioral Brain Research* 183 (1):31-42.

Korzan, W. J., Ø. Øverli, and C. H. Summers. 2006. Future social rank: Forecasting status in the green anole (*Anolis carolinensis*). *Acta Ethologica* 9:48-57.

Korzan, W. J., and C. H. Summers. Forthcoming. Behavioral diversity and neurochemical plasticity: Selection of stress coping strategies that define social status. *Brain Behavior and Evolution*.

Kossowska, M., and A. Van Hiel. 2003. The relationship between need for closure and conservative beliefs in Western and Eastern Europe. *Political Psychology* 24 (3): 501-18.

Kruk, M. R., J. Halász, W. Meelis, and J. Haller. 2004. Fast positive feedback between the adrenocortical stress response and a brain mechanism involved in aggressive behavior. *Behavioral Neuroscience* 118:1062-70.

Larson, E. T., and C. H. Summers. 2001. Serotonin reverses dominant social status. *Behavioral Brain Research* 121 (1-2): 95-102.

Lease, A. M., K. T. Musgrove, and J. L. Axelrod. 2002. Dimensions of social status in preadolescent peer groups: Likability, perceived popularity, and social dominance. *Social Development* 11 (4): 508-33.

Lidberg, L., J. R. Tuck, M. Asberg, G. P. Scalia-Tomba, and L. Bertilsson. 1985. Homicide, suicide and CSF 5-HIAA. *Acta Psychiatr.Scand.* 71 (3): 230-36.

Lippa, R., and S. Arad. 1999. Gender, personality, and prejudice: The display of authoritarianism and social dominance in interviews with college men and women. *Journal of Research in Personality* 33:463-93.

Loehlin, J. C. 1992. *Genes and environment in personality development*. Newbury Park, CA: Sage.

Loehlin, J. C., R. R. McCrae, P. T. Costa, and O. P. John. 1998. Heritabilities of common and measure-specific components of the Big Five personality factors. *Journal of Research in Personality* 32:431-53.

Lord, R. G., C. L. De Vader, and G. M. Allinger. 1986. A meta-analysis of the relation between personality traits and leadership perceptions: An application of validity generalization procedures. *Journal of Applied Psychology* 71:402-10.

Lowry, C. A. 2002. Functional subsets of serotonergic neurons: Implications for control of the hypothalamic-pituitary-adrenal axis. *J.Neuroendocrinol.* 14:911-23.

Ludwig, A. M. 2002. *King of the mountain: The nature of political leadership*. Lexington: University Press of Kentucky.

Mann, J. J., K. M. Malone, M. R. Psych, J. A. Sweeney, R. P. Brown, M. Linnoila, B. Stanley, and M. Stanley. 1996. Attempted suicide characteristics and cerebrospinal fluid amine metabolites in depressed inpatients. *Neuropsychopharmacology* 15 (6): 576-86.

Martinez, M., F. Guillen-Salazar, A. Salvador, and V. M. Simon. 1995. Successful intermale aggression and conditioned place preference in mice. *Physiol Behav.* 58 (2): 323-28.

McCann, S. J. H. 1997. Threatening times, "strong" presidential popular vote winners, and the victory margin, 1824-1964. *Journal of Personality and Social Psychology* 73 (1): 160-70.

McHoskey, J. W. 1996. Authoritarianism and ethical ideology. *Journal of Social Psychology* 136:708-17.

Mehlman, P. T., J. D. Higley, I. Faucher, A. A. Lilly, D. M. Taub, J. Vickers, S. J. Suomi, and M. Linnoila. 1994. Low CSF 5-HIAA concentrations and severe aggression and impaired impulse control in non-human primates. *Am.J.Psychiatry* 151 (10): 1485-91.

Melloni, R. H., D. F. Connor, P. T. Hang, R. J. Harrison, and C. F. Ferris. 1997. Anabolic-androgenic steroid exposure during adolescence and aggressive behavior in golden hamsters. *Physiol Behav.* 61 (3): 359-64.

Melloni, R. H., and C. F. Ferris. 1996. Adolescent anabolic steroid use and aggressive behavior in golden hamsters. *Ann.N.Y.Acad.Sci.* 794:372-75.

Mitman, G. 1990. Dominance, leadership, and aggression: Animal behavior studies during the Second World War. *Journal of the History of the Behavioral Sciences* 26 (1): 3-16.

Nelson, R. J., and S. Chiavegatto. 2001. Molecular basis of aggression. *Trends Neurosci.* 24 (12): 713-19.

Nemeroff, C. B. 1998a. The neurobiology of depression. *Sci.Am.* 278 (6): 42-49.

———. 1998b. Psychopharmacology of affective disorders in the 21st century. *Biol Psychiatry* 44 (7): 517-25.

Oliveira, R. F., V. C. Almada, and A. V. Canario. 1996. Social modulation of sex steroid concentrations in the urine of male cichlid fish *Oreochromis mossambicus*. *Hormones and Behavior* 30 (1): 2-12.

Oliveira, R. F., L. A. Carneiro, and A. V. Canario. 2005. No hormonal response in tied fights. *Nature* 437 (7056): 207-8.

Oliveira, R. F., K. Hirschenhauser, L. A. Carneiro, and A. V. Canario. 2002. Social modulation of androgen levels in male teleost fish. *Comp Biochem.Physiol B Biochem.Mol.Biol.* 132 (1): 203-15.

Oliveira, R. F., M. Lopes, L. A. Carneiro, and A. V. Canario. 2001. Watching fights raises fish hormone levels. *Nature* 409 (6819): 475.

Oliveira, R. F., P. K. McGregor, and C. Latruffe. 1998. Know thine enemy: Fighting fish gather information from observing conspecific interactions. *Proc.R.Soc Lond B Biol.Sci.* 265:1045-49.

Øverli, Ø., W. J. Korzan, E. Höglund, S. Winberg, H. Bollig, M. J. Watt, G. L. Forster, B. A. Barton, E. Øverli, K. J. Renner, and C. H. Summers. 2004. Stress coping style predicts aggression and social dominance in rainbow trout. *Hormones and Behavior* 45:235-41.

Øverli, Ø., C. Sørensen, K. G. Pulman, T. G. Pottinger, W. Korzan, C. H. Summers, and G. E. Nilsson. 2007. Evolutionary background for stress-coping styles: Relationships between physiological, behavioral, and cognitive traits in non-mammalian vertebrates. *Neurosci.Biobehav.Rev.* 31 (3): 396-412.

Ozer, D. J., and V. Benet-Martinez. 2006. Personality and the prediction of consequential outcomes. *Annual Review of Psychology* 57 (1): 401-21.

Piazza, P. V., and M. Le Moal. 1997. Glucocorticoids as a biological substrate of reward: Physiological and pathophysiological implications. *Brain Res.Brain Res.Rev.* 25 (3): 359-72.

Plomin, R. 1990. The role of inheritance in behavior. *Science* 248 (4952): 183-88.

Pottinger, T. G., and T. R. Carrick. 1999. Modification of the plasma cortisol response to stress in rainbow trout by selective breeding. *General and Comparative Endocrinology* 116 (1): 122-32.

———. 2001. Stress responsiveness affects dominant-subordinate relationships in rainbow trout. *Hormones and Behavior* 40 (3): 419-27.

Pratto, F., J. Sidanius, L. M. Stallworth, and B. F. Malle. 1994. Social dominance orientation: A personality variable predicting social and political attitudes. *Journal of Personality and Social Psychology* 67:741-63.

Pratto, F., L. M. Stallworth, J. Sidanius, and B. Siers. 1997. The gender gap in occupational role attainment: A social dominance approach. *Journal of Personality and Social Psychology* 72:37-53.

Raleigh, M. J., M. T. McGuire, G. L. Brammer, D. B. Pollack, and A. Yuwiler. 1991. Serotonergic mechanisms promote dominance acquisition in adult male vervet monkeys. *Brain Research* 559 (2): 181-90.

Ray, J. 1976. Do authoritarians hold authoritarian attitudes? *Human Relations* 29:307-25.

Ray, J., and R. M. Sapolsky. 1992. Styles of male social behavior and their endocrine correlates among high-ranking wild baboons. *American Journal of Primatology* 28:231-50.

Roccato, M., and L. Ricolfi. 2005. On the correlation between right-wing authoritarianism and social dominance orientation. *Basic and Applied Social Psychology* 27 (3): 187-200.

Rowe, R., B. Maughan, C. M. Worthman, E. J. Costello, and A. Angold. 2004. Testosterone, anti-social behavior, and social dominance in boys: Pubertal development and biosocial interaction. *Biological Psychiatry* 55:546-52.

Rushton, J. P. 1997. Race, IQ, and the APA report on the bell curve. *American Psychologist* 52 (1): 69-70.

Salgado, J. F. 2003. Predicting job performance using FFM and non-FFM personality measures. *Journal of Occupational and Organization Psychology* 76 (3): 323-46.

Salvadora, A., F. Suay, S. Martinez-Sanchis, V. M. Simon, and P. F. Brain. 1999. Correlating testosterone and fighting in male participants in judo contests. *Physiol Behav.* 68 (1-2): 205-9.

Sarason, I. 1986. Stress, anxiety, and cognitive interference: Reactions to stress. *Journal of Personality and Social Psychology* 86 (6): 929-39.

Savin-Williams, R. C. 1979. Dominance hierarchies in groups of early adolescents. *Child Development* 50 (4): 923-35.

Schaal, B., R. E. Tremblay, R. Soussignan, and E. J. Susman. 1996. Male testosterone linked to high social dominance by low physical aggression in early adolescence. *Journal of the Academy of Child and Adolescent Psychiatry* 34 (10): 1322-30.

Scheepers, D., and N. Ellemers. 2005. When the pressure is up: The assessment of social identity threat in low and high status groups. *Journal of Experimental Social Psychology* 37:93-103.

Sibley, C. G., A. Robertson, and M. S. Wilson. 2006. Social dominance orientation and right-wing authoritarianism: Additive and interactive effects. *Political Psychology* 27 (5): 755-68.

Sidanius, J., and F. Pratto. 1999. *Social dominance*. New York: Cambridge University Press.

Simon, N. G., A. Cologer-Clifford, S. F. Lu, S. E. McKenna, and S. Hu. 1998. Testosterone and its metabolites modulate $5HT_{1A}$ and $5HT_{1B}$ agonist effects on intermale aggression. *Neurosci.Biobehav.Rev.* 23 (2): 325-36.

Son-Hing, L. S., D. R. Bobocel, M. P. Zanna, and M. V. McBride. 2007. Authoritarian dynamics and unethical decision making: High social dominance orientation leaders and high right-wing authoritarianism followers. *Journal of Personality and Social Psychology* 92:67-81.

Sternberg, R. J. 2002. Creativity as a decision. *American Psychologist* 52 (10): 1030-57.
————. 2003. A broad view of intelligence: The theory of successful intelligence. *Journal of Consulting Psychology* 55 (3): 139-54.
Stogdill, R. M. 1948. Personal factors associated with leadership: A review of the literature. *Journal of Psychology* 25:35-71.
————. 1974. *Handbook of leadership*. New York: Free Press.
Stones, C. R. 2006. Antigay prejudice among heterosexual males: Right-wing authoritarianism as a stronger predictor than social dominance orientation and heterosexual identity. *Social Behavior and Personality* 34 (9): 1137-50.
Suay, F., A. Salvador, E. Gonzalez-Bono, C. Sanchis, M. Martinez, S. Martinez-Sanchis, V. M. Simon, and J. B. Montoro. 1999. Effects of competition and its outcome on serum testosterone, cortisol and prolactin. *Psychoneuroendocrinology* 24 (5): 551-66.
Summers, C. H., G. L. Forster, W. J. Korzan, M. J. Watt, E. T. Larson, Ø. Øverli, E. Höglund, P. J. Ronan, T. R. Summers, K. J. Renner, and N. Greenberg. 2005. Dynamics and mechanics of social rank reversal. *Journal of Comparative Physiology. A, Neuroethology, Sensory, Neural, and Behavioral Physiology* 191 (3): 241-52.
Summers, C. H., J. L. Kampshoff, P. J. Ronan, C. A. Lowry, A. A. Prestbo, W. J. Korzan, and K. J. Renner. 2003. Monoaminergic activity in subregions of raphe nuclei elicited by prior stress and the neuropeptide corticotropin-releasing factor. *J.Neuroendocrinol.* 15 (12): 1122-33.
Summers, C. H., W. J. Korzan, J. L. Lukkes, Ø. Øverli, E. Höglund, M. J. Watt, E. T. Larson, G. L. Forster, P. J. Ronan, T. R. Summers, K. J. Renner, and N. Greenberg. 2005. Does serotonin influence aggression? Comparing regional activity before and during social interaction. *Physiological and Biochemical Zoology* 78:679-94.
Summers, C. H., E. T. Larson, P. J. Ronan, P. M. Hofmann, A. J. Emerson, and K. J. Renner. 2000. Serotonergic responses to corticosterone and testosterone in the limbic system. *Gen.Comp Endocrinol.* 117 (1): 151-59.
Summers, C. H., T. R. Summers, M. C. Moore, W. J. Korzan, S. K. Woodley, P. J. Ronan, E. Höglund, M. J. Watt, and N. Greenberg. 2003. Temporal patterns of limbic monoamine and plasma corticosterone response during social stress. *Neuroscience* 116 (2): 553-63.
Summers, C. H., M. J. Watt, T. J. Ling, G. L. Forster, R. E. Carpenter, W. J. Korzan, J. L. Lukkes, and Ø. Øverli. 2005. Glucocorticoid interaction with aggression in non-mammalian vertebrates: Reciprocal action. *European Journal of Pharmacology* 526:21-35.
Summers, Cliff H., and Svante Winberg. 2006. Interactions between the neural regulation of stress and aggression. *Journal of Experimental Biology* 209 (23): 4581-89.
Summers, T. R., J. M. Matter, J. M. McKay, P. J. Ronan, E. T. Larson, K. J. Renner, and C. H. Summers. 2003. Rapid glucocorticoid stimulation and GABAergic inhibition of hippocampal serotonergic response: In vivo dialysis in the lizard *Anolis carolinensis*. *Horm.Behav* 43 (1): 245-53.
Swim, J. K., K. J. Aikin, W. S. Hall, and B. A. Hunter. 1995. Sexism and racism: Old-fashioned and modern prejudice. *Journal of Personality and Social Psychology* 68:199-214.
Tett, R. P., and D. D. Burnett. 2003. A personality trait-based interactionist model of job performance. *Journal of Applied Psychology* 88 (3): 500-517.
Thomas, C. A., and V. M. Esses. 2004. Individual differences in reactions to sexist humor. *Group Processes and Intergroup Relations* 7:89-100.
Tremblay, R. E., B. Schaal, B. Boulerice, R. G. Soussignan, D. Paquette, and D. Laurant. 1998. Testosterone, physical aggression, dominance, and physical development in early adolescence. *International Journal of Behavioral Development* 22:753-77.
Tupes, E. C., and R. E. Christal. 1961. Recurrent personality factors based on trait ratings. Technical Report ASD-TR-61-97. Lackland Air Force Base, TX: U.S. Air Force.
Udry, J. R., N. M. Morris, and J. Kovenock. 1995. Androgen effects on women's gendered behavior. *Journal of Biosocial Science* 27:359-69.
Valentino, R. J., L. Liouterman, and E. J. Van Bockstaele. 2001. Evidence for regional heterogeneity in corticotropin-releasing factor interactions in the dorsal raphe nucleus. *J.Comp Neurol.* 435 (4): 450-63.
Van Goozen, S. H., H. Snoek, G. Fairchild, and G. T. Harold. 2007. The evidence for a neurobiological model of childhood antisocial behavior. *Psychological Bulletin* 133 (1): 149-82.

Van Hiel, A., M. Pandelaere, and B. Duriez. 2004. The impact of need for closure on conservative beliefs and racism: Differential mediation by authoritarian submission and authoritarian dominance. *Personality and Social Psychology Bulletin* 30:824-37.

Van Praag, H. M. 1991. Serotonergic dysfunction and aggression control. *Psychol.Med.* 21 (1): 15-19.

Veenema, A. H., O. C. Meijer, E. R. de Kloet, and J. M. Koolhaas. 2003. Genetic selection for coping style predicts stressor susceptibility. *J Neuroendocrinol* 15 (3): 256-67.

Veenema, A. H., O. C. Meijer, E. R. de Kloet, J. M. Koolhaas, and B. G. Bohus. 2003. Differences in basal and stress-induced HPA regulation of wild house mice selected for high and low aggression. *Hormones and Behavior* 43 (1): 197-204.

Virkkunen, M., D. Goldman, D. A. Nielsen, and M. Linnoila. 1995. Low brain serotonin turnover rate (low CSF 5-HIAA) and impulsive violence. *J.Psychiatry Neurosci* 20 (4): 271-75.

Whitley, B. E. 1999. Right-wing authoritarianism, social dominance orientation, and prejudice. *Journal of Personality and Social Psychology* 77:126-34.

Wilson, M. S. 2003. Social dominance and ethical ideology: The end justifies the means? *Journal of Social Psychology* 143 (5): 549-58.

Wingfield, J. C. 1985. Short-term changes in plasma levels of hormones during establishment and defense of a breeding territory in male song sparrows, *Melospiza melodia*. *Hormones and Behavior* 19 (2): 174-87.

Wingfield, J. C., R. E. Hegner, A. M. Dufty, and G. F. Ball. 1990. The challenge hypothesis: Theoretical implications for patterns of testosterone secretion, mating systems, and breeding strategies. *Am.Nat.* 136:829-46.

The Political Consequences of Perceived Threat and Felt Insecurity

The authors draw on data from a national random digit dial (RDD) telephone sample of 1,549 adult Americans conducted between October 15, 2001, and March 2, 2002, to explore the impact of a need for security on support for national security policies in the aftermath of the 9/11 terrorist attacks. They examine support for protective government policies among individuals who vary in their ability to feel secure in the aftermath of terrorism, exploring the interaction between perceived threat and felt security. Most Americans reported a sense of security after the 9/11 attacks. But a sense of insecurity among a minority of Americans coupled with a perceived threat of future terrorism increased support for both domestic and international security policy—the curtailment of domestic civil liberties, tougher visa checks, and support for the war in Afghanistan. The authors' findings underscore the diverse ways in which individuals react politically to a common external threat.

Keywords: threat; public opinion; security; attachment theory

By
LEONIE HUDDY,
STANLEY FELDMAN,
and
CHRISTOPHER WEBER

Psychological reactions to terrorism play a pivotal role in understanding public support for government antiterrorist policies. As Crenshaw (1986, 400) argued, "The political effectiveness of terrorism is importantly determined by the psychological effects of violence on audiences." Psychological reactions to external threat differ, however, and these reactions shape support of government policies designed to combat terrorism. In our past research, we have explored the differing political implications of anxiety, anger, perceived personal threat, and perceived national threat (Huddy et al. 2005; Huddy, Feldman, and Cassese 2007; Huddy et al. 2002). In the current study, we take this research one step further to explore not only political

NOTE: This article was originally presented at the Hendricks Conference on Political Behavior, Lincoln, Nebraska, October 13-14. This research was supported by Grants SES-0201650 and SES-9975063 from the National Science Foundation. We wish to thank our colleagues Charles Taber and Gallya Lahav for permission to use data from the Threat and National Security Survey.

DOI: 10.1177/0002716207305951

reactions to threat but how a sense of security interacts with threat to influence support for national security policies.

Terrorists aim to threaten members of a target population directly by perpetrating random acts of violence on people engaged in everyday activities. Research on threats that involve the potential for physical harm such as crime, natural disasters, and violent conflicts provides clear evidence that personal threat increases one's sense of vulnerability and motivates action designed to minimize personal risk (Browne and Hoyt 2000; Ferraro 1996; Sattler, Kaiser, and Hittner 2000). We find similar evidence after 9/11. Individuals living in Queens and Long Island (in relatively close proximity to the World Trade Center) who felt personally threatened by terrorism used more caution in handling their mail, spent more time with their families, delayed or dropped their plans to travel by air, and used public transportation in Manhattan less frequently in the several months after the attacks. In this instance, perceived personal threat motivated cautionary action over and above the effects of any perceived risk of terrorism to Americans more generally (Huddy et al. 2002).

Threat not only motivates protective behaviors but also promotes support for protective government policies. Studies conducted to date find a clear link between national threat and support for national and domestic security policies (Davis and Silver 2004; Huddy et al. 2005). In our research on reactions to 9/11, we find that perceived future terrorist threat leads to greater support for an aggressive national security policy, including increased support for the war in Afghanistan (Huddy et al. 2005). Threat also heightens support for increased surveillance policies against current and potential Arab immigrants to the United States and policies that promise increased domestic safety but could threaten Americans' civil liberties. National threat leads to support for punitive action against terrorist groups (Bar-Tal and Labin 2001; Gordon and Arian 2001; Friedland and Merari 1985). And an adversary's degree of belligerence and the level of threat posed to U.S. interests increase public support for war and military action against a specific aggressor (Herrmann, Tetlock, and Visser 1999; Jentleson 1992; Jentleson and Britton 1998; Mueller 1973). Threat clearly increases support for aggressive foreign policy. It is less clear, however, whether this reaction serves a retaliatory function or is seen as a form of personal protection.

Leonie Huddy is a professor of political science and director of the Center for Survey Research at Stony Brook University, New York. She has written extensively on the application of psychological theories to the study of political beliefs, with a special emphasis on race, ethnic, and gender relations. She is the coeditor of the Oxford Handbook of Political Psychology *and coeditor of the journal* Political Psychology.

Stanley Feldman is a professor of political science at Stony Brook University. His interests include political ideology, political psychology, and methodology. He is a former president of the Methodology section of the American Political Science Association and a former member of the Board of Overseers for the American National Election Studies.

Christopher Weber is a graduate student in political science at Stony Brook University. His primary research interests include ideology, public opinion, political communication, and the role that emotions play in political persuasion and deliberation.

We further explore the link between threat and support of national security policy by examining the extent to which it depends on a person's degree of felt security. Our research stems from evidence that some individuals are able to maintain a sense of security even in the face of threatening events. This sense of security may undercut their need for protective personal and government policies in response to threatening events (Pyszczynski, Solomon, and Greenberg 2002; Mikulincer and Shaver 2003; Fraley et al. 2006).

A Need for Security: Attachment and Terror Management Theories

Social scientists broadly agree that a sense of security is a basic need in humans and other species (Fraley 2002; Goldberg 2000; Mikulincer and Shaver 2003). Psychologist Abraham Maslow (1943) placed security just above the satisfaction of basic physiological needs in his hierarchy of human needs (and below love and self-actualization). And political scientist Ronald Inglehart (1997), building on Maslow's work, viewed the fulfillment of basic economic and security needs as a necessary societal precondition to the pursuit of postmaterialist values that emphasize freedom, self-expression, and quality of life. Bowlby's attachment theory ([1969] 1982) represents an evolutionary–developmental account of social behavior that posits a need for social proximity to protective others, especially under conditions of threat and danger, to explain the development of felt security. According to this approach, the attachment system—a system that takes shape in early infancy—is activated in times of distress. Successful attachment is built on a foundation of secure parental relations, produces a lifelong ability to positively cope with negative events and their accompanying anxiety and stress, and leads to an enduring sense of security.

Building on Bowlby's notion ([1969] 1982) of a universal human need for attachment as a way to deal with insecurity, numerous scholars have explored the likely evolutionary advantage of adult attachment under conditions of threat (Ainsworth et al. 1978; Mikulincer and Shaver 2003; Fraley, Brumbaugh, and Marks 2005; Kirkpatrick 1998; Tancredy and Fraley 2006; Simpson et al. 2007). Several different possibilities have been raised. First, adult attachment could improve human reproductive fitness through the process of kin selection by promoting the protection of those with whom one shares similar genes (Hamilton 1964). Second, adult attachment could be a simple outgrowth of humans' protracted developmental period in infancy in which attachment is needed to protect offspring and stimulate complex social and cognitive skills (Bowlby [1969] 1982; Fernald 1992; Mikulincer and Shaver 2003; Fraley 2002). Third, adult attachment may foster long-lasting romantic and parenting relationships that may improve the fitness of one's offspring (Zeifman and Hazan 1997; although for alternative views, see Belsky 1999; Chisholm 1996; Buss and Schmitt 1993; Schmitt 2005; cf. Kirkpatrick 1998).

The primary goal of attachment behaviors is to reduce anxiety through an established sense of "felt security" (Sroufe and Waters 1977). The attachment system emerges in early infancy, particularly in the context of the caregiver–child relationship, and operates as a functional system organizing interpersonal beliefs throughout development (Bowlby [1969] 1982). While the *attachment system* is universal, operating in all humans and a host of other organisms (e.g., Fraley, Brumbaugh, and Marks 2005), individual differences often emerge from variations in attachment histories. Successful early attachment experiences establish one's *chronic* attachment style, operating as what Bowlby ([1969] 1982) referred to as an "internal working model" of the self and other (Bartholomew and Horowitz 1991). For instance, a secure attachment style—marked by self-confidence, empathy, and trust between the caregiver and child—stems from repeated episodes of successful attachment behavior. Insecure attachment patterns emerge in less responsive caregiving contexts (Mikulincer and Shaver 2003; Brennan and Shaver 1995; Mikulincer and Shaver 2001). While many scholars have distinguished between the various types of insecure attachment patterns (e.g., Weber and Federico 2007), and the stability of attachment patterns throughout development (e.g., Simpson et al. 2007), we are primarily concerned with the difference between a secure and insecure attachment as a moderating influence on emotional and political reactions to the September 11, 2001, terrorist attacks.

Once established, attachment styles are relatively constant across the lifespan, suggesting that they serve as a stable individual difference (Fraley 2002; Ainsworth 1991; Simpson et al. 2007) that may be mediated by distinct neural and hormonal reactions to threat. For instance, Kraemer (1992) found that physiological indicators of stress such as norepinephrine varied in rhesus monkeys depending on whether they were reared in isolation or with mothers and/or peers. Humans with an enduring sense of insecurity release higher levels of glucocorticoids in stressful situations than those with a secure attachment (Goldberg 2000). Moreover, in a major longitudinal study, Simpson et al. (2007) found that one's attachment pattern measured in infancy predicted social competence in adolescence, feelings of security in late adolescence and, ultimately, the ways in which romantic partners related to one another in early adulthood.

A good deal of research on attachment theory has been devoted to the assessment of individual differences in attachment style and the effects of this style on interpersonal relations and mental health. But the theory is broader than that and has been employed to understand individual differences in the development of political ideologies (Weber and Federico 2007), coping with the 9/11 terrorist attacks (Fraley et al. 2006), derogating out-groups (Mikulincer and Shaver 2003), engaging in risk-seeking behavior (Taubman Ben-Ari and Mikulincer 2007), and responding to stressful events. Typically, researchers examine the impact of attachment style on coping with various threats (for a review, see Mikulincer and Shaver 2003). Some of that research is very relevant to the study of reactions to terrorism. Mikulincer, Florian, and Weller (1993) examined the effects of the Gulf War and Iraqi Scud missile attacks on Israelis with different attachment styles and found that securely attached individuals perceived lower levels of threat, reported higher levels of self-efficacy, actively sought out social support, and pursued constructive problem-solving strategies. Former Israeli prisoners of war with a secure attachment style recalled positive memories or encounters with others to help cope with their imprisonment, in essence seeking symbolic proximity to internalized attachment figures (Solomon et al. 1998). The need for attachment can also be activated by a mortality salience manipulation typically employed in the study of terror management theory (Mikulincer et al. 2000). Secure individuals often react to mortality salience by seeking the closeness of others, whereas attachment insecurity tends to inhibit social interaction and can lead to harsh treatment of those who violate social conventions (Mikulincer and Florian 2000; Taubman Ben-Ari, Findler, and Mikulincer 2002; Florian, Mikulincer, and Hirschberger 2002; Fraley et al. 2006).

When taken together, research on attachment theory suggests that a long-standing sense of security derived from a secure attachment style and its associated active coping strategies may help to mitigate the negative effects of stressful events. The ability to cope well with stressful events may extend to politics, undermining the need among secure individuals for government policies designed to promote a sense of safety. This possibility has not yet received empirical support but offers an intriguing explanation of how long-standing dispositions interact with events to shape support for government security policies. As a consequence, the theory may help to explain why threat is likely to drive one person to demand more powerful safety and security policies from the federal government while another is able to maintain a sense of personal security in the absence of government action.

The ability to cope well with stressful events may extend to politics, undermining the need among secure individuals for government policies designed to promote a sense of safety.

In a popular competing view of how humans maintain a sense of ongoing security, terror management theorists (Pyszczynski, Solomon, and Greenberg 2002) provide a related but distinct account of how individuals restore a sense of security in the face of threat, especially existential threats linked to one's morality. From this perspective, coping involves adherence to a cultural worldview linked, for example, to religion, moral conduct, or patriotism that boosts self-esteem and often involves the derogation of outsiders who do not share the same view. Terror management researchers have paid less attention to differences in the ways in which individuals restore a sense of security, but recent research by Hart, Shaver, and Goldenberg (2005) suggests that differences in attachment style also moderate responses to existential threats. In their research, insecure individuals were most likely to respond to existential threat with more positive ratings of an in-group member.

In this research, we closely examine whether a sense of felt security provides a buffer against threatening events and reduces the need for government action to maintain a sense of safety. We focus on both domestic and international government security policies. In essence, we test whether perceived threat coupled with a feeling of insecurity promotes support for policies that enhance domestic security but may reduce civil liberties and leads to increased support for overseas military action.

Anxiety: A Needed Control

In turning to security as an important moderating influence on perceived threat, it is important to distinguish its effects from that of anxiety, with which it is related. Our past work demonstrates that personal threat is strongly tied to a sense of heightened anxiety. Individuals who felt anxious after 9/11 experienced higher levels of personal threat and were more likely to live in New York City and to have known someone who was killed or injured in the attacks (Huddy et al. 2005). This highlights a key facet of anxiety. It is, in part, situational (Eysenck 1992). But this stands in marked contrast to a sense of security, which, unlike anxiety, is grounded in a long-standing sense of personal safety that is unlikely to be affected by a specific stressful event. Anxiety is a product of a stressful event whereas a sense of security mitigates negative psychological reactions to such an event (Mikulincer and Shaver 2003).

Research on attachment theory makes clear that anxiety and a secure attachment style are negatively related. A secure attachment predicts better mental health under stressful circumstances and decreased symptoms of depression and anxiety (Fraley et al. 2006). A sense of felt security is likely to dampen anxious reactions to the events of 9/11 and so be negatively related to it, but we expect the relationship to be modest because other situational factors such as proximity to the events or the severity of their personal impact also shape a sense of personal threat and concomitant levels of anxiety.

We expect anxiety and security to have differing effects on domestic and national security policies. Recent psychological research demonstrates that threat-induced anxiety tends to elevate risk perceptions and risk aversion (Lerner and Keltner 2000, 2001; Lowenstein et al. 2001; Raghunathan and Pham 1999). The link between anxiety and risk aversion has important implications for support of national but not domestic security policies. Anxiety is likely to elevate the perceived risks associated with a given military intervention and decrease support for the deployment of military troops, potentially undercutting a desire for retaliation. But it is unlikely to undercut support for domestic security policies that are not inherently risky. We have confirmed these predictions in our prior research on reactions to 9/11 and the Iraq war (Huddy et al. 2005; Huddy, Feldman, and Cassese 2007). In contrast, both domestic and international security policies should provide a sense of security to threatened individuals who lack a strong sense of internal safety.

Research on attachment theory makes clear that anxiety and a secure attachment style are negatively related.

Hypotheses

We supplement past findings from research on terrorism with recent psychological insights from attachment and terror-management theories on the importance of felt security in dealing with stressful events. We focus specifically on the degree to which the political effects of threat depend on a sense of insecurity. We contrast the origins of felt security with other reactions to the 9/11 terrorist attacks and expect security to be less influenced by the details of the immediate event than anxiety and depression. Consistent with the predictions of attachment theory, we also expect felt security to moderate the influence of threat on anxiety. We examine whether a sense of security moderates the desire to bolster self-esteem through an increase in American patriotism and heightened denigration of outsiders, consistent with the expectations of a blended attachment–terror management approach.

Finally, we evaluate whether felt security decreases the political effects of perceived threat on support of national security policy. Felt security should also decrease the impact of threat on support for overseas military action. In contrast, insecure individuals who perceive pervasive threat should be most inclined to support both domestic and international security policy.

Methods and Results

Sample

Our data are drawn from a national telephone survey conducted between early October 2001 and early March 2002 and includes interviews with 1,549 randomly selected adults aged eighteen or older. A sample of random digit dial

(RDD) telephone numbers was generated by Genesys Inc. from telephone blocks with at least one listed residential number (one-plus). Respondents were selected randomly within the household using the last-birthday method (Lavrakas 1993). The sample was drawn as a weekly rolling cross-section with roughly one hundred individuals interviewed each week throughout this period. Numbers from each randomly selected sample were in use for a two-week period. The first month of data was collected by Shulman, Ronca, and Bukuvalis; the remainder of the data was collected by the Stony Brook University Center for Survey Research. Up to fifteen callbacks were made at each number and an attempt was made to convert individuals who initially refused. The overall response rate was 32 percent (calculated as American Association of Public Opinion Research [AAPOR] Response Rate 3), and the cooperation rate was 52 percent (AAPOR Cooperation Rate 3; for more details on response rate calculations, see http://www.aapor.org/pdfs/standarddefs_4.pdf).[1]

Threat and security

We begin by examining the *perceived threat* of terrorism in the aftermath of the attacks of 9/11. The survey included four items designed to measure the perceived threat of terrorism, which are presented in Table 1. Levels of national threat were quite high. More than 85 percent of Americans reported that they were very or somewhat concerned about another attack, and 84 percent were very or somewhat concerned about the threat of biological or chemical attacks. Levels of personal threat were lower, although still surprisingly high given the very small percentage of the population killed in the attacks. More than two-thirds (68 percent) of respondents reported being very or somewhat concerned about being personally affected by a terrorist attack; 31 percent were very concerned. More than half (52 percent) said that the attacks had shaken their sense of personal safety and security a great deal or some. This latter item appears to tap security, but in reality it is more closely aligned with perceived personal and national threat. These four items are highly intercorrelated with a mean correlation .48, and a simple additive scale has an estimated reliability (coefficient alpha) of .79. The perceived threat scale ranges from 0 to 1 and has a mean of .66 and standard deviation of .24.

It is clear from these responses that Americans saw considerable future terrorist threat to the nation in the months after 9/11. Despite this, levels of *felt security* were high. The majority of respondents reported feeling secure and confident when asked to "think about the terrorist attacks and the U.S. response." About 45 percent of respondents said they felt secure and confident "very often," a little over a third said they felt this way "sometimes," and only 16 percent said "not very often" or "never." Thus, even when asked about their feelings in the context of the 9/11 attacks, Americans reported high levels of felt security. The two security items were highly correlated ($r = .53$) and were combined into a scale ranging from 0 to 1 (high security) with a mean of .75.

TABLE 1
FREQUENCY DISTRIBUTIONS OF THREAT AND SECURITY ITEMS
(IN PERCENTAGES)

	Very Concerned	Somewhat Concerned	Not Very Concerned	Not At All Concerned	Don't Know/ Not Applicable
Threat					
How concerned are you that there will be another terrorist attack on U.S. soil in the near future?	49.8	36.5	9.7	3.5	0.4
How concerned are you that terrorists will attack the U.S. with biological or chemical weapons?	47.3	37.4	10.2	3.8	1.3
How concerned are you personally about you yourself, a friend, or a relative being the victim of a future terrorist attack in the United States?	30.8	37.1	19.8	11.2	1.2

	A Great Deal	Some	A Little	Not At All	Don't Know/ Not Applicable
How much, if any, have the terrorist attacks shaken your own sense of personal safety and security?	17.8	34.2	23.4	23.8	0.9

	Very Often	Sometimes	Not Very Often	Never	Don't Know/ Not Applicable
Security					
As you think about the terrorist attacks and the U.S. response, how often have you felt . . .					
Secure?	45.0	36.2	10.8	6.4	1.7
Confident?	46.4	35.6	9.5	5.6	2.9

As noted earlier, security is expected to be distinct from other emotional reactions to the attacks such as anxiety. The two security items were asked in the same battery as four *anxiety* questions. Respondents were again asked, "As you think about the terrorist attacks and the U.S. response, how often have you felt" anxious, scared, worried, and frightened. These four responses were highly correlated (mean $r = .59$) and combined into a scale with an estimated reliability of .85. A confirmatory factor analysis of all six emotional reactions (anxiety and security) indicates that a two-factor solution is a much better fit to the data than a single-factor model. With the inclusion of a methods factor to account for the common response alternatives, the estimated correlation for the latent anxiety and security factors is −.35. It is thus clear that the anxiety and security measures are negatively related but are also empirically distinct.

As can be seen in Figure 1, security and anxiety also have noticeably different distributions in this sample. Consistent with previous research on secure attachments, a large fraction of the respondents score at the upper end of the security measure. Typically, roughly 75 percent of adults have a secure attachment style when assessed with a standard measure based on questions about romantic relationships (Hazan and Shaver 1987). The mean of the felt security scale in this study is .75 and the median is .83, indicating that feeling secure is the modal response among respondents. While most data center on the high end of the scale, there is a definite lower tail to the distribution that extends to its lowest reaches (3.5 percent of the respondents obtained a value of 0). In contrast, anxiety is more widely distributed with a mean of .39 and a median of .33. High scores on anxiety are much more common in these data than low scores on security, as can be seen in Figure 1.

Determinants of anxiety, depression, and security

The nature of security can be seen more clearly when we examine its predictors along with the determinants of anxiety and reported symptoms of depression. To measure feelings of *depression*, respondents were asked, "In the past week, how depressed have you felt, if at all, about the terrorist attacks and the events since then?" with response options ranging from *very* to *not at all*. Similar questions were asked about how much difficulty respondents had in concentrating on their job and sleeping. Responses to these questions had a mean interitem correlation of .58 and were combined into an additive scale ranging from 0 to 1. We estimated two models to assess the respective determinants of anxiety, feelings of depression, and felt security. The first model includes demographic variables (age, education, gender, race/ethnicity), political variables (partisan and ideological identification and authoritarianism), and physical and emotional proximity to the 9/11 attacks (living in the Northeast and knowing someone hurt or killed in the attacks). Perceived threat was added to these equations in a second set of models. Estimates of these regression equations are shown in Table 2.

At the outset, we expected anxiety and depression to be closely linked to different aspects of the terrorist attacks but did not hold the same expectations of felt

FIGURE 1
KERNEL DENSITY PLOTS FOR ANXIETY AND SECURITY

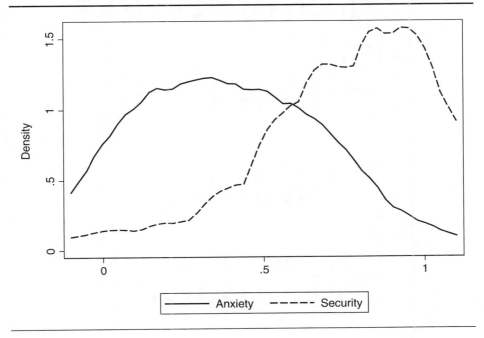

security because of its theoretical status as a more enduring and stable individual difference. This expectation is largely supported in Table 2. Physical proximity to the 9/11 attacks, as indicated by living in the Northeast of the United States, had a significant effect on both anxiety and depression. Knowing someone who was killed in the attacks also increased levels of both variables.[2] In contrast, physical and emotional proximity to the attacks did not decrease feelings of personal security. Indeed, there were few other significant predictors of security. Most notably, women reported feeling less secure than men, older people felt more secure than younger respondents, and blacks felt slightly less secure than whites. Political beliefs and allegiances also influenced anxiety and depression. Republicans felt less anxious and depressed, and authoritarians felt more so. But once again felt security was unrelated to partisanship, political ideology, or authoritarianism.

The relative stability of feelings of security is also suggested by the results of a second set of estimates obtained by adding perceived threat to each of the models in Table 2. As seen in the table, threat has large effects on anxiety and symptoms of depression. Anxiety in particular rises rapidly with increases in perceived threat. While the effect of threat is significant in the security equation, it is small compared to its coefficients in the other two equations. The effect of threat on security is less than a fourth the size of its effect on anxiety (coefficients can be

TABLE 2
DETERMINANTS OF ANXIETY, DEPRESSION, AND SECURITY

	Anxiety		Depression		Security	
	Model 1	Model 2	Model 1	Model 2	Model 1	Model 2
Know someone killed	**.07** (.02)	.04 (.01)	**.06** (.01)	.04 (.01)	-.01 (.02)	.00 (.02)
Live in Northeast	**.05** (.02)	.01 (.02)	**.06** (.02)	.03 (.02)	-.02 (.02)	-.01 (.02)
Threat		**.61** (.02)		**.45** (.02)		**-.14** (.03)
Age	-.013 (.004)	-.014 (.003)	.006 (.004)	.006 (.004)	**.008** (.004)	.008 (.004)
Education	**-.014** (.003)	-.006 (.002)	**-.016** (.003)	-.011 (.002)	.002 (.003)	.000 (.003)
Gender (female)	**.18** (.01)	.12 (.01)	**.06** (.01)	.02 (.01)	**-.09** (.01)	-.07 (.01)
Black	-.00 (.03)	**-.05** (.02)	**.08** (.02)	.05 (.02)	**-.06** (.03)	-.05 (.03)
Hispanic	.04 (.03)	.00 (.02)	**.11** (.03)	.08 (.02)	.02 (.03)	.01 (.02)
Other	.01 (.03)	-.01 (.02)	.05 (.03)	.04 (.03)	-.02 (.03)	-.01 (.03)
Party ID (Republican)	**-.05** (.02)	-.03 (.02)	**-.06** (.02)	-.04 (.02)	.03 (.02)	.03 (.02)
Ideology (conservative)	.04 (.02)	.02 (.02)	.03 (.02)	.02 (.02)	.02 (.02)	.02 (.02)
Authoritarianism	**.05** (.02)	-.02 (.02)	**.08** (.02)	.03 (.02)	-.02 (.02)	-.00 (.02)
Constant	**.49** (.05)	.08 (.04)	**.31** (.05)	.01 (.05)	**.72** (.05)	.81 (.05)
N	1,478	1,478	1,478	1,478	1,474	1,474
R^2	.16	.42	.10	.26	.04	.06

NOTE: Entries are unstandardized regression coefficients with standard errors in parentheses. Coefficients in bold are at least two times the size of their standard errors. Variables are coded to range from 0 to 1 except for age (in tens of years) and education (in years). White is the excluded category for the race/ethnicity dummy variables.

simply compared because each variable is measured on a 0 to 1 scale). Thus, while anxiety and depression were strongly related to the threat of terrorism, those same threat perceptions only slightly reduced feelings of security.

In general, there is much less variation in security across social and political variables than is seen for anxiety or depression, and it has no obvious relationship to variables that convey the impact of physical or social proximity to the attacks and its victims. Overall, threat and demographic factors accounted for 6 percent of the variance in felt security compared to 26 percent of the variance in depression and an impressive 42 percent of variance in anxiety. When taken together, these findings provide suggestive evidence that feelings of security may be a long-standing reaction that is relatively unaffected by ongoing events or standard political attitudes and beliefs, although we do not have conclusive evidence on this point.

Emotional consequences of security

According to attachment theory, one of the key functions of a secure attachment is to promote active coping that helps to deal with stress and mitigate its negative psychological consequences. Thus, among people who perceive themselves to be personally at threat from terrorism, feeling secure should result in lower levels of psychological distress than among the insecure. To test the buffering hypothesis, we estimated a regression model for anxiety and depression that included perceived threat, security, and their interaction along with other standard demographic predictors. As shown in Table 3, there is a sizable coefficient for both threat and its interaction with security. With threat and security both ranging from 0 to 1, the coefficient for security indicates its effect when security is at its minimum. Its impact is large. Among the least secure, perceived threat produces considerable anxiety and depression. There is also a significant interaction between threat and security. The impact of threat among the most secure can be calculated by adding the coefficient for threat to that of the interaction. This indicates that the psychological impact of threat is reduced substantially among the most secure and is almost halved for depression. These findings lend support to the notion that security minimized the psychological impact of the 9/11 terrorist attacks.

According to a blended terror-management attachment theory approach, threat should produce heightened in-group attachments and increased out-group derogation among insecure individuals as another way in which to restore their sense of security (Hart, Shaver, and Goldenberg 2005). We examine the extent to which threat, security, and their interaction influence levels of symbolic patriotism and negative stereotyping of Arabs in regression equations presented in Table 3. In this analysis, symbolic patriotism is a scale made up of two items: pride in being American and good feelings in response to the flag ($r = .61$). Arab stereotyping is assessed with four items asking how well the words trustworthy, honest, violent, and extremist described most Arabs (mean $r = .36$, alpha $= .7$).

As seen in Table 3, the coefficient for threat and its interaction with security are statistically significant for symbolic patriotism. The coefficient for threat indicates the impact of threat when felt security is at zero. And the impact on

TABLE 3
PSYCHOLOGICAL EFFECTS OF THREAT AND SECURITY

	Anxiety	Depression	Symbolic Patriotism	Negative Arab Stereotypes
Threat	**.80** (.07)	**.66** (.07)	**.41** (.07)	**.25** (.09)
Security	.09 (.06)	.08 (.06)	**.29** (.06)	.01 (.07)
Threat × Security	**−.25** (.08)	**−.29** (.09)	**−.32** (.09)	−.11 (.10)
Anxiety	—	—	−.01 (.03)	−.03 (.03)
Age	**−.015** (.003)	.006 (.004)	.001 (.003)	.005 (.004)
Education	**−.005** (.002)	**−.010** (.002)	−.003 (.002)	**−.011** (.003)
Gender (female)	**.11** (.01)	.00 (.01)	.00 (.01)	.02 (.01)
Black	**−.05** (.02)	.04 (.02)	**−.09** (.02)	.01 (.02)
Hispanic	−.01 (.02)	**.08** (.02)	**−.06** (.02)	.08 (.03)
Other	−.01 (.02)	.04 (.03)	**−.06** (.02)	−.03 (.03)
Party ID (Republican)	−.02 (.02)	−.03 (.02)	**.04** (.02)	.03 (.02)
Ideology (conservative)	.02 (.02)	.02 (.02)	**.08** (.02)	**.05** (.02)
Authoritarianism	−.02 (.02)	.03 (.02)	**.07** (.02)	**.11** (.02)
Constant	.00 (.05)	−.04 (.06)	**.43** (.05)	**.36** (.08)
N	1,473	1,472	1,423	1,224
R^2/R^2	.42	.27	.13	.13

NOTE: Entries are unstandardized regression coefficients with standard errors in parentheses. Coefficients in bold are at least twice the size of their standard error. Variables are coded to range from 0 to 1 except for age (in tens of years) and education (in years). White is the excluded category for the race/ethnicity dummy variables.

patriotism is clearly sizable. Threat produces a substantial increase in symbolic patriotism among insecure individuals but has a much more modest positive effect on patriotism among the most secure. Threat also enhances negative Arab stereotypes, but its interaction with security is not significant. The absence of a significant interaction between threat and security means that perceived threat promotes negative stereotypes of Arabs regardless of felt security. Overall, it appears that insecure individuals respond to the threat of terrorism with enhanced in-group attachment as reflected in higher levels of reported patriotism. But out-group derogation is driven simply by threat. These findings highlight the importance of patriotism and in-group attachments as a way to restore a sense of security in the face of threat. In contrast, out-group derogation may simply reflect the vilification of a threatening out-group that has little to do with a sense of personal security.

Domestic security policies

We now turn to an examination of the effects of threat on support for domestic security policies. The survey included two specific proposals to limit general civil liberties to reduce the threat of terror: requiring national identity cards and

TABLE 4
DETERMINANTS OF CIVIL LIBERTY PREFERENCES

	Support National ID Card	Monitor Phones and E-Mail	Antiterrorism Laws vs. Civil Liberties
Threat	**1.50** (.40)	**0.85** (.40)	**1.82** (.54)
Security	0.46 (.33)	0.42 (.34)	**1.14** (.46)
Threat × Security	−0.85 (.47)	−0.25 (.47)	**−1.32** (.64)
Anxiety	0.15 (.14)	0.20 (.15)	−0.03 (.18)
Age	0.011 (.018)	**0.063** (.018)	0.035 (.025)
Education	**−0.046** (.013)	**−0.035** (.013)	−0.000 (.017)
Gender (female)	0.04 (.06)	−0.01 (.06)	0.06 (.08)
Black	−0.17 (.12)	−0.07 (.12)	−0.20 (.15)
Hispanic	0.06 (.12)	0.22 (.12)	−0.23 (.16)
Other	−0.02 (.14)	0.13 (.14)	0.06 (.17)
Party ID (Republican)	−0.04 (.10)	**0.21** (.10)	**0.46** (.12)
Ideology (conservative)	**0.21** (.10)	**0.46** (.10)	**0.26** (.13)
Authoritarianism	0.11 (.09)	**0.21** (.10)	**0.25** (.12)
Threshold 1	−0.11 (.35)	1.00 (.36)	2.23 (.48)
Threshold 2	0.43 (.35)	1.69 (.36)	
Threshold 3	1.24 (.35)	2.50 (.36)	
N	1,431	1,439	1,200
Pseudo-R^2	.03	.04	.05

NOTE: Entries are maximum likelihood probit coefficients with standard errors in parentheses. Coefficients in bold are at least twice the size of their standard error. Variables are coded to range from 0 to 1 except for age (in tens of years) and education (in years). White is the excluded category for the race/ethnicity dummy variables.

allowing the government to monitor personal phone calls and e-mails of ordinary Americans. We also asked respondents if they were more concerned that the country would fail to enact strong antiterrorism laws or if they were more worried that new laws would restrict civil liberties.

Three additional questions focused on activities designed to monitor and restrict the activities of people who might be considered threatening. Questions included whether Arabs and Arab Americans in the United States should be put under special surveillance, support for greater restrictions on visas for foreign students and other visitors to the United States, and whether Arabs should undergo more intensive security checks than visitors from other countries. Probit estimates for the first three domestic security measures are shown in Table 4, and estimates for the second set of security restrictions are presented in Table 5. In all equations, we include as predictors threat, security, and the interaction between threat and security, along with demographic controls.

The results in Table 4 show that increasing perceptions of threat predict greater support for both domestic security measures and lesser concern with civil

TABLE 5
DETERMINANTS OF PREFERENCES ON POLICIES TARGETING ARABS

	Surveillance for Arabs and Arab Americans	Tougher Restrictions on Visas	Stricter Security Checks for Arabs
Threat	**1.69** (.53)	**2.25** (.57)	**1.29** (.45)
Security	0.83 (.44)	0.66 (.44)	0.24 (.29)
Threat × Security	**−1.38** (.62)	**−1.47** (.68)	−0.91 (.54)
Anxiety	0.09 (.18)	−0.31 (.21)	0.21 (.17)
Age	**0.059** (.024)	**0.157** (.028)	**0.064** (.022)
Education	−0.021 (.016)	0.019 (.019)	−0.021 (.015)
Gender (female)	**−0.21** (.08)	−0.08 (.09)	**−0.26** (.08)
Black	**−0.32** (.15)	**−0.47** (.15)	0.05 (.13)
Hispanic	**−0.34** (.16)	**−0.41** (.16)	0.13 (.15)
Other	**−0.44** (.21)	0.00 (.20)	0.05 (.16)
Party ID (Republican)	**0.24** (.12)	0.19 (.14)	0.00 (.11)
Ideology (conservative)	**0.36** (.13)	**0.51** (.15)	**0.41** (.12)
Authoritarianism	**0.39** (.12)	**0.29** (.14)	**0.26** (.11)
Threshold 1	2.05 (.46)	1.46 (.48)	1.00 (.40)
N	1,334	1,419	1,429
Pseudo-R^2	.07	.11	.05

NOTE: Entries are maximum-likelihood probit coefficients with standard errors in parentheses. Coefficients in bold are at least twice the size of their standard error. Variables are coded to range from 0 to 1 except for age (in tens of years) and education (in years). White is the excluded category for the race/ethnicity dummy variables.

liberties. With the inclusion of an interaction term between threat and security, the coefficient for perceived threat yields its effect when security is 0. In all three equations there are large, significant effects of threat when security is low, indicating that perceived threat has a sizable influence on policy support among the least secure. The interaction term is also substantively large, significant at the .05 level with a one-tailed test, and in the predicted direction for national identity cards and concerns about a failure to enact strong antiterrorism laws. In both instances, the effect of threat on support for domestic security policies decreases as security increases. The size of the interaction term indicates that the effect of threat, while smaller for those high in security, does not fully decline to 0. There is no interaction between security and threat for monitoring phones and e-mails, however. The estimates for that equation indicate that the effect of threat is not reduced by felt security.

Among the other independent variables, the most consistent predictors of support for internal security measures are political orientations: conservatives and Republicans are more likely to support these policies than liberals and Democrats, and authoritarianism is associated with greater support. In addition, support for these policies decreases somewhat as education increases.

The three policies just examined involve security measures that would directly impact most Americans. The second set of policies assess support for more targeted "threats" to security by focusing on Arabs and other foreign visitors to the United States. The estimates for these equations, shown in Table 5, are broadly similar to those just discussed, with some significant differences. Notice first that, for all three equations, the interaction between personal threat and security is in the predicted direction, significant at the .05 level in a one-tailed test, and substantively large. As before, when security is at its lowest value, the effect of personal threat on support for security policies is large. In two of these cases, surveillance and stricter security checks, the interaction between personal threat and felt security is sufficiently large that personal threat has no impact among those who feel completely secure. Thus, security reduces the effects of threat on support for these targeted policies to a greater degree than for more general domestic surveillance policies.

As an illustration of the magnitude of the political effects of threat, we present predicted probabilities at differing levels of threat and security for two of the domestic security policies—the national ID card and special surveillance for Arabs and Arab Americans. Predicted probabilities are calculated for white males who score at the midpoint on all other independent variables in Tables 4 and 5. Among those scoring at the lowest level of felt security, less than 20 percent are predicted to support national ID cards at the lowest level of perceived threat; this goes up to almost 80 percent among those who see maximum threat. This is a massive difference. The effects of threat are more muted among those high in security, ranging from a predicted low of 38 percent when threat is low to 64 percent when it is high. A similar trend is observed on support for increased surveillance of Arabs and Arab Americans. Among those low in security, predicted support for increased surveillance goes from a low of 9 percent to a high of 58 percent as threat ranges from its lowest to highest value. Among those high in security, predicted support for surveillance varies less dramatically with level of threat, ranging from 26 to 37 percent. It is also clear that those with a high sense of felt security who see little terrorist threat are more supportive of security policies than their less secure counterparts, a somewhat puzzling finding that requires further investigation.

Threat and support for military action

We also examined the impact of threat and security on support for overseas military action in response to the events of 9/11. Three questions tapped support for military intervention in Afghanistan, the general level of U.S. military action in response to the terrorist attacks, support for "increasing the level of military action even if it means that U.S. armed forces might suffer a substantial number of casualties," and whether "the U.S. should limit its military action to Osama bin Laden and the Taliban or should it broaden its action to include other countries that harbor and support terrorists." Ordered probit analyses were conducted to assess the determinants of support for each one of these questions; findings are reported in Table 6.

TABLE 6
DETERMINANTS OF SUPPORT FOR MILITARY ACTION

	Level of Military Action	Support Greater Military Action	Expand Military Action against Terrorism
Threat	**1.70** (.44)	**1.13** (.41)	**2.70** (.59)
Security	0.56 (.36)	**0.68** (.34)	**1.49** (.47)
Threat × Security	**−1.29** (.52)	−0.52 (.49)	**−2.24** (.71)
Anxiety	−0.25 (.17)	**−0.42** (.15)	**−0.55** (.21)
Age	−0.040 (.021)	0.021 (.020)	−0.021 (.028)
Education	−0.008 (.015)	−0.008 (.014)	0.011 (.019)
Gender (female)	**−0.25** (.07)	**−0.36** (.07)	**−0.30** (.09)
Black	**−0.38** (.13)	**−0.50** (.12)	**−0.44** (.15)
Hispanic	−0.20 (.14)	**−0.43** (.13)	**−0.40** (.17)
Other	0.01 (.16)	−0.26 (.14)	−0.24 (.19)
Party ID (Republican)	**0.17** (.11)	**0.62** (.10)	**0.57** (.14)
Ideology (conservative)	**0.32** (.12)	**0.30** (.11)	0.02 (.15)
Authoritarianism	**0.30** (.11)	**0.24** (.11)	0.27 (.14)
Threshold 1	−0.80 (.39)	−0.04 (.36)	0.75 (.51)
Threshold 2	1.65 (.39)	0.52 (.36)	
Threshold 3		1.64 (.37)	
N	1,381	1,309	1,369
Pseudo-R^2	.05	.07	.08

NOTE: Entries are maximum-likelihood probit coefficients with standard errors in parentheses. Coefficients in bold are at least twice the size of their standard error. Variables are coded to range from 0 to 1 except for age (in tens of years) and education (in years). White is the excluded category for the race/ethnicity dummy variables.

Previous analyses of these data provide evidence that threat has a substantial, positive impact on support for overseas military action (Huddy et al. 2005). This finding is confirmed in the current analysis but is further qualified by evidence of a sizable interaction between threat and security. As seen in Table 6, threat has substantial impact on all three indicators of support for military action when security is at its lowest level. In addition, the interaction between threat and security is sizable and significant for level of military action and a desire to expand action beyond Osama bin Laden and the Taliban. In both instances, the effects of threat on support for military action are greatly reduced among the most secure. There is also a sizable but nonsignificant interaction between threat and security that almost halves the impact of threat on support for increased military action even with casualties among the most secure.

As for domestic policy, felt security has a sizable moderating influence on the degree to which threat increases support for national security policy. Based on the analyses presented in Table 6, we calculated the predicted probability that respondents rated the U.S. level of military action in response to 9/11 as "too little." Among those who felt insecure, roughly 6 percent who perceived little threat thought the response had been inadequate compared to 54 percent of those who perceived maximum future threat to the United States. In contrast, threat had a much reduced effect on policy support among those who felt the most secure. Fifteen percent of the most secure who perceived little terrorist threat thought the U.S. response had been inadequate compared to 27 percent of those who perceived the United States as facing the highest level of threat, a far more muted difference. Felt security clearly moderates the influence of threat on American support for overseas military action.

Finally, a number of other factors influenced support for an aggressive foreign policy. Men, nonblacks, Republicans, conservatives, and authoritarians were generally more supportive of overseas military intervention than others, as seen in Table 6.

Conclusion

Not everyone responds to the threat of terrorism in the same way. In this study, we have highlighted the powerful moderating influence of felt security on the extent to which perceived threat leads to support for restrictive domestic security policy and aggressive international action. We have shown in past research that feelings of threat promote support for an aggressive foreign policy (Huddy et al. 2005). The current findings temper that conclusion by demonstrating that the greatest impact of threat is concentrated among individuals who had difficulty maintaining a sense of security in the months following the terrorist attacks of 9/11. We also highlight the powerful influence of security and threat on support for domestic national security policies that potentially curtail American civil liberties. For both domestic and international security policy, feeling insecure can profoundly influence whether individuals turn to government policy to restore a sense of personal security.

For both domestic and international security policy, feeling insecure can profoundly influence whether individuals turn to government policy to restore a sense of personal security.

Our research not only sheds light on reactions to the events of 9/11 but also provides an important extension to existing research on tolerance and civil liberties

by demonstrating the powerful and distinct effects of threat. Past tolerance studies have typically found a strong desire to curtail the rights and liberties of
members of groups that pose a broad societal threat (Marcus et al. 1995;
Sullivan, Piereson, and Marcus 1982). But researchers have paid much less
attention to the willingness of study participants to forgo their own liberties and
freedoms. Findings from the current study suggest that this depends centrally
on the combined experience of threat and insecurity. In our data, a sense of personal insecurity plays a central role in a willingness to forfeit personal liberties
in response to an external threat, suggesting new avenues for research on political tolerance.

Drawing on psychological attachment theory, we suggest that feelings of security are a long-standing individual characteristic that may derive from early childhood attachment experiences. Attachment theory indicates that most adults
achieve a secure attachment, and this, in turn, improves their ability to deal with
stress through imagined or real proximity to attachment figures. But more is
needed to establish the links between felt security as measured in a survey context and standard measures of attachment in order to verify that felt security has
many of the same properties. We uncover suggestive evidence consistent with
attachment theory that felt security was not greatly affected by the terrorist
attacks of 9/11 and was much less affected than other reactions such as anxiety or
depression. Felt security helped to minimize feelings of anxiety and mitigated the
need to elevate feelings of symbolic patriotism as a way to cope with threat.[3]
When taken together, these findings suggest that felt security plays a central role
in how people cope with stressful events and whether this translates into support
for protective government policies.

But more information is needed on a sense of felt security to ensure that it
fully conforms to the expectations of attachment theory. How well does a sense
of felt security correlate with other, more standard measures of attachment style
within romantic relationships? What evidence is there that a sense of felt security
is stable over time and relatively immune to the impact of ongoing events? And
is there evidence that the impact of felt security can be observed in response to
other government policies designed to handle frightening events such as avian flu
or food contamination? Further research into felt security will help to determine
the kinds of individuals most likely to support aggressive government action to
deal with threatening events.

Notes

1. There was no difference in response rate between the two survey organizations, and response rates
were similar to those obtained in recent random digit dial (RDD) surveys using a different sampling frame
but similar methodology (Steeh et al. 2001; Losch et al. 2002).

2. The exact question wording is, "Do you, any of your friends, or relatives know someone who is missing, hurt, or killed in the terrorist attacks of September 11?"

3. In additional analyses not reported here, we also find, consistent with the predictions of attachment
theory, that felt security is a significant predictor of how much people trust other Americans.

References

Ainsworth, M. D. S. 1991. Attachments and other affectional bonds across the life cycle. In *Attachment across the life cycle*, ed. C. M. Parkes, J. Stevenson-Hinde, and P. Marris, 33-51. London: Tavistock/Routledge.

Ainsworth, M. D. S., M. C. Blehar, E. Waters, and S. Walls. 1978. *Patterns of attachment: Assessed in the strange situation and at home.* Hillsdale, NJ: Erlbaum.

Bar-Tal, D., and D. Labin. 2001. The effect of a major event on stereotyping: Terrorist attacks in Israel and Israeli adolescents' perceptions of Palestinians, Jordanians and Arabs. *European Journal of Social Psychology* 31:265-80.

Bartholomew, K., and L. M. Horowitz. 1991. Attachment styles among young adults: A test of a four-category model. *Journal of Personality and Social Psychology* 61:226-44.

Belsky, J. 1999. Modern evolutionary theory and patterns of attachment. In *Handbook of attachment: Theory, research, and clinical applications*, ed. J. Cassidy and P. R. Shaver, 141-61. New York: Guilford.

Bowlby, J. [1969] 1982. *Attachment and loss: Attachment (Volume 1).* New York: Basic Books.

Brennan, K. A., and P. R. Shaver. 1995. Dimensions of adult attachment, affect regulation, and romantic relationship functioning. *Personality and Social Psychology Bulletin* 21:267-83.

Browne, M. J., and R. E. Hoyt. 2000. The demand for flood insurance: Empirical evidence. *Journal of Risk and Uncertainty* 20:271-89.

Buss, D. M., and D. P. Schmitt. 1993. Sexual strategies theory: An evolutionary perspective on human mating. *Psychological Review* 100:204-32.

Chisholm, J. S. 1996. The evolutionary ecology of attachment organization. *Human Nature* 7 (1): 1-38.

Crenshaw, Martha. 1986. The psychology of political terrorism. In *Political psychology*, ed. Margaret G. Hermann. New York: Jossey-Bass.

Davis, D. W., and B. D. Silver. 2004. Civil liberties versus security in the context of the terrorist attacks on America. *American Journal of Political Science* 48:28-46.

Eysenck, M. W. 1992. *Anxiety: The cognitive perspective.* London: Lawrence Erlbaum.

Fernald, A. 1992. Human maternal vocalizations to infants as biologically relevant signals: An evolutionary perspective. In *The adapted mind: Evolutionary psychology and the generation of culture*, ed. J. H. Barkow, L. Cosmides and J. Tooby, 391-428. Oxford: Oxford University Press.

Ferraro, K. A. 1996. Women's fear of victimization: Shadow of sexual assault? *Social Forces* 75:667-90.

Florian, V., M. Mikulincer, and G. Hirschberger. 2002. The anxiety-buffering function of close relationships: Evidence that relationship commitment acts as a terror management mechanism. *Journal of Personality and Social Psychology* 82: 527-542.

Fraley, R. C. 2002. Attachment stability from infancy to adulthood: Meta-analysis and dynamic modeling of developmental mechanisms. *Personality and Social Psychology Review* 6 (2): 123-51.

Fraley, R. C., C. C. Brumbaugh, and M. J. Marks. 2005. The evolution and function of adult attachment: A comparative and phylogenetic analysis. *Journal of Personality and Social Psychology* 89:731-46.

Fraley, R. C., D. A. Fazzari, G. A. Bonanno, and S. Dekel. 2006. Attachment and psychological adaptation in high exposure survivors of the September 11th attack on the World Trade Center. *Personality and Social Psychology Bulletin* 32 (4): 538-51.

Friedland, N., and A. Merari. 1985. The psychological impact of terrorism: A double-edged sword. *Political Psychology* 6:591-604.

Goldberg, S. 2000. *Attachment and development.* London: Oxford University Press.

Gordon, C., and A. Arian. 2001. Threat and decision making. *Journal of Conflict Resolution* 45:197-215.

Hamilton, W. D. 1964. The genetic evolution of social behaviour. *Journal of Theoretical Biology* 7:1-52.

Hart, J., P. Shaver, and J. Goldenberg. 2005. Attachment, self-esteem, worldviews, and terror management: Evidence for a tripartite security system. *Journal of Personality and Social Psychology* 88:999-1013.

Hazan, C., and P. R. Shaver. 1987. Romantic love conceptualized as an attachment process. *Journal of Personality and Social Psychology* 52:511-24.

Herrmann, Richard K., Philip E. Tetlock, and Penny S. Visser. 1999. Mass public decisions to go to war: A cognitive-interactionist framework. *American Political Science Review* 93 (3): 553-73.

Huddy, L., S. Feldman, T. Capelos, and C. Provost. 2002. The consequences of terrorism: Disentangling the effects of personal and national threat. *Political Psychology* 23:485-509.

Huddy, L., S. Feldman, and E. Cassese. 2007. On the distinct political effects of anxiety and anger. In *The political dynamics of feeling and thinking*, ed. A. Crigler, M. MacKuen, G. E. Marcus, and W. R. Neuman. Chicago: University of Chicago Press.

Huddy, L., S. Feldman, C. Taber, and G. Lahav. 2005. Threat, anxiety, and support of anti-terrorism policies. *American Journal of Political Science* 49:610-25.

Inglehart, R. 1997. *Modernization and post-modernization: Political, cultural, and economic change in 43 societies*. Princeton, NJ: Princeton University Press.

Jentleson, B. 1992. The pretty prudent public: Post post-Vietnam American opinion on the use of force. *International Studies Quarterly* 36:49-74

Jentleson, B. W., and R. L. Britton. 1998. Still pretty prudent: Post–cold war American public opinion on the use of military force. *Journal of Conflict Resolution* 42:395-417.

Kirkpatrick, L. A. 1998. Evolution, pair-bonding, and reproductive strategies: A reconceptualization of adult attachment. In *Attachment theory and close relationships*, ed. J. A. Simpson and W. S. Rholes, 353-93. New York: Guilford.

Kraemer, G. W. 1992. A psychobiological theory of attachment. *Behavioral and Brain Sciences* 15 (3): 493-541.

Lavrakas, P. J. 1993. *Telephone survey methods: Sampling, selection and supervision*. Newbury Park, CA: Sage.

Lerner, J. S., and D. Keltner. 2000. Beyond valence: Toward a model of emotion-specific influences on judgment and choice. *Cognition and Emotion* 14 (4): 473-93.

———. 2001. Fear, anger, and risk. *Journal of Personality and Social Psychology* 81:146-59.

Losch, M. E., A. Maitland, G. Lutz, P. Mariolis, and S. Gleason. 2002. The effect of time of year of data collection on sample efficiency. *Public Opinion Quarterly* 66:594-607.

Lowenstein, G. F., E. U. Weber, C. K. Haste, and N. Welch. 2001. Risk as feelings. *Psychological Bulletin* 127:267-86.

Marcus, G. E., J. L. Sullivan, E. Theiss-Morse, and S. L. Wood. 1995. *With malice toward some: How people make civil liberties judgments*. Cambridge: Cambridge University Press.

Maslow, Abraham H. 1943. A theory of human motivation. *Psychological Review* 50 (4): 370-96.

Mikulincer, M., G. Birnbaum, D. Woddis, and O. Nachmias. 2000. Stress and accessibility of proximity-related thoughts: Exploring the normative and intraindividual components of attachment theory. *Journal of Personality and Social Psychology* 78 (3): 509-23.

Mikulincer, M., and V. Florian. 2000. Exploring individual differences in reactions to mortality salience— Does attachment style regulate terror management mechanisms? *Journal of Personality and Social Psychology* 79:260-73.

Mikulincer, M., V. Florian, and A. Weller. 1993. Attachment styles, coping strategies, and posttraumatic psychological distress: The impact of the Gulf War in Israel. *Journal of Personality and Social Psychology* 64 (5): 817-26.

Mikulincer, M., and P. Shaver. 2001. Attachment theory and intergroup bias: Evidence that priming the secure base schema attenuates negative reactions to out-groups. *Journal of Personality and Social Psychology* 81:97-115.

———. 2003. The attachment behavioral system in adulthood: Activation, psychodynamics, and interpersonal processes. In *Advances in experimental social psychology*, vol. 35, ed. M. P. Zanna, 53-152. San Diego, CA: Elsevier Academic Press.

Mueller, J. E. 1973. *War, presidents, and public opinion*. New York: John Wiley.

Pyszczynski, T., S. Solomon, and J. Greenberg. 2002. *In the wake of 9/11: The psychology of terror*. Washington, DC: APA.

Raghunathan, R., and M. T. Pham. 1999. All negative moods are not equal: Motivational influences of anxiety and sadness on decision making. *Organizational Behavior and Human Decision Processes* 79:56-77.

Sattler, D. N., C. F. Kaiser, and J. B. Hittner. 2000. Disaster preparedness: Relationships among prior experience, personal characteristics, and distress. *Journal of Applied Social Psychology* 37:1396-1420.

Schmitt, D. P. 2005. Is short-term mating the maladaptive result of insecure attachment? A test of competing evolutionary perspectives. *Personality and Social Psychology Bulletin* 31 (6): 747-68.

Simpson, J. A., W. A. Collins, S. S. Tran, and K. C. Haydon. 2007. Attachment and the experience and expression of emotions in romantic relationships: A developmental perspective. *Journal of Personality and Social Psychology* 92:355-67.

Solomon, Z., K. Ginzburg, M. Mikulincer, Y. Neria, and A. Ohry. 1998. Coping with war captivity: The role of attachment style. *European Journal of Personality* 12:271-85.

Sroufe, L. A., and E. Waters. 1977. Attachment as an organizational construct. *Child Development* 48:1184-99.

Steeh, C., N. Kirgis, B. Cannon, and Jeff DeWitt. 2001. Are they really as bad as they seem? Nonresponse rates at the end of the twentieth century. *Journal of Official Statistics* 17:227-47.

Sullivan, J. L., J. Piereson, and G. E. Marcus. 1982. *Political tolerance and American democracy*. Chicago: University of Chicago Press.

Tancredy, C. M., and R. C. Fraley. 2006. The nature of adult twin relationships: An attachment-theoretical perspective. *Journal of Personality and Social Psychology* 90 (1): 78-93.

Taubman Ben-Ari, O., L. Findler, and M. Mikulincer. 2002. The effects of mortality salience on relationship strivings and beliefs: The moderating role of attachment style. *British Journal of Social Psychology* 41:419-41.

Taubman Ben-Ari, O., and M. Mikulincer. 2007. The effects of dispositional attachment orientations and contextual priming of attachment security on reckless driving. *Transportation Research Part F: Traffic Psychology and Behaviour* 10:123-38.

Weber, C., and C. Federico. 2007. Interpersonal attachment and patterns of ideological belief. *Political Psychology* 28 (4): 389-416.

Zeifman, D., and C. Hazan. 1997. Attachment: The bond in pair-bonds. In *Evolutionary social psychology*, ed. J. A. Simpson and D. T. Kenrick, 237-63. Mahwah, NJ: Lawrence Erlbaum.

A Dual-Edged Sword: Empathy and Collective Action in the Prisoner's Dilemma

By
JOHN A. SAUTTER,
LEVENTE LITTVAY,
and
BRENNEN BEARNES

Researchers guided by evolutionary psychology have theorized that in an iterated prisoner's dilemma, reciprocal behavior is a product of evolutionary design, where individuals are guided by an innate sense of fairness for equal outcomes. Empathy as a prosocial emotion could be a key to understanding the psychological underpinnings of why and who tends to cooperate in a collective act. In short, why are some individuals more prone to participate in collective action? The authors test the hypothesis that a prosocial psychological disposition, stemming from self-reported empathy, will lead to group-oriented behavior in an iterated prisoner's dilemma game. Results suggest that an empathetic disposition does not lead to a higher rate of cooperation but interacts with environmental conditioning to produce either a highly cooperative or highly uncooperative personality type.

Keywords: collective action; egalitarian outcomes; empathy; evolutionary psychology; phenotypic variation; prisoner's dilemma

This study investigates the effects of an empathetic emotional disposition in decision making by using the iterated prisoner's dilemma (PD) framework. It is theorized that an empathetic disposition is an important guide to an individual's decision-making process when faced with a collective action problem. Evolutionary theory posits that group-level

John A. Sautter received his PhD in political science from the University of Nebraska–Lincoln. He currently attends Vermont Law School in South Royalton and is a first lieutenant in the United States Marine Corps.

Levente Littvay is a visiting assistant professor of the Central European University in Budapest, Hungary. He received his PhD in political science from the University of Nebraska–Lincoln and is finishing a degree in survey research.

Brennen Bearnes received his BA in history from the University of Nebraska–Lincoln. He has acted as project designer, programmer, and implementation consultant for a number of human-subject experimental projects. He is currently an independent information technology consultant in Boulder, Colorado.

DOI: 10.1177/0002716207306360

ANNALS, AAPSS, 614, November 2007

selection has endowed humans with a propensity for cooperative behavior in the absence of selective incentives by equipping the human mind with prosocial emotions (Field 2004; Bowles and Gintis 2003; Sober and Wilson 1998). However, some people get more satisfaction than others out of political participation or paying attention to civic issues. This is likely due to differences in behavioral traits that are partly genetically innate and partly socially conditioned (Alford and Hibbing 2004; Kagan 2003). We hypothesize that a higher level of self-reported empathy will lead to a more explicit demonstration of group-oriented egalitarian behavior in the iterated PD.

Evolution and Empathy

Research in behavioral psychology and neuroscience suggests an alternative approach to the PD in human interactions. Instead of envisioning each individual as a rational being with merely different preferences as compared to others, innate genetic and socialized personality differences are understood to be an ultimate cause of preferences for cooperative behavior. In other words, the Olsonian free rider is not just a theoretical concept but is a personality type with distinct characteristics (Hibbing and Alford 2004). Evolution has cultivated a multitude of personality traits that vary among humans. This phenotypic variation allows for selective advantages on the group level (Wilson 2002). Whether an individual is more of a rational calculator or an empathetic altruist, both would have played an important role in collective success in humans' distant past. Indeed, geneticists have found important links between genes and behavior (Davis, Luce, and Kraus 1994). Studies of autism, violent behavior, and other asocial disorders indicate that genetic inheritance is an important determinant of patterns of behavior (Ebstein, Benjamin, and Belmaker 2003; Pericak-Vance 2003).

Prosocial personality traits have also been connected to an individual's genetic makeup. Most important among prosocial personality traits is empathy. Empathy can be defined and interpreted under the auspices of three main subcharacteristics: concern for others, perspective taking (also called theory of mind empathy) and personal distress, or the ability to have emotional reactions to others in need. A study of eight hundred twin-pairs that compared monozygotic to dizygotic dyads estimated the combined inheritance of these three components of empathy at 32 percent (Davis, Luce, and Kraus 1994). In light of this sort of finding and those concerning antisocial behavior, it is likely that genetic inheritance of behavioral traits affects the preferences that individuals form for cooperative social behavior.

The study of the manner in which individuals attempt to understand and place themselves emotionally in the place of another is of great importance in contemplating how social groups and networks are motivated to carry out prosocial behavior. Thoits (1989, 328) stated that "empathetic role-taking emotions, or vicarious emotions, result from mentally placing oneself in another's position and feeling what the other might feel in that situation." Empathy is arguably one of the most important socioemotional experiences because it provides the impetus and mental processes involved in "the effort to understand the internal mental and emotional events of other human beings" (Rosenberg 1990, 8). Indeed, this sort of emotional capacity has been important to researchers looking at what motivates moral and prosocial actions, finding that higher levels of empathy tend to make individuals more likely to be morally outraged or to take action to prevent unjust acts (Davis 1996; Smith-Lovin 1995). A heightened sense of morality or an active vigilance in regards to justice are exactly the sorts of behavioral tendencies that evolutionary theory would suggest should be present in those individuals with an inclination for group-orientated outcomes.

> *A heightened sense of morality or an active vigilance in regards to justice are exactly the sorts of behavioral tendencies that evolutionary theory would suggest should be present in those individuals with an inclination for group-oriented outcomes.*

The Prisoner's Dilemma as Collective Action

The PD represents, in a simplified manner, the continual problems of reciprocity, trust, and collective action (Rapoport and Chammah 1965; Hardin 1971; Axelrod 1984; Ridley 1996; Fehr and Schmidt 1999; Dawes et al. 2007) that are ever-present in iterated interactions between human beings. This makes the PD framework ideal for a test of prosocial emotional disposition in an incentive-based game because it is simple enough for those first exposed to it in an experimental setting to comprehend, yet theoretically sophisticated so as to allow a rich interpretation of the results.[1]

Although empathy has not been tested in the PD, altruism has been modeled in many different ways. Andreoni and Miller (1993) found that altruists even exist in the finitely repeated PD, where individuals are aware of when the game will end. In their experiment, they defined two groups: those who can build reputations for altruistic acts and those who are not able to build reputations because of behavioral constraints. In the group that cannot build reputations, they found that after two hundred rounds of single-shot PD games, there is a persistent pattern of cooperation that does not deteriorate. In the other group, where reputation building is possible, individuals also tend to cooperate. By separating the two groups, Andreoni and Miller were able to show that reputation is not as important to altruistic behavior as might be thought. Indeed, their findings suggest that people probably have what they refer to as "homemade" altruistic preferences, or, in other words, people tend to have individual dispositions making them more likely to cooperate.

Fehr and Schmidt (1999) looked at the PD in an entirely different way. Similar to Hibbing and Alford's (2004) notion of people as wary cooperators, they saw individuals as being inequality averse (Smith et al. 2007). In this conception of the PD, people have an expressed preference for equal payoffs. Framing becomes the key in this case. If players are more optimistic about the other player's probability of cooperating, then inequality-averse players will cooperate more often than the standard, theoretical, completely rational, agent. They presented this idea as a social utility function, where each player calculates his or her payoff in regards to how that payoff relates to the other player's payoff, thus making inequality-averse players conditional cooperators.

The alpha and beta terms in Table 1 reflect the relative disposition for fairness of each player. Under this scheme, both players prefer equal outcomes, unless one of the players acts unfairly: The further the outcome from the equal payoff, the more guilt or anger that each player will feel. If an inequality-averse player knowingly met a selfish player, then he or she would defect because the selfish player would not likely reciprocate his or her cooperation. Therefore, the most equal payoff for both parties, in the eyes of the inequality-averse player, would be the Nash equilibrium outcome (P,P). The inequality-averse player is not altruistic, but egalitarian.

Emotion and Cooperation

This notion of egalitarianism coincides with the way that evolutionary psychology theorizes that individuals have innate preferences for fairness. Absolute outcomes are not as important as relative outcomes. The way the game is played in relation to the other player becomes the most important aspect. Both evolutionary theories of multilevel selection and reciprocal altruism reflect this focus on relative outcomes. In the case of collective action, individuals should be disposed toward equal and fair outcomes that reflect an innate desire to achieve what is implicitly best for the group, rather than the individual (Fehr and Gachter 2000). This is in line with Hibbing and Alford's (2004) notion that people are wary cooperators, who want to be neither suckers nor leeches in their relations to others. Indeed, the very emotions that Fehr and Schmidt (1999) suggested are elicited (anger and guilt) when an individual receives or dictates what he or she perceives to be an unequal payoff are theorized to have evolved from a sort of reciprocal necessity over millions of years of protohuman existence. Evolutionary

TABLE 1
PAYOFF MATRIX AS DEVISED BY FEHR AND SCHMIDT (1999)

		Player II	
		Cooperate (C)	Defect (D)
Player I	Cooperate (C)	2,2	$0 - 3\alpha, 3 - 3\beta$
	Defect (D)	$0 - 3\beta, 3 - 3\alpha$	1,1

pressure equipped humans with emotions to guide their decision making in the group context (Bowles and Gintis 2003). From this perspective, it is not rationality per se that a researcher should be investigating, but the emotions that lead to intragroup rationality that have evolved to deal with conflict and compromise.

[I]t is not rationality per se that a researcher should be investigating, but the emotions that lead to intragroup rationality that have evolved to deal with conflict and compromise.

Empathy becomes an important element in attempting to understand this innate and evolved group-related behavior. Most mammals, and certainly non-mammalian species, do not have the scope or breadth of complexity in emotion that humans demonstrate in their everyday interaction. At the base of this emotional temperament is a prosocial empathetic disposition that varies from individual to individual. As Sober and Wilson (1998) implied throughout their polemic, empathy is the veritable context with in which all choices are made.[2] Indeed, McCabe et al. (2001) found that different parts of the brain are used when a player is competing against a computer versus another human. When playing against another human, a large part of the prefrontal cortex becomes activated; while in contrast, when playing a computer, only a small area in the rear of the brain that is used in mental calculation, like arithmetic, becomes activated. This suggests that the empathetic context of social interaction actually provokes a completely different sort of "rationality" than interaction with nonhuman subjects.

These findings, along with the aforementioned studies on empathy and past experimental work using the PD posed the following hypotheses:

> *Hypothesis 1:* A more robust empathetic psychological disposition will lead to higher rates of "punishment" (or mutual defection) in the face of defection by an opposing player.
> *Hypothesis 2:* Empathy will predict more forgiving behavior in a player during a period when the opposing player attempts to reestablish mutual cooperation.

In short, it is hypothesized that more empathy will lead to a more explicit display of group-oriented egalitarian behavior. Empathy should heighten an individual's awareness of being the Hibbian/Alfordian leech or sucker (Hibbing and Alford 2004).

The Experiment

An experiment was undertaken to test the hypotheses suggested above. The experiment involved replicating a PD situation where defection and cooperation are hypothesized to occur. We then gathered psychological information using a battery of self-reported empathy questions to measure each respondent's empathetic disposition.

Using 133 undergraduate students (57 females and 76 males) as participants, a fifteen round, three-stage game was used to test the hypothetical relationship between group-oriented behavior and empathy. Two separate groups of undergraduates participated. One group consisted of 81 students from a finance class, and the other consisted of 52 College of Arts and Sciences students taken from a psychology and a political science class. Students made their decisions simultaneously with their opponent. They were told and given every indication that they were playing another person, when in reality they were playing a computer programmed with scripted actions. The first stage of mixed cooperation and defection by the computer was followed by a second stage of complete defection, which in turn, was followed by a final stage of complete cooperation. The experiment allowed the investigator to analyze how participants reacted to the complete defection in the second stage as well as complete cooperation in the third stage.

Students were not informed when the game would end but were told that it would end randomly at some unknown round. Participants played for extra credit. At the beginning of the game, students were told that the winner of the game would receive the full amount of extra credit, while the loser would only receive half of the amount of extra credit promised. At the end of the game, students were debriefed and told that no matter the outcome, all students would receive the full amount of extra credit promised. The payoff regime followed the ordering presented in Table 2, where there is a collective benefit of 4 points, divided by both players equally to cooperate, but an individual incentive of 3 to defect.

Stage 1

Round	1	2	3	4	5
Computer	C	D	C	C	C

TABLE 2
PAYOFF REGIME FOR THE PRISONER'S DILEMMA EXPERIMENT

	Cooperate (C)	Defect (D)
Cooperate (C)	2,2	0,3
Defect (D)	3,0	1,1

NOTE: Numbers indicate hypothetical "dollars" that participants were told they needed to accumulate to gain extra credit.

In stage 1, the computer was programmed to cooperate except for a single second round defection. The second round defection was felt necessary to imbibe into students a sense of randomness and uncertainty that should accompany playing another human being. Complete cooperation followed by complete defection in the second stage of the experiment, it was felt, might induce a feeling in the participant that he or she was playing with an artificial opponent, which would of course pollute the results.

Stage 2

Round	6	7	8	9	10
Computer	D	D	D	D	C

In stage 2 of the experiment, the computer was programmed to defect for four rounds, beginning in round 6 and ending in round 9. It was during this stage that it was expected that a strong majority of participants would begin to consistently defect on their computer opponent. However, the hypothesis for this experiment is that those with a higher level of empathy will defect at a higher rate than those with lower levels because of their group-oriented leanings. The final cooperation in round 10 was necessary to allow a full five rounds of informed decision making by the participant during the next and final stage. Cooperation in the tenth round should hypothetically begin to sway a participant toward mutual cooperation in the eleventh round.

Stage 3

Round	11	12	13	14	15
Computer	C	C	C	C	C

The third stage in the experiment is the most interesting part. According to Hibbing and Alford's (2004) theory of humans as wary cooperators who want to be neither leeches (take advantage of others) nor suckers (to be taken advantage of), when the computer begins cooperating, individuals should feel as though they are being leeches on a cooperative person. If, indeed, empathy is motivating human participants' guilt (as Fehr and Schmidt [1999] might suggest) or motivation in cooperation, then individuals with higher levels of empathy should begin to establish mutual cooperation to a higher degree during the final stage of the experiment.

Analysis

Respondents' decisions during each round were recorded as either 1 (cooperation) or 0 (defection). The dependent variable used for analysis was the summed up responses for the entire game for each participant.

Independent variables used in analysis included age, gender, income, population of hometown, race, and grade point average. Respondents' round 1 decision to cooperate or defect was also used as an independent predictor. Because this decision was made in the absence of information on the other player, it was taken as an indication of each participant's general willingness to cooperate.[3]

It was necessary to control for socioeconomic status to isolate the effects of empathy. As Schieman and Van Gundy (2000) showed, empathy is a context-specific phenomenon that is particular to one's socioeconomic status. By documenting the relationship between education, age, income, and gender over an entire community, they were able to demonstrate that empathy levels are in some part relative to social position. For instance, Shieman and Van Gundy presented evidence that empathy tends to decrease with age but that increases in higher education, income, and being female can mitigate this general trend. If these factors were not taken into account, it would lead to a misguided analysis of the role that a particular individual's relative level of empathy plays in his or her decision-making process. Therefore, controlling for these differences through independent predictors, such as age, gender, and GPA, allows for a statistical analysis that looks for relative rates of empathy for an individual in their socioeconomic group.

Factor analysis was used to create a factor score of empathy for each participant from the eight empathy questions from Goldberg (1999) that were asked in the postexperiment questionnaire. The eight empathy questions are presented in Table 3 with their respective factor loadings.[4] Empathy questions were recorded on a 7-point Likert scale. Items were coded in a manner such that higher scores reflect more empathy.

Results

The first hypothesis presented was that empathy would be a significant predictor of participants' defection in the second stage of the experiment. Table 4 shows that a participant's empathetic disposition was a significant predictor of defection in retaliation to the opposing player's second stage defections, albeit at the $p < .10$ level. Therefore, we can say that empathy was an important predictor of defection, but not to the degree that we expected.

TABLE 3
EMPATHY SCALE ITEMS AND FACTOR ANALYSIS LOADINGS

Empathy Question	Loading
1. I make people feel welcome.	.758
2. I anticipate the needs of others.	.626
3. I love to help others.	.769
4. I am concerned about others.	.558
5. I have a good word for everyone.	.628
6. I am sensitive to the feelings of others.	.760
7. I make people feel comfortable.	.798
8. I take time for others.	.785

TABLE 4
ORDINARY LEAST SQUARES (OLS) REGRESSION OF STAGE II RESPONSES

Variable	B (Unstandardized)	SE	Beta (Standardized)	p-Value
Constant	3.890	1.651		.020
Round 1	1.043	0.250	.350	.000
Gender (0 = male, 1 = female)	0.445	0.219	.184	.044
Age	0.002	0.048	.003	.973
Income	−0.039	0.122	−.029	.750
Population of home	−0.102	0.081	−.117	.211
Race (0 = white, 1 = ethnic origin other than white)	−0.015	0.398	−.003	.970
Grade point average	−0.444	0.257	−.147	.087
Empathy	−0.028	0.017	−.144	.100
F	3.995			.000
Adjusted R^2 = .16				
N = 126				

NOTE: The dependent variable, Stage II Responses, is a summation of a participant's responses during the second stage of the experiment, including responses during rounds 7 through 10. Analysis was run on SPSS 12.

The second hypothesis that an empathetic disposition would lead to higher rates of recooperation in the final stage of the experiment proved to be incorrect. A null result occurred. Indeed, in looking closely at the third stage regression results presented in Table 5, one should note that the empathy factor variable carries a negative coefficient. Though not significant in the regression, it indicates that even marginal levels of empathy led to more defection in the final rounds of the experiment. Truly, empathy was not a facilitator of restoring cooperation after reciprocal trust had been broken.

TABLE 5
ORDINARY LEAST SQUARE (OLS) REGRESSION OF STAGE III RESPONSES

Variable	B (Unstandardized)	SE	Beta (Standardized)	p-Value
Constant	2.037	2.345		.387
Round 1	1.425	0.355	.351	.000
Gender (0 = male, 1 = female)	0.078	0.310	.024	.802
Age	0.002	0.068	.002	.979
Income	−0.267	0.173	−.147	.126
Population of home	0.112	0.115	.095	.332
Race (0 = white, 1 = ethnic origin other than white)	0.072	0.565	.012	.899
Grade point average	0.278	0.365	.068	.447
Empathy	−0.024	0.024	−.089	.328
F	2.505			.015
Adjusted R^2 = .087				
N = 126				

NOTE: The dependent variable, Stage III Responses, is a summation of a participant's responses during the third stage of the experiment, including responses during rounds 11 through 15. Analysis was run on SPSS 12.

Uncovering the Dual Edge of Empathy

After reviewing the experimental results, we decided to conduct an exploratory analysis of the data to investigate other relationships between empathy and participants' actions. In Figure 1, the number of individuals is compared with the number of times he or she cooperated during the entire experiment. The normal distribution of cooperative decisions over the course of the game is near ideal. Participants could have cooperated anywhere from 0 to 15 times during the course of the experiment and the mean of this distribution is 7.78, or nearly 7.5, which would be the mean of a perfectly normal distribution across this sample of students.

What is intriguing is the display of the mean factor score of empathy across the sample shown in Figure 2. There is a bimodal distribution (two peaks) across the sample in regards to the mean factor score of empathy per incidences of cooperation during the experiment. Those individuals at the extremes of the distribution have, on average, very low empathy scores.[5] Those in the middle of the distribution tended to have higher scores than those in the tails but, on average, were far lower than the individuals present in either peak, where the empathy scores were the highest. This indicates that there is a "J-curve" to empathy, or that high levels of empathy can produce either more defection or more cooperation depending on the individual, but that participants with a median level of empathy converged toward cooperating about 50 percent of the time.[6]

FIGURE 1
NUMBER OF PARTICIPANTS PER INCIDENCES OF COOPERATION

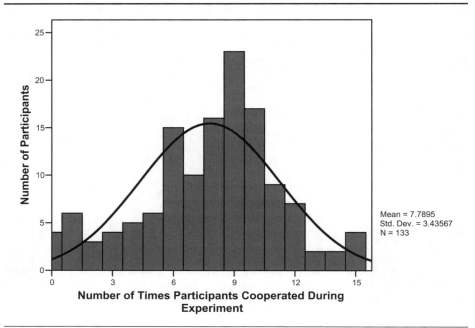

Figure 3 shows this relationship over the entire game. The Y-axis has the percentage of each group that cooperated, with each round and the computer's action denoted on the X-axis. Notice, those participants in the higher, "more cooperative" empathy peak acted as we might expect according to our hypotheses. These individuals with high levels of empathy all cooperated in the first round. A majority of them then defected by round 8. Finally, 100 percent of this group reestablished cooperation by round 13 in response to the computer's cooperative actions. However, the lower, "less cooperative" empathy peak acted in an opposite fashion. The only moment in the game when they acted in near unanimity was to defect in round 8. Indeed, at no point in the entire game did a majority of the "less cooperative," high-empathy peak cooperate with the opposing computer player. The evidence of play over the entire game supports the J-curve theory of empathy.

A binary probit regression model was estimated to test the statistical significance of the J-curve relationship. The regression was used to account for differences between the two groups of participants with high empathy when controlling for important independent variables that might also explain difference in behavior. The results appear in Table 6. The binary dependent variable is coded 1 (being present in an empathy peak) and 0 (the rest of the sample). The

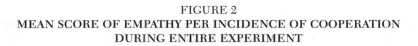

FIGURE 2
MEAN SCORE OF EMPATHY PER INCIDENCE OF COOPERATION
DURING ENTIRE EXPERIMENT

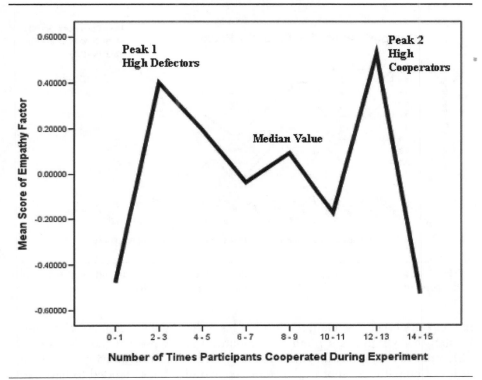

NOTE: Each data point represents the mean value of the two incidences of cooperation indicated on the X-axis.

empathy factor variable is significant at the $p < .05$ level and positive. The probit estimation eliminates the possibility that another socioeconomic factor (like gender, age, or race) that correlates with empathy could be causing the unique distribution of individuals with higher rates of empathy. Thirty-six participants inhabited the bimodal high-empathy peaks, with eighteen participants in the less cooperative peak and eighteen individuals in the more cooperative peak of the bimodal distribution. In other words, 50 percent of those with high empathy levels that did not converge toward the median range of cooperation tended to be the highest defectors.

Finally, an analysis of the possible differences between individuals with high levels of empathy residing in the more cooperative empathy peak and the less cooperative empathy peak was conducted. All possible variables that were gathered from the survey after the experiment were investigated. The size of a

FIGURE 3
COMPARISON OF PERCENTAGE COOPERATING IN EACH ROUND BETWEEN
HIGH-EMPATHY PEAKS AND TOTAL

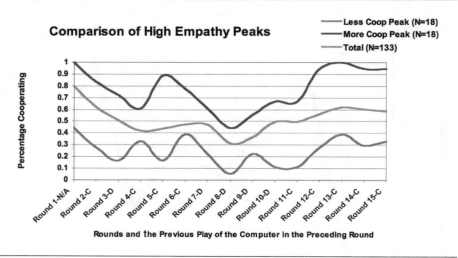

NOTE: Y-axis: percentage of group cooperating per round. X-axis: round and the previous play of the computer in the preceding round. C = cooperation; D = defection.

participant's home town and the level of his or her family income were found to be statistically significant predictors. Figures 4 and 5 present the results of the difference of means test for each variable. Essentially, those individuals with high levels of empathy present in the "more cooperative peak" tended to have been raised in smaller towns and come from families with a relatively lower level of income. In contrast, individuals present in the "less cooperative peak" were raised in a large city environment and came from families with a relatively higher level of income.

The results of this experiment suggest social conditioning could be very important to the way an empathetic disposition manifests itself in social decision making. Being from a larger urban area during an individual's childhood would likely diminish the reputation effects of continued social interaction. In a large city, it is less likely that an individual would cross paths with the same person again and again in an iterative manner where one's reputation would affect social interaction. On the other hand, growing up in a small town diminishes anonymity. Individuals would place a stronger emphasis on initial interactions because the likelihood of encountering the same person repeatedly is much greater due to a lower population density. Thus, these two opposite social environments may interact with an individual's genetically predisposed level of empathy to create different other-regarding tendencies.

TABLE 6
BINARY PROBIT REGRESSION OF ALL ROUND BIMODAL

Variable	B (Unstandardized)	SE	Z-Score	p-Value
Constant	0.395278	1.802669	0.219274	.8264
Round 1	−0.522978	0.301229	−1.736147	.0825
Gender (0 = male, 1 = female)	0.169787	0.268907	0.631398	.5278
Age	0.015265	0.058234	0.262126	.7932
Income	−0.014955	0.148860	−0.100461	.9200
Population of home	−0.029947	0.102471	−0.292251	.7701
Race (0 = white, 1 = ethnic origin other than white)	−0.002640	0.470379	−0.005613	.9955
Grade point average	−0.256563	0.320598	−0.800263	.4236
Empathy	0.305954	0.138090	2.215611	.0267

McFadden R^2 = .07
N = 127
Observations with dependent
  variable coded 0 = 92
Observations with dependent
  variable coded 1 = 35

NOTE: The dependent variable, All Round Bimodal, is a binary (0, 1) variable. Participants with incidences of cooperation throughout the entire experiment that numbered 2, 3, 4, and 5, as well as 11, 12, and 13, were coded as 1. All other participants were coded as 0. Analysis was run on Eviews 5.

Conclusion

It is important to note that this experiment only included a sample of under-graduate students. Future research should be conducted to duplicate the results. However, judging by this experiment, empathy seems to have a bipolar nature. Higher rates of empathy tended to have two contrary effects by either making an individual more likely to defect or more likely to cooperate, but not to converge toward the median level of cooperation as the majority of participants in this experiment. The line graph presented in Figure 2 demonstrates the J-curve phe-nomenon with empathy and cooperation over the entire experiment. Contrary to the hypotheses originally being tested, it is not that empathy has a simple positive linear relationship with a desire for egalitarian outcomes. Rather, an empathetic emotional disposition likely cultivates a sensitivity to social decisions, which, depending on an individual's social conditioning, leads to a more intense display of cooperation and defection.

FIGURE 4
DIFFERENCE OF MEANS TEST COMPARING SIZE OF HOME TOWN
FOR PARTICIPANTS FALLING INTO THE "LESS COOPERATIVE EMPATHY"
PEAK AND THOSE IN THE "MOST COOPERATIVE EMPATHY" PEAK

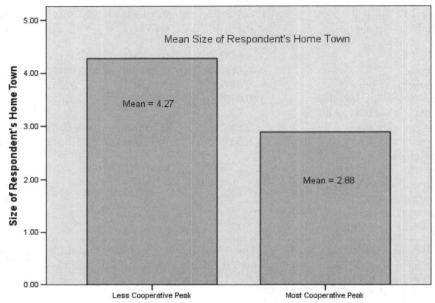

NOTE: 1 = rural area; 2 = village (population less than 1,000); 3 = town (1,000 to 10,000); 4 = city (10,000-100,000); 5 = large city (greater than 100,000). Mean for entire sample: 3.73 ($N = 133$). Bimodal empathy peaks ($N = 36$). $t = 3.32$, $p < .01$.

[E]mpathy tended to have two contrary effects by either making an individual more likely to defect or more likely to cooperate, but not to converge toward the median level of cooperation.

FIGURE 5
DIFFERENCE OF MEANS TEST COMPARING SIZE OF FAMILY INCOME FOR
PARTICIPANTS FALLING INTO THE "LESS COOPERATIVE EMPATHY" PEAK
AND THOSE IN THE "MOST COOPERATIVE EMPATHY" PEAK

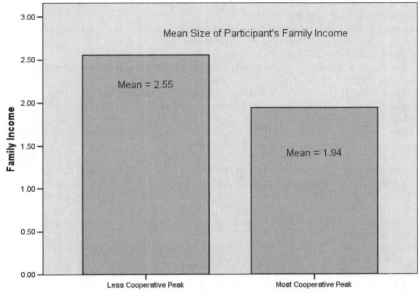

Bimodal Peaks of High Empathy: Less Cooperative (N=18) and More
Cooperative (N=17)

NOTE: 1 = less than \$40,000; 2 = \$40,000 to \$80,000; 3 = \$80,000 to \$120,000; 4 = greater than \$120,000. Mean for entire sample: 2.32 ($N = 133$). For this test only, seventeen individuals are present in the "more cooperative" peak because of the absence of a survey answer to this question. Bimodal empathy peaks ($N = 36$). $t = 1.908$, $p < .10$.

Notes

1. Originally designed by the Rand Corporation in the 1950s to test cold war nuclear exchange strategies, the incentive structure is such that mutual defection, or noncooperation, is the rational choice, but cooperation is the mutually beneficial response for both participants (Poundstone 1992).

2. See chapter 3 especially.

3. Out of the 133 undergraduate students who participated, 79.7 percent cooperated on the first round and 20.3 percent defected.

4. A reliability analysis was conducted on the responses to the empathy questions with a Cronbach's alpha score of $\alpha = .853$.

5. Individuals in the tails of the distribution of cooperative behavior had lower empathy levels than the rest of the sample. Whether their opponent defected or cooperated, these individuals were indifferent and can be seen as having adopted a strategy to use throughout the entire game. A difference of means was estimated and significant at the $p < .05$ level, indicating that those participants who cooperated or defected to the extreme actually had significantly lower levels of empathy than the rest of the sample.

6. The J-curve concept is aptly illustrated by a study regarding testosterone and depression. It has been found that testosterone levels conform to a J-curve in regards to depression in men (Booth, Johnson, and

Granger 1999) where extremely high and low levels of testosterone correlate with depression while median levels of testosterone (which encompasses a majority of males) correlates with lower rates of depression.

References

Alford, John R., and John R. Hibbing. 2004. The origin of politics: An evolutionary theory of political behavior. *Perspectives on Politics* 2:707-23.

Andreoni, James, and John H. Miller. 1993. Rational cooperation in the finitely repeated prisoner's dilemma: Experimental evidence. *The Economic Journal* 103:570-85.

Axelrod, Robert. 1984. *The evolution of co-operation.* New York: Basic Books.

Booth, Alan, David R. Johnson, and Douglas A. Granger. 1999. Testosterone and men's depression: The role of social behavior. *Journal of Health and Social Behavior* 40:130-40.

Bowles, Samuel, and Herbert Gintis. 2003. Origins of human cooperation. In *Genetic and cultural evolution of cooperation,* ed. P. Hammerstein. Cambridge, MA: MIT Press.

Davis, Mark H. 1996. *Empathy: A social psychological approach.* Boulder, CO: Westview.

Davis, Mark, Carol Luce, and Stephen J. Kraus. 1994. The heritability of characteristics associated with dispositional empathy. *Journal of Personality* 62:371-91.

Dawes, Christopher, James Fowler, Tim Johnson, Richard McElreath, and Oleg Smirnov. 2007. Egalitarian motives in humans. *Science* 446:794-796.

Ebstein, Richard P., Jonathan Benjamin, and Robert H. Belmaker. 2003. Behavioral genetics, genomics, and personality. In *Behavioral genetics in the postgenomic era,* ed. Robert Plomin, John C. Defries, Ian W. Craig, and Peter McGuffin. Washington, DC: American Psychological Association.

Fehr, Ernst, and Simon Gachter. 2000. Fairness and retaliation: The economics of retaliation. *Journal of Economics Perspectives* 14:159-81.

Fehr, Ernst, and Klaus M. Schmidt. 1999. A theory of fairness, competition and cooperation. *Quarterly Journal of Economics* 114:817-68.

Field, Alexander J. 2004. *Altruistically inclined?* Ann Arbor: University of Michigan Press.

Goldberg, L. R. 1999. A broad-bandwidth, public-domain, personality inventory measuring the lower-level facets of several five-factor models. In *Pers. psychology in Europe,* vol. 7, ed. I. Mervielde, I. Deary, F. De Fruyt, and F. Ostendorf, 7-28. Tilburg, the Netherlands: Tilburg University Press.

Hardin, Russell. 1971. Collective action as an agreeable N-prisoner's dilemma. *Behavioral Science* 16:472-81.

Hibbing, John R., and John R. Alford. 2004. Accepting authoritative decisions: Humans as wary cooperators. *American Journal of Political Science* 48:62-76.

Kagan, Jerome. 2003. A behavioral science perspective. In *Behavioral genetics in the postgenomic era,* ed. Robert Plomin, John C. Defries, Ian W. Craig, and Peter McGuffin. Washington, DC: American Psychological Association.

McCabe, Kevin, Daniel Houser, Lee Ryan, Vernon Smith, and Theodore Trouard. 2001. A functional imaging study of cooperation in two-person reciprocal exchange. *Proceedings of the National Academy of Sciences* 98:11832-835.

Pericak-Vance, Margaret. 2003. The genetics of autistic disorder. In *Behavioral genetics in the postgenomic era,* ed. Robert Plomin, John C. Defries, Ian W. Craig, and Peter McGuffin. Washington, DC: American Psychological Association.

Poundstone, William. 1992. *Prisoner's dilemma.* New York: Doubleday.

Rapoport, Anatol, and Albert M. Chammah. 1965. *Prisoner's dilemma: A study in conflict and cooperation.* Ann Arbor: University of Michigan Press.

Ridley, Matt. 1996. *The origin of virtue.* New York: Penguin.

Rosenberg, Morris. 1990. Reflexivity and emotions. *Social Psychology Quarterly* 53:3-12.

Schieman, Scott, and Karen Van Gundy. 2000. The personal and social links between age and self-reported empathy. *Social Psychology Quarterly* 63:152-74.

Sober, Eliot, and David Sloan Wilson. 1998. *Unto others.* Cambridge, MA: Harvard University Press.

Smith, Kevin, Christopher Larimer, Levente Littvay, and John Hibbing. 2007. Evolutionary theory and political leadership: Why certain people do not trust decision makers. The *Journal of Politics* 69:283-297.

Smith-Lovin, Lynn. 1995. The sociology of affect and emotion. In *Sociological perspectives on social psychology*, ed. Karen S. Cook, Gary A. Fine, and James S. House. Boston: Allyn & Bacon.
Thoits, Peggy A. 1989. The sociology of emotion. In *Annual review of sociology*, ed. W. R. Scott and J. Blake. Palo Alto, CA: Annual Reviews.
Wilson, David S. 2002. *Darwin's cathedral: Evolution, religion and the nature of society*. Chicago: University of Chicago Press.

Personality and Emotional Response: Strategic and Tactical Responses to Changing Political Circumstances

By
JENNIFER WOLAK
and
GEORGE E. MARCUS

Emotions enable people to navigate various political environments, differentiating familiar situations where standard operating procedures are suitable from unfamiliar terrain when more attention is needed. While previous research identifies consequences of emotion, we know less about what triggers affective response. In this article, the authors investigate what role personality has in the operation of the systems of affective intelligence. Using experimental data as well as responses from the 2000 and 2004 American National Election Studies, the authors first consider whether personality affects the activation of emotional response. Next, they explore the degree to which citizen attitudes like openness to information and compromise are explained by personality characteristics and subconscious emotional response. Finally, they consider the implications of these results for our normative understanding of democratic citizenship.

Keywords: personality traits; emotional response; political involvement; citizen attitudes; anxiety

Emotions serve people by enabling them to navigate the diverse political environments they encounter. According to the theory of affective intelligence, people respond to political situations by relying on the initial preconscious appraisals provided by a dual system of emotional appraisal (Marcus, Neuman, and MacKuen 2000). When confronted with familiar friends or foes, people rely on an appraisal system that uses variations in the emotions of enthusiasm and anger to deliver assessments of the situation and guide habitual routines to manage such recurring events. These feelings guide our reliance on existing habits. But when people encounter unfamiliar circumstances, they rely on a second appraisal system that makes use of the emotional dimension of anxiety. As anxiety increases, people become more attentive to the immediate circum-

NOTE: An earlier version of this article was presented at the Hendricks Conference on Biology, Evolution, and Political Behavior, University of Nebraska–Lincoln, October 13-14, 2006. We thank Stanley Feldman and Elizabeth Theiss-Morse for their helpful comments.

DOI: 10.1177/0002716207306086

stances and rely on expressly deliberative strategies rather than continued reliance on habitual responses. Thus, preconscious affective appraisal systems provide a potent dual capacity, distinguishing the situations when previously learned routines are suitable from the contexts where greater attentiveness and consideration are needed (Marcus 2002; Marcus, Neuman, and MacKuen 2000).

> *As anxiety increases, people become more attentive to the immediate circumstances and rely on expressly deliberative strategies rather than continued reliance on habitual responses.*

The idea that people rely on both habitual and deliberative strategies depending on the circumstances conflicts with the accounts offered by theorists that require deliberative approaches applied to all political choices (Benhabib 1996; Bohman and Rehg 1997; Fishkin 1991; Habermas 1996). However, we argue against the notion that each and every political decision needs to be the result of a deliberative process to secure a legitimate authoritative result (Gutmann and Thompson 1996; Marcus 2002; Sanders 1997; Young 2000). First, this requirement presumes that deliberative decision-making mechanisms are always superior to more automatic processes, a claim that is generally false (Gigerenzer, Todd, and ABC Research Group 1999; Bargh and Chartrand 1999; Bargh and Ferguson 2000). Second, claiming deliberation as the sole determinant of citizen competence obscures the distinction between familiar circumstances wherein previously mastered routines offer speed of execution and predictability of result and unfamiliar circumstances where habituated responses are likely to produce unreliable and potentially disastrous results. Deliberative approaches are indeed

Jennifer Wolak is Assistant Professor of Political Science at the University of Colorado at Boulder. Her research interests include political psychology and public opinion. She has published research on the causes of attitudinal ambivalence, the role of emotion in politics, and the effects of campaigns on political learning.

George E. Marcus is a professor of political science at Williams College. His research interests include democratic theory, public opinion, electoral behavior in democratic societies, political psychology with special interest on the role of emotions in politics, philosophies of science, and methodology. He has published numerous articles and chapters on American political behavior, as well as on political tolerance, the role of issues and emotions in the American electorate, appraisal of candidates, dynamics of electoral campaigns, and political psychology.

important, but only in those circumstances wherein prior information provides an inappropriate guide.

Prior research shows that anxiety helps determine how people practice citizenship, identifying when to move from standard routines and cues to engage in greater issue learning and more deliberative reasoning (MacKuen et al. 2001). But do the systems of affective intelligence operate in the same fashion across all people? Or are some people more receptive to threats and more likely to be cued to attentiveness by anxious reactions? While previous research explores the consequences of emotional reactions to politics (Brader 2006; Marcus, Neuman, and MacKuen 2000; Rudolph, Gangl, and Stevens 2000), less is known about what engages people emotionally in politics. Brader (2006) found that visual and audio cues can influence how people react emotionally to politics. Other research suggests that differences in issue framing have only a modest effect on emotional response, where emotional engagement is better explained by individual differences in the direction and intensity of prior preferences (Wolak et al. 2003). In this article, we consider the personality roots of emotional response. Emotions react with particular speed, generating appraisals within 80 to 120 milliseconds of exposure to some stimuli, far faster than the 500 milliseconds for perceptions that become consciously apparent. As such, the swift modulations of affective states may be governed not so much by conscious consideration of the current circumstances but by personality differences and individual predispositions to be more or less emotional and reactive.

In this article, we investigate what role personality has in the operation of the emotional systems of affective intelligence and the practice of citizenship to see whether emotional reactions are best understood as contemporary responses to current circumstances or instead spurred by underlying personality traits. Using experimental data as well as responses from the 2000 and 2004 American National Election Studies, we explore whether personality affects the activation of emotional response. Next, we consider whether political attitudes like openness to information are better predicted by personality characteristics or emotional response. Investigating the roots of civic behavior informs normative concerns about promoting civic competence. If some are more predisposed to become emotionally engaged in politics than others, this suggests that some people will be more reactive to changes in their contemporary political environment, moving from habitual processing to more deliberative consideration. Similarly, those who are less likely to become anxious about politics will be less responsive to changes in immediate political environments. But if personality differences in emotional response are slight, it suggests that most individuals are able to adaptively use emotions to navigate political environments.

Sources of Political Citizenship

Traditionally, the roots of good citizenship are thought to be in political socialization, where civics lessons help people assume the norms of citizenship. People must learn how to be good citizens (Almond and Verba 1963; Galston 2001). Through education, people become more politically knowledgeable and engaged and supportive of principles of democracy (Nie, Junn, and Stehlik-Barry 1996). The barriers to deliberative citizenship are usually seen as attitudinal. Active partisans and those with strong prior preferences seek out information that supports their priors and resist consideration of alternative viewpoints (Redlawsk 2002; Taber and Lodge 2006). These studies suggest that those interested in promoting deliberation and voter participation should focus their energies on programs of civic education. Programs in secondary schools can instill norms of good citizenship, and the effects of bias might be limited by urging people to be fair-minded and balanced in contemplating alternatives.

Other evidence suggests, however, that the practice of good citizenship has deeper roots than personal issue preferences and socialized views of citizenship. While good citizenship can be learned, some are perhaps more predisposed to support such principles than others. Personality has not been at the forefront of most research into political behavior (although see Sniderman 1975). Still, a modest body of research is worth noting. Personality differences can drive candidate evaluations and party preferences (Caprara, Barbaranelli, and Zimbardo 1999; Caprara et al. 2006), and genetic dispositions can influence ideological leanings (Alford, Funk, and Hibbing 2005). People's willingness to extend rights to disliked groups can also depend on personality. Marcus et al. (1995) found personality-based differences in tolerance, where greater neuroticism and extroversion limits tolerance and greater openness promotes it. Stenner (2005) also connected authoritarianism with political tolerance, where authoritarian predispositions combine with perceptions of threat to influence views on civil liberties and race. Dogmatism associated with authoritarianism can limit political tolerance and lead people to selectively search for information that supports and reinforces prior preferences (Feldman 2003; Feldman and Stenner 1997; Lavine, Lodge, and Freitas 2005).

While good citizenship can be learned, some are perhaps more predisposed to support such principles than others. Personality has not been at the forefront of most research into political behavior.

Beyond their effect on issue preferences, personality differences have also been shown to influence people's levels of political engagement. Fowler (2006) connected altruism to the inclination to turn out to vote, where those with greater concern for others report greater electoral participation. Individual differences in the need to evaluate help explain political activism and opinionation (Bizer et al. 2004). Bekkers (2005) also found personality differences in political engagement, particularly for empathy but also for extroversion and conscientiousness. These accounts suggest important individual differences in reactivity to political signals. Faced with the same political threat, some will be more likely to become interested and be driven to act on this issue, while others will remain unresponsive—depending on underlying differences in traits.

Emotion, Personality, and Citizenship

Citizenship activities can be both internal, when we turn away from our private concerns to ponder matters from a political perspective, as well as public, when we engage in public discourse and political activities. In this study, we select three dimensions of citizenship that are central to most accounts of democratic citizenship. First, people become citizens when they turn away from the mundane affairs that consume their lives and shift their attention to some political issue that commands their attention. This requires consideration of new information and a desire to learn more about the stakes involved. Second, once they become attentive, people need to speak up and become active citizens. And third, once engaged by a political conflict, they have to determine whether to engage in compromise, to seek some middle ground that might resolve the dispute by mutual accommodation, or remain steadfastly loyal to the cause until victory is obtained.

We have elsewhere shown that these citizenship features have their roots in emotionality (Marcus and MacKuen 1993; Marcus, Neuman, and MacKuen 2000; MacKuen et al. 2001). Here we take up the question of whether adding personality into the mix adds and alters our understanding of citizenship. Our prior work on tolerance suggests that the effects of personality are "encapsulated" in factors more proximal rather than being direct (Marcus et al. 1995). That is to say, basic individual differences in personality influence the standing decisions people acquire, rather than directly affecting how they made tolerance decisions.

Here, we are particularly interested in another situation most vital and central to democratic politics—what engages people to become active citizens and consider an issue that asserts a position contrary to one they hold. When challenged, people may either respond or remain disengaged and focused on their private pursuits. If what shapes their engagement is largely due to historical factors like personality, then democratic politics will be practiced not on the basis of the merits of the contemporary issue challenge but rather by preexisting appetite for or aversion to the demands of democratic engagement (Hibbing and Theiss-Morse 2002; Mansbridge 1980). For the most part, the normative expectation diverges from the more normal empirical expectation. Weak effects of personality and robust effects of emotional response are the desired normative result. Such a pattern would enable most, if not all, citizens to battle to a result based on the character of the conflict, rather than the deep personality suitability for politics that is not evenly distributed in the population.

Given the formulation of the theory of affective intelligence (Marcus 2002), we expect that the extent to which personality influences emotional engagement, these traits will influence some emotional reactions more than others. In the taxonomy of preconscious emotions, the emotions of enthusiasm and aversion are managed by the disposition system. It is here we expect to see the greatest expression of personality traits, to influence the standing dispositions of like and dislike in response to familiar political stimuli. The second emotional system, the surveillance system, depends less on the information of one's subjective state and more on assessments of the external environment to determine the suitability of habitual responses. Thus, personality dispositions ought to be less influential on the operation of the surveillance system than on the action of the disposition system.[1]

The Effects of Personality

Personality can be seen as an evolutionary adaptation that provides variations in reactions and responses, which ensures that the population has available a wider repertoire of options to new and old challenges (Alford, Funk, and Hibbing 2005). Jeffery Gray (1981, 1985, 1987a, 1987b, 1990) suggested that these affective systems have personality or trait features, such that people will respond not only to the changing circumstances through emotional assessments but also by virtue of their personality differences.[2] Those who are more inhibited or neurotic will tend to become more anxious in the face of threats, while extroverts and those who are more sensitive to rewards will respond with greater enthusiasm when encountering favorable outcomes (Carver, Sutton, and Scheier 2000; Carver and White 1994; Elliot and Thrash 2002). The idea that some people are, by their nature, more inclined to attend to politics and be interested by political debates is suggested in a number of studies. We consider whether inherent differences in learning and engagement depend on deep-rooted personality differences.

We focus on four personality characteristics: neuroticism, extroversion, openness, and authoritarianism. The first three traits are components of the five-factor model of personality. Neuroticism is the personality trait most closely connected to emotionality, representing emotional stability. Those high on neuroticism can be characterized as moody, anxious, self-conscious, or insecure, while those low in neuroticism are described as unemotional—relaxed, calm, and secure. We expect that those who tend to be neurotic will be more sensitive to political threats and more likely to report emotional responses, particularly the negative emotions of aversion and anxiety. The consequences of the trait anxiety of neuroticism for citizenship are less clear. On one hand, studies of affective intelligence show a relationship between policy anxiety and the desire to learn more about the issue (MacKuen et al. 2001). This suggests that those who are more neurotic may be more likely to seek out information to ease their feelings of anxiety. But, to the extent that neurotic individuals feel not just anxiety but also hostility or distress, neuroticism may instead close the door to consideration, discouraging consideration of compromise and political action.

Extroversion and openness to experience, however, will likely have a positive relationship with citizenship behaviors of learning and compromise. Extroverts are outgoing and optimistic, more likely to be emotionally expressive and interested in political participation than reserved, introverted individuals. We expect that extroverts will also be more likely to consider new information and express a desire for greater personal political engagement. Those high in openness are more curious and will be more likely to express interest in learning more about policy issues than those who prefer to avoid unfamiliar or new experiences. We expect those who are low in openness to be less likely to embrace new information or political action. Gray's (1987b) work on personality and emotional response suggests one key interaction. Gray argued that those who are simultaneously high on extroversion and neuroticism are most likely to be attentive and responsive to unanticipated changes in the environment. This is premised on the expectation that those high on extroversion are more likely to be active in the social environment and more confident in their abilities to meet the challenges that are evoked by confronting conditions of risk. Those high on neuroticism are most attentive and responsive to circumstances of uncertainty. Thus, it is likely that those who are most capable in performing, those high in extroversion, and those high in responsiveness to circumstances of uncertainty—those high in neuroticism—are most likely to be anxious in conditions of risk (Rudolph, Gangl, and Stevens 2000).

Authoritarianism is a personality trait associated with support for social conventions and respect for authorities (Adorno et al. 1950; Altemeyer 1988). Those high in authoritarianism are less likely to challenge the views of authorities. We expect that people high in authoritarianism will be more likely to respond to threats with aversion rather than anxiety. In terms of the behavioral consequences, we expect that authoritarian individuals will be less open to consideration of new information and less interested in political action.

Personality and Emotional Reactions to Policy Issues

We explore these questions first using responses from an experimental study. Participants were undergraduates at a public university in the south who participated for course credit. In total, 162 individuals participated. First, participants completed a pretest questionnaire. Several days later, they were sent a link that directed them to a policy story in the style of an online newspaper article and a questionnaire about what they read. Participants later read two more policy stories and completed two more questionnaires over the next few weeks.

The policy articles concerned one of four issues—affirmative action programs at universities, mental health budget cuts, tuition costs, and music downloading policies. Three different issue frames were also used in addition to a neutral presentation—one that emphasized this policy change as extreme, one that described the policy change as within one's own state of residence rather than some distant setting, and one that varied whether the policy change was proposed or passed into law. The issues were selected to challenge the prior preferences of most, where the issue is contrary to pretest preferences in 89 percent of these cases. In 11 percent of the cases, participants were sent a link that presented an issue presentation that affirmed their position. This enables us to contrast responses to reassuring circumstances (affirmation) and disturbing circumstances (confrontation). To measure personality, we used the battery of items developed by Costa and MacRae (1985, 1992) that assess neuroticism, extroversion, and openness. Each personality trait was assessed with twelve items, as described in Marcus et al. (1995, 251-52). To measure authoritarianism, we use a scale of nine items concerning matters such as support for traditional values and respect for authorities.[3]

To assess people's emotional reactions, we asked them how the policy changes made them feel—*very anxious, somewhat anxious, not very anxious*, or *not at all anxious*. Responses about feelings of anxiety, unease, and fear were summed to create a measure of anxiety. The measure of enthusiasm reflects sentiments of pride, hopefulness, and enthusiasm, while aversion concerns the degree to which the policy made one feel contemptuous, bitter, angry, and disgusted (Marcus et al. 2006). Because emotions are used differently depending on the character of the contemporary environment, we consider the roots of emotion and citizenship separately depending on whether one saw a policy article that challenged or complemented people's prior issue preferences. In this study, most people were presented with a policy issue that challenged their prior positions, so we must be cautious in generalizing from the reassuring condition, as our sample size here is quite low.

First, we consider the degree to which personality traits explain emotional reactions to political issues. Because each participant viewed three different stimuli, we report standard errors clustered by individual. In the first two columns of Table 1, we consider the roots of policy anxiety. While it is reasonable to expect that those high on neuroticism will be more sensitive to policy change and more likely to have their surveillance systems activated, we find no significant differences in anxiety by level of neuroticism.[4] This is surprising given previous research connecting neuroticism to anxious reactions (Cassese and Feldman 2005). However, the expected interaction between neuroticism and extroversion are interactive, as suggested by Gray (1987b), is significant. While the interaction of extroversion and neuroticism has limited explanatory power across most of our models, it is a significant explanation of anxiety under conditions of policy challenge. Those high in both neuroticism and extroversion are significantly more likely to express anxiety in response to a challenging policy change but not a reassuring policy change. Those open to experiences are slightly more likely to become anxious when confronted by a policy that challenges their prior preferences but no more prone to feelings of fear when that policy change favors prior attitudes. Among those viewing issue challenges at the lowest level of openness,

180   THE ANNALS OF THE AMERICAN ACADEMY

TABLE 1
THE EFFECTS OF PERSONALITY ON EMOTIONAL RESPONSE

	Anxiety		Aversion		Enthusiasm	
	Challenge	Reassure	Challenge	Reassure	Challenge	Reassure
Neuroticism	.048	−.002	.096*	.038	.032	−.116
	(.043)	(.053)	(.043)	(.075)	(.033)	(.083)
Extroversion	.033	−.167*	.102*	.126	.084	−.191*
	(.052)	(.063)	(.048)	(.078)	(.053)	(.100)
Openness	.106*	.108	−.088*	−.032	−.020	.017
	(.054)	(.083)	(.046)	(.152)	(.054)	(.135)
Authoritarianism	.029	.138	−.035	−.141	−.003	−.053
	(.036)	(.084)	(.036)	(.147)	(.040)	(.096)
Anxiety	—	—	.514*	.851*	−.082	−.533*
			(.050)	(.128)	(.055)	(.184)
Aversion	.522*	.575*	—	—	−.336*	.080
	(.048)	(.106)			(.053)	(.166)
Enthusiasm	−.087	−.362*	−.352*	.080	—	—
	(.058)	(.149)	(.060)	(.176)		
Constant	.301*	.427*	.313*	−.092	.455*	.605*
	(.039)	(.084)	(.043)	(.132)	(.032)	(.082)
N	384	45	384	45	384	45
R^2	.38	.71	.45	.59	.22	.39

NOTE: Regression estimates. Standard errors in parentheses.
*$p < .05$.

the predicted level of anxiety is .49, compared to .64 for those with the highest level of openness, all else equal. While extroversion has no effect on anxiety among those facing challenging policies, extroverted individuals faced with a favorable policy change do see a decrease in levels of anxiety. Authoritarian predispositions have no significant influence on levels of issue anxiety for those viewing either reassuring or challenging stimuli.[5] On the whole, personality differences play only a modest role in the activation of the emotional surveillance system, and these traits operate differently depending on whether circumstances challenge or support prior preferences.

Next, we consider the roots of feelings of anger. For those who read about policies that support personal preferences, personality traits fail to have a significant effect on levels of policy aversion. Under the condition of policy challenge, however, the association between personality and policy anger is more substantial. Authoritarianism fails to be a significant predictor of anger, but neuroticism, extroversion, and openness all predict policy aversion. Neuroticism and extroversion are positively associated with anger. Those higher in neuroticism are more sensitive to emotional signals and become more angry when faced with a policy change opposed to prior preferences. Extroverts are also more likely to react in anger in the face of policy challenges than those who are more introverted.

Openness to experience, however, is negatively correlated with policy anger. Those open to new experiences are less likely to become angry at challenging policies than those closed to experiences, perhaps because they are more able to engage with diverse settings than those who are less open to new experiences. The magnitude of the effect size is similar across the three personality traits. Overall, personality traits have greater power in explaining differences in people's dispositions than in explaining the activation of the surveillance system. The cuing of personality to drive dispositions also appears to depend on the context, where personality roots to policy anger emerge in the face of policy threats. But the contribution of personality in explaining the variance of policy aversion is more modest than the overall explanatory contribution from the emotional reactions of anxiety and enthusiasm. Enthusiasm is negatively related to aversion, while increasing anxiety predicts greater policy aversion. Moving from the lowest level of anxiety to the highest increases aversion by half a point, compared to about a .15 predicted point increase from a similar size movement on any of the three personality dimensions.

The other emotion of the disposition system, enthusiasm, is also predicted by levels of extroversion. Extroverts who encounter reassuring policy changes are less likely to become enthusiastic. When faced with policy challenges, the effect is in the opposite direction (though not significant), where extroverts are more likely to become enthusiastic. Personality differences in authoritarianism, neuroticism, and openness appear unrelated to levels of policy enthusiasm regardless of whether the issue favors or opposes a person's prior issue predispositions.

Overall, personality traits do affect emotional engagement in policy issues, but only to a limited degree. The greatest effects of personality are in the generation of policy anger in the face of policy threats.

Overall, personality traits do affect emotional engagement in policy issues, but only to a limited degree. The greatest effects of personality are in the generation of policy anger in the face of policy threats. While we have only a limited sample from which to generalize, the effects of personality in the face of reassuring policy changes are slight, confined to the effects of extroversion—which can promote anxiety and limit enthusiasm. For the most part, personality operates to promote additional engagement—openness triggers the surveillance system and limits the expression of aversion. The exceptions are in the case of policy anger, where neuroticism and extroversion promote aversion in the face of policy challenges. On the whole, we find that personality features influence dispositions more than the activation of political anxiety, suggesting that all are able to use the surveillance system to identify the political circumstances that require greater consideration.

Personality and the Practice of Citizenship

Next, we consider the effects of personality on three citizenship behaviors—the willingness to learn more about the issue, interest in political participation, and consideration of policy compromise. We explain citizenship behavior as a function of emotion and personality, controlling for attitude strength and personal issue salience.[6] If emotions are the primary predictors of citizenship behavior, this indicates the importance of the operation of the system of affective intelligence. If personality measures are significant, this indicates that the practice of citizenship also depends on innate differences to engage and disengage in political life. By testing both as explanations for citizenship behaviors, we can explore the relative strength of each in explaining learning and participation, as well as the general importance of these psychological processes for the practice of citizenship.

We assess people's willingness to learn more with three measures that ask people whether they would like to learn more about the views of issue proponents, the perspectives of issue opponents, and more about the issue generally. People respond yes, maybe, or no, where responses are summed to create a 7-point scale of the willingness to learn more about the issue.[7] We interact personality with seeing a reassuring or challenging policy issue, to see if personality operates differently in the presence of policy threat. First, we find that anxiety prompts greater interest in learning more about the policy issue, confirming prior affective intelligence findings (Marcus, Neuman, and MacKuen 2000, MacKuen et al. 2001). Enthusiasm is also positively associated with the desire to learn more.[8]

We also find significant direct effects of personality on citizenship behavior beyond any contribution via emotional engagement. Those who are open to experiences are more likely to report a desire to learn more about policy issues. Moving from the lowest level of openness to the highest level of openness predicts a 30 percent increase in the desire to learn more about the issue among those who see a challenging issue, all else equal. Earlier we found no connection between trait differences in neuroticism and the activation of the surveillance system. Here, we find effects for neuroticism only in the condition of when people confront a familiar and affirming issue position, where those high in neuroticism express a heightened desire to learn more about the policy. For those who see reassuring policy change, levels of extroversion are also positively associated with a willingness to learn about public policy. These effects come in addition to significant positive effects on learning from attitude strength and personal issue salience. Thus, personality plays a modestly greater role when subjects are in a reassuring familiar context and a lesser role when, in the confrontational disturbing condition, as we find significant interactions with neuroticism and extroversion and this treatment condition.

Next, we consider the role of emotional engagement and trait differences in people's desire to engage in politics. Anxiety can promote a desire for more information—does it also encourage political participation? Study participants were asked if they would be interested in participating in the issue in one of several ways—sending a letter to the editor, signing an online petition, writing to legislators, donating money, participating in a rally, or receiving additional information by e-mail from groups. Study participants checked as many or as few of these activities as they would be interested in engaging in. We sum responses to create a measure of one's overall willingness to commit to political action. Negative binomial regression results are shown in the second column of Table 2.

We find first that anxiety relates to a desire to politically engage in the issue. Moving from the lowest to the highest level of anxiety predicts an increase of interest in one additional political act, all else equal. Here, we find no significant effects for anger or enthusiasm on interest in participation once we control for trait differences and variations in issue strength and salience. Personality traits like openness and extroversion also have little effect on the willingness to consider political action. The main personality effect is among those viewing reassuring policy change, where high authoritarianism limits interest in political participation. When confronted with a reassuring policy change, those who are highest in authoritarianism are predicted to express interest in two fewer political acts than those lowest in authoritarianism, all else equal. This is consistent with Feldman and Stenner's (1997) work, which suggests that authoritarianism is expressed differently depending on whether circumstances are threatening. On the whole, however, personality plays little role in motivating a desire to act.

Last, we consider people's endorsement of policy compromise to see whether personality predispositions leave people resistant to consideration of middle-ground policy remedies. In the posttest, participants were asked what they preferred as a policy outcome—the policy they read about, a reversal of this policy, or a compromise remedy. Results of probit estimation are shown in the third column of Table 2. Again, we find emotional roots to deliberative behavior. Those who become anxious about the policy change report greater willingness to support some sort of policy compromise as a solution. Those who react with anger, however, resist middle-ground remedies and are less likely to support a compromise.

While personality traits play only a modest role in directing learning and participation, we find a number of personality differences in the willingness to endorse policy compromise. Those high in authoritarianism support convention and here resist policy compromise. Those with the lowest-level authoritarianism are predicted to support compromise 80 percent of the time in the face of policy challenge, all else equal. For those highest in authoritarianism, this prediction drops to a 55 percent likelihood of supporting compromise. We also find that openness to experience surprisingly also acts to limit compromise. Levels of extroversion relate to support for compromise, with effects that vary depending

TABLE 2
**EMOTIONS AND PERSONALITY AS EXPLANATIONS
OF CITIZENSHIP BEHAVIORS**

	Learn More	Interest in Participation	Compromise
Neuroticism	−0.078	−0.144	0.245
	(0.064)	(0.202)	(0.251)
Extroversion	0.002	−0.022	0.524*
	(0.078)	(0.253)	(0.306)
Openness	0.212*	0.394	−0.756*
	(0.084)	(0.276)	(0.347)
Authoritarianism	0.065	0.145	−0.452*
	(0.064)	(0.203)	(0.250)
Reassuring policy change	0.050	−0.280	−0.458*
	(0.054)	(0.176)	(0.229)
Reassure × Neuroticism	0.301*	0.622	−0.109
	(0.153)	(0.569)	(0.555)
Reassure × Extroversion	0.299*	0.275	−1.657*
	(0.163)	(0.643)	(0.689)
Reassure × Openness	0.012	0.010	0.912
	(0.201)	(0.909)	(0.780)
Reassure × Authoritarianism	−0.154	−1.475*	1.023
	(0.140)	(0.592)	(0.674)
Anxiety	0.227*	0.968*	0.658*
	(0.082)	(0.249)	(0.389)
Aversion	0.073	0.273	−0.882*
	(0.077)	(0.256)	(0.392)
Enthusiasm	0.151*	0.394	−0.247
	(0.071)	(0.262)	(0.410)
Attitude strength	0.112*	0.414*	−0.385
	(0.049)	(0.177)	(0.264)
Personal issue salience	0.094*	0.204*	−0.073
	(0.028)	(0.084)	(0.154)
Constant	0.283*	−0.791	0.894*
	(0.068)	(0.258)	(0.332)
N	414	414	382
R^2/pseudo-R^2	.14	—	.04
χ^2	—	72.68*	24.21*

NOTE: Regression estimates, first column; negative binomial regression, second column; probit estimates, last column. Standard errors in parentheses.
*$p < .05$.

on whether the issue favors or challenges people's prior predispositions. Under the condition of issue challenge, extroverts support compromise, while extroverts who see reassuring policy change are less likely to endorse compromise. Here, personality traits have significant explanatory power over people's willingness to support compromise, beyond any indirect influence through emotional response.

While trait differences play only a modest role in emotional engagement in policy issues, they play a somewhat greater role in explaining people's propensity to learn more about public policy. In the case of policy learning, the effects are generally positive, where openness, neuroticism, and extroversion if anything predict a stronger desire to find out more about the policy issue. In the case of participation and compromise, however, the effects of trait differences are primarily in the opposite direction—openness limits compromise, and high levels of authoritarianism discourage compromise and political action. The effects of policy anxiety are robust. Greater anxiety predicts all three citizenship behaviors—those who are made anxious by policy change are more interested in learning about the issue, more inclined to participate politically, and more open to compromise remedies. The effects of personality traits on the whole are less consistent. Trait dispositions do little to influence one's propensity for political action, and appear most influential in the decision to compromise or stay fast.

Greater anxiety predicts all three citizenship behaviors—those who are made anxious by policy change are more interested in learning about the issue, more inclined to participate politically, and more open to compromise remedies.

Emotion, Authoritarianism, and Evaluations of Presidential Candidates

Next, we consider the connections between personality characteristics and emotional reactions to the presidential candidates, to see whether trait differences underlie reactions to politicians. We rely on responses from the 2000 and 2004 American National Election Studies. While the sample is more representative than the respondents in our above experiment, unfortunately the surveys do not include general measures of personality. Thus, we can consider only the effects of authoritarianism and not neuroticism, extroversion, or openness. We proceed in a similar fashion as the previous analyses. First, we consider the effects of personality differences on emotional response. Those high in authoritarianism are more responsive to political threats, so we expect that authoritarians will be more likely to experience the negative emotion of aversion. Second,

TABLE 3
AUTHORITARIANISM AND EMOTIONAL REACTIONS
TO PRESIDENTIAL CANDIDATES

	Anxiety		Aversion		Enthusiasm	
	2000	2004	2000	2004	2000	2004
Authoritarianism	−.027	−.031	−.110*	−.168*	.089*	.059*
	(.031)	(.041)	(.032)	(.043)	(.035)	(.036)
Candidate anxiety	—	—	.494*	.478*	.051*	.127*
			(.023)	(.030)	(.029)	(.027)
Candidate aversion	.474*	.419*	—	—	.163*	.026
	(.022)	(.026)			(.029)	(.026)
Candidate enthusiasm	.040*	.168*	.134*	.039	—	—
	(.023)	(.036)	(.023)	(.039)		
Strength of partisanship	.006	−.008	.001	.026*	.080*	.077*
	(.009)	(.012)	(.009)	(.013)	(.010)	(.011)
Constant	.089*	.116*	.205*	.405*	.240*	.393*
	(.027)	(.041)	(.027)	(.042)	(.030)	(.034)
N	1,470	1,007	1,470	1,007	1,470	1,007
R^2	.25	.23	.27	.23	.09	.09

NOTE: Regression estimates, standard errors in parentheses.
*$p < .05$.

we consider whether authoritarianism has unique effects on political learning and participation beyond any indirect effects through emotion. We expect authoritarians to resist accumulating political information and avoid political engagement and to report less campaign learning and participation.

In Table 3, we consider the effects of authoritarianism on emotional engagement. Emotional reactions to the presidential candidates are assessed with a set of four items, asked about both the Democratic and Republican candidate. To measure enthusiasm, respondents were asked about whether the candidates made them feel hopeful or proud. Anxiety is measured by asking if the candidates made the respondent afraid, and aversion is measured with responses about anger toward the candidates.[9] Because we are interested in the general emotional reactivity of people, we sum reactions to the Democratic and Republican presidential candidates to consider cumulative levels of emotional response. Authoritarianism is measured with a set of four items about the ideal qualities for children (Feldman and Stenner 1997).[10] We also control for strength of partisanship, measured as a folded version of the 7-point party identification scale.

We find that authoritarianism is not significantly related to activation of the emotional surveillance system. Those high in authoritarianism are no more likely to experience anxiety than those low in authoritarianism. Authoritarianism is, however, correlated with the operation of the emotional disposition system. Authoritarians are more likely to report enthusiasm about the candidates in both 2000 and 2004. Those high in authoritarianism express greater hope and pride and are less likely to report

TABLE 4
THE EFFECTS OF AUTHORITARIANISM AND EMOTION
ON LEARNING AND PARTICIPATION

	Number of Comments about Presidential Candidates		Campaign Participation	
	2000	2004	2000	2004
Authoritarianism	−1.047*	−1.178*	−0.429*	−0.236*
	(0.297)	(0.357)	(0.140)	(0.122)
Candidate anxiety	1.389*	0.361	0.332*	0.266*
	(0.229)	(0.253)	(0.100)	(0.086)
Candidate aversion	1.084*	1.256*	0.381*	0.412*
	(0.223)	(0.234)	(0.100)	(0.084)
Candidate enthusiasm	1.698*	1.689*	0.535*	0.593*
	(0.204)	(0.291)	(0.098)	(0.108)
Strength of partisanship	0.303*	0.221*	0.186*	0.287*
	(0.080)	(0.101)	(0.039)	(0.037)
Education	0.522*	0.357*	0.105*	0.101*
	(0.052)	(0.063)	(0.025)	(0.022)
Age	0.008*	0.011*	0.004	−0.001
	(0.005)	(0.006)	(0.002)	(0.002)
Female	−0.530*	−0.311	−0.327*	−0.151*
	(0.156)	(0.191)	(0.074)	(0.067)
Black	−0.676*	−0.686*	−0.049	−0.260*
	(0.259)	(0.278)	(0.130)	(0.109)
Constant	0.796*	1.688*	−1.504*	−1.495*
	(0.433)	(0.513)	(0.217)	(0.190)
N	1,434	1,002	1,431	999
R^2/pseudo-R^2	.27	.18	.06	.08

NOTE: Regression estimates, first two columns; negative binomial regression, last two columns. Standard errors in parentheses.
*$p < .05$.

angry reactions to the candidates. While authoritarianism was unrelated to people's emotional reactions to policy issues, here we find a greater connection between authoritarian personality characteristics and candidate emotions. But, as in the case of policy issues, we find personality traits to be better predictors of the emotions of the disposition system than the emotions of the surveillance system.

In Table 4, we consider the effects of emotion and personality on political learning and participation to examine the relative contributions of each in explaining citizenship behaviors in campaign seasons. To measure learning, we sum the number of likes and dislikes people mention about the Democratic and Republican presidential candidates. Again, we control for strength of partisanship, also adding controls for education, age, gender, and race. Considering the role of personality, we find that those high in authoritarianism are significantly

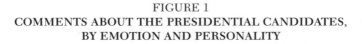

FIGURE 1
COMMENTS ABOUT THE PRESIDENTIAL CANDIDATES,
BY EMOTION AND PERSONALITY

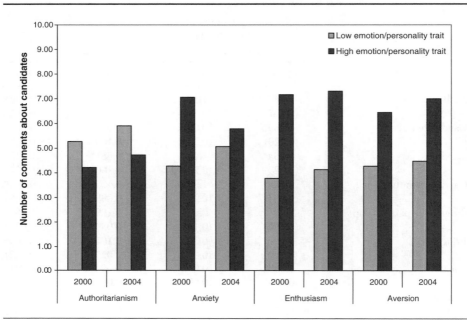

less likely to recall candidate details. As shown in Figure 1, moving from the lowest level of authoritarianism in 2000 to the highest level predicts one fewer recalled consideration about the candidates, all else equal, a significant effect given that the average respondent recalls about five pieces of information about the presidential candidates. Emotional reactions also relate to levels of candidate recall. We find that anxious respondents report greater campaign knowledge in 2000, where moving from the lowest level of anxiety to the highest level predicts an increase in candidate recall of nearly three comments, all else equal. Thus, the effects of emotion on candidate knowledge are more sizeable than the effects of personality. In 2004, the relationship between anxiety and knowledge is also positive, but not statistically significant. Anger and enthusiasm are also correlated with the number of likes and dislikes mentioned. Those with the higher level of anger about the candidates name two more candidate likes and dislikes than those expressing the least candidate anger. Those who are enthusiastic also recall more details, where moving from the lowest to the highest level of candidate enthusiasm predicts an increase of three candidate comments, all else equal.[11]

Next, we consider the effects of personality and emotion on campaign participation. To measure participation, we sum responses to questions that asked whether people donated to a candidate, party, or other group during the campaign;

FIGURE 2
PARTICIPATION IN THE CAMPAIGN, BY EMOTION AND PERSONALITY

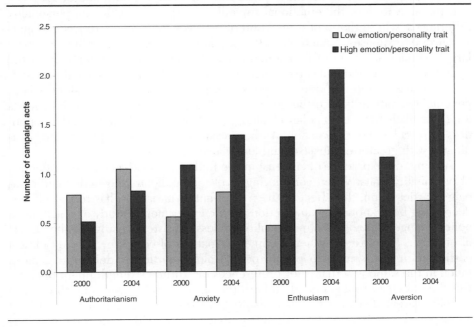

attended a rally; worked for a candidate; displayed a campaign sign; or tried to persuade another how to vote. We find a similar pattern of results, as illustrated in Figure 2. Anxious voters are more likely to participate, as are angry and aversive voters. Those high in authoritarianism however, are less likely to report campaign activity. Again, the magnitude of the effects of personality is more modest compared to the influence of emotional reactions. Moving from the lowest level of authoritarianism to the highest predicts a decrease in political participation of about .25 political acts, all else equal. For anxiety, a similar size movement predicts an increase in political participation of about .5 political acts. Overall, those with higher levels of authoritarianism are less likely to report anger about the candidates and more likely to express enthusiasm. But when it comes to campaign engagement, authoritarians are less involved, reporting less recall and lower levels of campaign participation.

Conclusions

When the political environment presents familiar friends and foes, the disposition system has particular importance and capability. When the unexpected or the unfamiliar arises, the emotional surveillance system is triggered to spur people to engage in more deliberative processing. Overall, we find modest evidence that the activation of the emotional surveillance system depends on personality differences, where the joint interaction of extroversion and neuroticism heightens anxiety responses. Nonetheless, the activation of these systems appears to be largely similar across most individuals, such that most people benefit from the operation of the emotional surveillance system. Trait differences have their greatest influence on the emotional responses of people's disposition system, where personality traits influence the generation of anger and enthusiasm. Extroverts are more likely to react to policy challenges with anger, while those high in openness express less policy aversion. Authoritarians respond to the presidential candidates with greater enthusiasm and lower levels of anger.

Turning to the practice of citizenship, we find mixed evidence of the influence of personality traits. When considering levels of candidate knowledge and campaign participation, the effect of the trait of authoritarianism has robust effects, decreasing both knowledge and action. In the experimental study of reactions to policy change, the effects of personality are less consistent relative to the effects of emotions like anxiety. When it comes to matters of compromise and political participation, traits tend to propel people along particular deliberative paths much in the same way that prior preferences or attitude strength might operate. But the effects of traits depend on both the citizenship behavior and the nature of policy threat. The effects of personality traits vary depending on whether they are exposed to reassuring or challenging policy issues, with traits serving as better explanations for the decision to compromise than the desire to politically engage. Overall, while we find some influence of personality traits in the triggering of emotional response and the practice of political citizenship, neither is determined by these prior predispositions.

Research is often taken to be significant when robust results are obtained. More rare is when insignificant empirical findings warrant greater attention. The recurring and seemingly stable existence of individual differences raises an interesting normative issue. If democratic citizenship requires an array of talents and orientations and these are not uniformly distributed within the population, then some will find themselves less well suited to and perhaps disinclined to engage in democratic politics. Thus, if personality had robust effects on citizenship practices, then some would be well prepared and others ill prepared to engage in citizenship—a result that obviously would undermine the equalitarian presumptions of democracy. Democracy requires that citizens are able and willing to articulate and defend their interests but, even more, to attend and be available to respond to the plight of others in securing the rights of all and the public good. A considerable number of studies show that the demands of democratic politics and engagement in conflicted situations is discomforting to some (Adorno et al. 1950; Fromm 1965; Mansbridge 1980; Altemeyer 1988; Hibbing and Theiss-Morse 2002). If personality had robust relationships to such factors as we study here, or some other features such as intolerance and support for authoritarian regimes, then democracy's normative appeal is diminished.

Appendix

Authoritarianism items

- A lot of rules regarding modesty and sexual behavior are just customs that are not necessarily any better or holier than those which other people follow.
- The situation in our country is getting so serious that stronger methods would be justified if they eliminated the troublemakers and got us back to our true path.
- People should pay less attention to the Bible and the other old traditional forms of religious guidance and instead develop their own personal standards of what is moral and immoral.
- The only way our country can get through the crisis ahead is to get back to our traditional values, put some tough leaders into power, and silence the troublemakers spreading bad ideas.
- Obedience and respect for authority are the most important virtues children should learn.
- Atheists and others who have rebelled against the established religions are no doubt every bit as good and virtuous as those who attend church regularly.
- It is always better to trust the judgment of the proper authorities in government and religion than to listen to the noisy rabble-rousers in our society who are trying to create doubt in people's minds.
- Our country will be destroyed someday if we do not smash the perversions eating away at our moral fiber and traditional beliefs.
- We should treat protestors and radicals with open arms and open minds, since new ideas are the lifeblood of progressive change.
- The facts on crime, sexual immorality, and the recent public disorders all show we have to crack down harder on deviant groups and troublemakers if we are going to save our moral standards and preserve law and order.

Question wordings of citizenship behaviors in policy experiment

Desire to learn more (response options: yes, maybe, no):

- Thinking about what you have read, would you like to learn more about the ideas of [groups who oppose the policy change]?
- Would you like to learn more about the ideas of [groups who favor the policy change]?
- And more generally, would you like to learn more about debates over [the policy] and ways to handle the issue?

Desire to participate:

Would you be interested in getting involved in this issue in any of the following ways? [*Check all that apply.*]

- Send a letter to the editor in response to this article.
- Sign an online petition in support of your view.
- Receive additional information by e-mail from groups that support your position.
- Send e-mail or write a letter to legislators to express your opinions.
- Donate money to help groups that advocate your position.
- Participate in a rally or protest held by groups that support your position.

Desire to compromise:

- Now taking into account everyone's views, as well as the general principles involved, what should happen? (Response options [wording varies depending on policy]: The policy should be supported, The policy should be repealed, Authorities should try to work out a compromise.)

TABLE A1
AUTHORITARIANISM, EMOTIONS, AND REACTIONS TO PRESIDENTIAL CANDIDATES

	Negativity		Enthusiasm		Comments about Presidential Candidates		Campaign Participation	
	2000	2004	2000	2004	2000	2004	2000	2004
Authoritarianism	-0.132*	-0.177*	0.087*	0.064*	-1.039*	-1.209*	-0.431*	-0.243*
	(0.031)	(0.040)	(0.035)	(0.036)	(0.296)	(0.358)	(0.140)	(0.122)
Candidate negativity	—	—	0.216*	0.149*	2.467*	1.665*	0.713*	0.681*
			(0.029)	(0.028)	(0.231)	(0.257)	(0.103)	(0.089)
Candidate enthusiasm	0.168*	0.190*	—	—	1.688*	1.639*	0.537*	0.584*
	(0.023)	(0.035)			(0.203)	(0.291)	(0.098)	(0.107)
Strength of partisanship	0.007	0.016	0.080*	0.076*	0.303*	0.233*	0.186*	0.289*
	(0.009)	(0.012)	(0.010)	(0.011)	(0.080)	(0.101)	(0.039)	(0.037)
Education	—	—	—	—	0.522*	0.354*	0.105*	0.101*
					(0.052)	(0.063)	(0.025)	(0.022)
Age					0.008*	0.011*	0.004	-0.001
					(0.005)	(0.006)	(0.002)	(0.002)
Female					-0.529*	-0.344*	-0.327*	-0.157*
					(0.156)	(0.191)	(0.074)	(0.067)
Black					-0.669*	-0.727*	-0.050	-0.267*
					(0.259)	(0.278)	(0.130)	(0.109)
Constant	0.285*	0.466*	0.245*	0.386*	0.780*	1.783*	-1.502*	-1.473*
	(0.027)	(0.038)	(0.030)	(0.034)	(0.433)	(0.512)	(0.217)	(0.189)
N	1,470	1,007	1,470	1,007	1,434	1,002	1,431	999
R^2	.05	.05	.08	.08	.27	.18	.06	.08

NOTE: Regression estimates, first six columns. Negative binomial regression, last two columns. Standard errors in parentheses.
*$p < .05$.

Notes

1. The disposition system, unlike the surveillance system, requires knowledge of the current state of the subject as well as information about the goals and relevant habitual routines (Marcus, Neuman, and MacKuen 2000). Hence, differences in introversion-extroversion that provide more—or less—energy and capability to engage in social activity ought to influence state responsiveness (Kagan 1994; Kagan and Snidman 2004).

2. We offer a fuller elaboration of Gray's (1987b) personality model and its application to emotional response in Marcus et al. (1995).

3. The items scale together well. The Cronbach's alpha for neuroticism was .88, .85 for extroversion, .77 for openness, and .86 for authoritarianism. The question wordings of the neuroticism items can be found in the appendix.

4. The pattern of results is robust to inclusion of controls for issue type, issue frame, attitude strength, and personal issue salience.

5. While openness to experience and authoritarianism are correlated ($r = .58$), authoritarianism fails to significantly predict emotional response to policy issues even when openness to experience is excluded from the specification.

6. Attitude strength is a 4-point measure of the strength of one's prior issue preference. Issue salience reflects one's personal connection to the issue. For the affirmative action issue, this is coded 1 if the respondent was nonwhite. For the mental health issue, respondents were asked if they knew a close friend or family member treated for mental health issues. For the music downloading issue, participants were asked about how frequently they used the Web to download music. And for the tuition issue, responses about whether the student helped pay for the costs of college were considered.

7. The specific question wordings to measure these can be found in the appendix.

8. Interactions of emotional reactions and personality predispositions are not significant explanations of the desire to learn more. Similarly, the directional effects of anxiety and enthusiasm are not conditioned on whether one views a reassuring or challenging policy change.

9. Not all circumstances generate aversion, and when they do not, "anger" measures act as measures of anxiety (Marcus et al. 2006). Unfortunately, the limited set of emotion items in the American National Election Studies do not allow us to distinguish whether the candidates in 2000 and 2004 generate the distinct negative emotions of both anxiety and aversion. Absent a means of establishing whether the anger items measure aversion or anxiety, we conducted the analyses in two conditions. In the body, we use the two negative emotion items to differentiate between anxiety and aversion, as it is likely that such a distinction emerges in the highly polarized climate of the 2000 and 2004 elections. Second, in Table A1 in the appendix, we show the same analyses, but with anger and anxiety treated as two measures of the same concept, anxiety. We find authoritarianism predicts candidate negativity as well as candidate enthusiasm. Whether we differentiate anxiety and aversion or not, we find high authoritarianism predicts lower knowledge and participation.

10. The four items ask respondents to choose one value as more important, independence versus respect for elders, curiosity versus good manners, obedience versus self-reliance, being considerate, or being well behaved. Those who choose the authoritarian response are coded 1, those who choose the other option are coded 0, and those who volunteer answers of "both" or "neither" are coded 0.5. Responses are summed to create our authoritarianism measure.

11. In Table 4, we report summary results for likes and dislikes of both candidates. If we model favorable recall and disliked considerations for each candidate separately, a few differences emerge. First, candidate anxiety prompts greater recall of disliked attributes about the Republican and Democratic candidates, while the number of favorable comments about the candidates falls for those who experience greater anxiety about the candidates. We also find that candidate aversion is negatively associated with recalled likes of the Democratic and Republican presidential candidates and positively associated with recalled dislikes of the candidates. Regarding the other emotion of the disposition system, we find the opposite pattern of effect, where candidate enthusiasm is positively associated with recalled likes and negatively related to candidate dislikes. The negative effect of authoritarianism on candidate recall is greatest for recalled likes of Democratic candidates and recalled dislikes of Republican candidates.

References

Adorno, Theodor W., Else Frenkel-Brunswik, Daniel J. Levinson, and R. Nevitt Sanford. 1950. *The authoritarian personality*. New York: Harper & Row.

Alford, John R., Carolyn L. Funk, and John R. Hibbing. 2005. Are political orientations genetically transmitted? *American Political Science Review* 99:153-67.

Almond, Gabriel A., and Sidney Verba. 1963. *The civic culture*. Princeton, NJ: Princeton University Press.

Altemeyer, Bob. 1988. *Enemies of freedom: Understanding right-wing authoritarianism*. San Francisco: Jossey-Bass.

Bargh, John A., and Tanya L. Chartrand. 1999. The unbearable automaticity of being. *American Psychologist* 54 (7): 462-79.

Bargh, John A., and Melissa L. Ferguson. 2000. Beyond behaviorism: On the automaticity of higher mental processes. *Psychological Bulletin* 126:925-45.

Bekkers, René. 2005. Participation in voluntary associations: Relations with resources, personality, and political values. *Political Psychology* 26:439-54.

Benhabib, Seyla. 1996. Toward a deliberative model of democratic legitimacy. In *Democracy and difference: Contesting the boundaries of the political*, ed. S. Benhabib. Princeton, NJ: University of Princeton Press.

Bizer, George Y., Jon A. Krosnick, Allyson L. Holbrook, S. Christian Wheeler, Derek D. Rucker, and Richard E. Petty. 2004. The impact of personality on cognitive, behavioral, and affective political processes: The effects of need to evaluate. *Journal of Personality* 72 (5): 995-1028.

Bohman, James, and William Rehg, eds. 1997. *Deliberative democracy: Essays in reason and politics*. Cambridge, MA: MIT Press.

Brader, Ted. 2006. *Campaigning for hearts and minds: How emotional appeals in political ads work*. Chicago: University of Chicago Press.

Caprara, Gian Vittorio, Claudio Barbaranelli, and Philip G. Zimbardo. 1999. Personality profiles and political parties. *Political Psychology* 20:175-97.

Caprara, Gian Vittorio, Shalom Schwartz, Cristina Capanna, Michele Vecchione, and Claudio Barbaranelli. 2006. Personality and politics: Values, traits, and political choice. *Political Psychology* 27:1-28.

Carver, Charles S., Steven K. Sutton, and Michael F. Scheier. 2000. Action, emotion, and personality: Emerging conceptual integration. *Personality and Social Psychology Bulletin* 26 (6): 741-51.

Carver, Charles S., and Teri L. White. 1994. Behavioral inhibition, behavioral activation, and affective responses to impending reward and punishment: The BIS/BAS scales. *Journal of Personality and Social Psychology* 67:319-33.

Cassese, Erin, and Stanley Feldman. 2005. Exploring the dynamics of threat: The consequences of personality and affect for threat perception and policy preferences. Paper presented at the annual meeting of the Midwest Political Science Association, Chicago.

Costa, P. T., Jr., and R. R. McCrae. 1985. *The NEO Personality Inventory Manual: Form S and Form R*. Odessa, FL: Psychological Assessment Resources.

—————. 1992. Revised NEO Personality Inventory (NEO-PI-R) and NEO Five Factor Inventory (NEO-FFI) professional manual. Odessa, FL: Psychological Assessment Resources.

Elliot, Andrew J., and Todd M. Thrash. 2002. Approach–avoidance motivation in personality: Approach and avoidance temperaments and goals. *Journal of Personality and Social Psychology* 82:804-18.

Feldman, Stanley. 2003. Enforcing social conformity: A theory of authoritarianism. *Political Psychology* 24:41-74.

Feldman, Stanley, and Karen Stenner. 1997. Perceived threat and authoritarianism. *Political Psychology* 18:741-70.

Fishkin, James. 1991. *Democracy and deliberation*. New Haven, CT: Yale University Press.

Fowler, James H. 2006. Altruism and turnout. *Journal of Politics* 68:674-83.

Fromm, Erich. 1965. *Escape from freedom*. New York: Avon.

Galston, William A. 2001. Political knowledge, political engagement, and civic education. *Annual Review of Political Science* 4:217-34.

Gigerenzer, Gerd, Peter M. Todd, and ABC Research Group. 1999. *Simple heuristics that make us smart*. New York: Oxford University Press.

Gray, Jeffrey A. 1981. The psychophysiology of anxiety. In *Dimensions of personality: Papers in honor of H. J. Eysenck*, ed. Robert Lynn. Elmsford, NY: Pergamon.

———. 1985. The neuropsychology of anxiety. *Stress and Anxiety* 10:201-27.

———. 1987a. The neuropsychology of emotion and personality. In *Cognitive neurochemistry*, ed. S. M. Stahl, Susan D. Iversen, and Elisabeth C. Goodman. Oxford: Oxford University Press.

———. 1987b. *The psychology of fear and stress*. 2nd ed. Cambridge: Cambridge University Press.

———. 1990. Brain systems that mediate both emotion and cognition. *Cognition & Emotion* 4 (3): 269-88.

Gutmann, Amy, and Dennis Thompson. 1996. *Democracy and disagreement*. Cambridge, MA: Harvard University Press.

Habermas, Jürgen. 1996. Three normative models of democracy. In *Democracy and difference: Contesting the boundaries of the political*, ed. S. Benhabib. Princeton, NJ: University of Princeton Press.

Hibbing, John R., and Elizabeth Theiss-Morse. 2002. *Stealth democracy*. New York: Cambridge University Press.

Kagan, Jerome. 1994. *Galen's prophecy: Temperament in human nature*. New York: Basic Books.

Kagan, Jerome, and Nancy C. Snidman. 2004. *The long shadow of temperament*. Cambridge, MA: Belknap Press of Harvard University Press.

Lavine, Howard, Milton Lodge, and Kate Freitas. 2005. Threat, authoritarianism, and selective exposure to information. *Political Psychology* 26:219-44.

MacKuen, Michael B., George E. Marcus, W. Russell Neuman, Luke Keele, and Jennifer Wolak. 2001. Emotions, information, and political cooperation. Presented at the annual meeting of the American Political Science Association, San Francisco.

Mansbridge, Jane J. 1980. *Beyond adversary democracy*. New York: Basic Books.

Marcus, George E. 2002. *The sentimental citizen: Emotion in democratic politics*. University Park: Pennsylvania State University Press.

Marcus, George E., and Michael MacKuen. 1993. Anxiety, enthusiasm and the vote: The emotional underpinnings of learning and involvement during presidential campaigns. *American Political Science Review* 87 (3): 688-701.

Marcus, George E., Michael MacKuen, Jennifer Wolak, and Luke Keele. 2006. The measure and mismeasure of emotion. In *Feeling politics: Emotion in political information processing*, ed. David Redlawsk. New York: Palgrave Macmillan.

Marcus, George E., W. Russell Neuman, and Michael B. MacKuen. 2000. *Affective intelligence and political judgment*. Chicago: University of Chicago Press.

Marcus, George E., John L. Sullivan, Elizabeth Theiss-Morse, and Sandra L. Wood. 1995. *With malice toward some: How people make civil liberties judgments*. New York: Cambridge University Press.

Nie, Norman H., Jane Junn, and Kenneth Stehlik-Barry. 1996. *Education and democratic citizenship in America*. Chicago: University of Chicago Press.

Redlawsk, David. 2002. Hot cognition or cool consideration? Testing the effects of motivated reasoning. *Journal of Politics* 64:1021-44.

Rudolph, Thomas J., Amy Gangl, and Dan Stevens. 2000. The effects of efficacy and emotions on campaign involvement. *Journal of Politics* 62 (4): 1189-97.

Sanders, Lynn M. 1997. Against deliberation. *Political Theory* 25 (3): 347-77.

Sniderman, Paul. 1975. *Personality and democratic politics*. Berkeley: University of California Press.

Stenner, Karen. 2005. *The authoritarian dynamic*. Cambridge: Cambridge University Press.

Taber, Charles, and Milton Lodge. 2006. Motivated skepticism in the evaluation of political beliefs. *American Journal of Political Science* 50 (3): 755-69.

Wolak, Jennifer, Michael MacKuen, Luke Keele, George E. Marcus, and W. Russell Neuman. 2003. How the emotions of public policy affect citizen engagement, public deliberation, and the quality of electoral choice. Paper presented at the annual meeting of the American Political Science Association, Philadelphia.

Young, Iris Marion. 2000. *Inclusion and democracy*. New York: Oxford University Press.

Personal, Interpersonal, and Political Temperaments

Are political liberals generous? Are political conservatives conscientious? Are generous people personally agreeable? Research in behavioral genetics and elsewhere increasingly indicates a biological basis for the manner in which people behave in personal, interpersonal, and political situations, but this biological basis does not mean behavior in these three very different contexts is correlated. In this article, using an original data set obtained from nearly three hundred subjects, the authors are able to test for the degree to which personal, interpersonal, and political temperaments are related. As expected, the overall correlations are quite low. Standard personality traits do not predict political attitudes, and neither political attitudes nor personality predicts the extent to which subjects are generous in interpersonal situations. Human behavior is partially biological, but the systems involved in shaping political behavior seem to be largely but not completely distinct from those involved in shaping personal and interpersonal behavior.

Keywords: temperament; political attitude; personality traits; behavior; ideology

By
JOHN R. ALFORD
and
JOHN R. HIBBING

The study of personality remains a controversial subfield in psychology, and it is doubtful there will ever be universal agreement on its essential component parts. The five-factor model—extroversion, agreeableness, conscientiousness, neuroticism (sometimes called emotional stability), and intellect/imagination (sometimes called openness)—is increasingly believed to capture the essence of personality (McCrae and Costa 1999; DeYoung, Peterson, and Higgins 2005; Mondak and Halperin forthcoming), but other personal temperaments such as risk-taking and harm avoidance are also frequently invoked. Still other constructs such as right-wing authoritarianism and social dominance orientation fight for recognition along with numerous other alleged dimensions; the overall result is a conceptual mishmash. Some observers would say this confusion is unavoidable given the complexities of the human condition, but we think progress can be made by

DOI: 10.1177/0002716207305621

recognizing that not all predispositions are best thought of as stemming from personal temperament. In this article, we argue and provide empirical evidence that the behaviors of an individual are not influenced solely by the personal temperaments traditionally studied by psychologists but also by reasonably distinct interpersonal and political temperaments that operate alongside personal temperament.

Distinguishing the Personal from the Interpersonal and the Political

Conceptually, personal temperament is quite different from interpersonal temperament, and interpersonal temperament, in turn, is quite distinct from political temperament. Personal temperament does not require other people to be in evidence. Risk-taking could manifest itself while an individual climbs a tree far from any other person (though it could also be in evidence in interactions with other people). Interpersonal temperament by definition requires another person. It is impossible to know whether a person is generous, trusting, or punitive unless other individuals are involved. But modern society has given rise to a third temperament, namely, political temperament. Like interpersonal, political temperament requires other people; unlike interpersonal, political temperament operates on a mass scale. Interpersonal involves those in the immediate social unit—fellow players in an economic game, office mates at work, or relatives at a family reunion. Political temperament, on the other hand, deals with the structure and organization of large-scale social life. The issues shift from whether a person nearby should be punished for being self-serving to whether in general it is preferable for misbehaving individuals to be punished and whether that punishment should be severe and automatic or mild and flexible. Politics involves the norms, mores, and statutes that govern large-scale social life, norms and statutes that do not only apply to people well known and close by but also to people unknown and far away.

John R. Alford is an associate professor of political science at Rice University in Houston, Texas. He has been published in the American Political Science Review, *the* American Journal of Political Science, *and* Perspectives on Politics. *His work addresses congressional elections, political parties, and, most recently, the influence of biological variables, including genetics, on political orientations and behaviors.*

John R. Hibbing is the Foundation Regents University Professor of Political Science at the University of Nebraska–Lincoln. With Elizabeth Theiss-Morse, he is the author of Congress as Public Enemy *as well as* Stealth Democracy, *both dealing with public attitudes toward government, governors, and governing. His recent work, primarily with John Alford but also with Kevin Smith and others, attempts to integrate biological concepts and the social sciences.*

NOTE: Financial support provided by the National Science Foundation (SES-350387). This article was written during a time when both authors were visiting fellows at the Hoover Institution, Stanford University, Stanford, California. The authors thank David Brady and others at Hoover for their hospitality.

The term *politics* is frequently used to refer to maneuvering in the immediate social environment. De Waal (1982, 1996) pointed out that primate troops can be seen playing politics of this type; humans will often write off unfavorable decisions at work or elsewhere as being shaped by "politics." Despite this common usage, we suggest that politics at the mass level can be distinguished from the interpersonal machinations that are often referred to as political. Thus, for our purposes, personal temperaments are predispositions (fastidiousness, for example) that can manifest themselves even when other people are not present. Interpersonal temperaments (being generous, for example) are at least dyadic in that they involve at a minimum one person in the immediate social environment. And political temperaments are those that apply to the governance of large-scale social life, life that extends beyond one's immediate social environment.

Whereas personal temperament has been studied mainly by psychologists and political temperament mainly by political scientists, interpersonal temperament is of interest to social psychologists as well as to sociologists and behavioral economists. Personal and political temperaments are usually assessed by survey questions, while for interpersonal temperament, experiments are often employed to determine the extent to which people share with others, trust others, and punish those who have behave selfishly. Trust, generosity, and interpersonal sanctioning are inherently social; as such they are distinct from risk taking or paranoia as well as from liberal or conservative political attitudes.

But are these three temperaments empirically as well as conceptually distinct? Our operating hypothesis is that they are largely but perhaps not completely uncorrelated, that individuals' preferences for the conduct of their personal lives are only weakly predictive of their preferences for both large-scale societal organization and behaviors in concrete, small-scale social situations. Casual observation would seem to support this hypothesis. When Rush Limbaugh was found to be addicted to drugs, his vast radio audience did not desert him even though his behavior seemed inconsistent with his political arguments in favor of personal responsibility and harsh punishment of lawbreakers. His behavioral lapse was viewed as a personal indiscretion. But if he began condoning permissiveness and forgiveness as a political philosophy, his audience quite likely would evaporate quickly. While political liberals may take this as evidence of hypocrisy on the right, the truth of the matter is that those on the left also separate the political from the personal (and the interpersonal). The real message is that people's personal behaviors are quite different from the behaviors they advocate for society as a whole. The contention that the personal, interpersonal, and political are reasonably separate receives support from neuroscience studies indicating that the neural systems involved with basic personal emotions such as anger, frustration, joy, and excitement are quite different from the neural systems involved in emotions that cannot exist except in the context of other people, such as guilt, shame, and embarrassment. Our suspicion is that politics, at least in part, may tap into yet another neural system.

*[P]eople's personal behaviors are quite
different from the behaviors they advocate for
society as a whole.*

Though we believe there is support for our expectation of relative indepen-dence across the temperaments, other expectations are possible. Perhaps inter-personal and political temperaments are merely spin-offs of personal temperament. Or perhaps the political is easily predicted from the interpersonal. The purpose of this article is to determine the extent to which these three core temperaments are related to each other. This is an important issue because if the personal is predictive of the political (and also the interpersonal), understanding personal temperament is all that is necessary for the understanding of interper-sonal. Political behavior and the other social sciences would therefore become a subfield of psychology. But to the extent that political and interpersonal tem-peraments do not correlate with personal temperament, these areas of study must be undertaken with separate approaches, theories, and expectations. This situation becomes especially important for those interested in identifying the bio-logical systems pertinent to temperaments and behaviors. Much is known about the genetic and biological precursors of personal temperament (see van Gestel and van Broeckhoven 2003; Comings et al. 2000; Bouchard and McGue 2003; Bachner-Melman et al. 2005; Carmen 2007 [this volume]), but little is known about the extent to which this information also informs us of the genes and bio-logical systems pertinent to interpersonal and political temperaments. Thus, information on the overlap of personal, interpersonal, and political phenotypes is loaded with implications for our understanding of human behavior as well as for identifying the best methods for studying that behavior.

Previous Research on the Connection of the Three Different Temperaments

Given our formulation of three categories of temperaments, we can make three possible links among these categories: the link between the personal and the political, the link between the personal and the interpersonal, and the link between the interpersonal and the political. Previous research has looked into each of these links, although not always as intensely as the topic deserves and with a surprising amount of variance in the answers obtained. We take each of the links in turn.

Personal temperament and political temperament

Of the three links, this is the one that has been analyzed the most. Academics have long suspected that particular personal temperaments may be the reason some individuals are, for example, politically conservative. Adorno et al.'s (1950) assertion that there is an "authoritarian personality" is perhaps the best-known early attempt to link personal and political temperaments. The claim is that people who prefer to live their own lives in an authoritarian fashion also prefer authoritarian political arrangements; that some people have a need for structure, hierarchy, and clarity; and that this need is manifested in all aspects of their lives from personal to political. Altemeyer (1981, 1996) extended these ideas, suggested measurement changes, and termed it "right-wing authoritarianism," much to the consternation of those who believe hierarchy and structure are advocated as much by those on the political left as the political right (think Lenin; for an example of such a critique, see Shils 1954).

McClosky (1958, 28) also asserted that there is a "conservative personality," that conservatism is a position "around which individuals of certain habitual outlooks, temperaments, and sensibilities can comfortably come to rest and be united with others of like disposition." And the temperaments and dispositions McClosky found to be associated with conservatism are not particularly desirable. His data led him to conclude that conservatism is typically the philosophy of "social isolates, of people who think poorly of themselves, who suffer personal disgruntlement and frustration, who are submissive, timid, and wanting in confidence, who lack a clear sense of direction and purpose, who are uncertain about their values, and who are generally bewildered by the alarming task of having to thread their way through a society which seems to them too complex to fathom" (p. 37).

More recent research continues to identify the personality traits of conservatism— usually unfavorable traits. Using an imaginative research design, Block and Block (2005) reported that personality traits of nursery school children are predictive of political beliefs held by those same individuals when grown up. According to these findings, as children, adult conservatives tend to be "easily offended, indecisive, fearful, rigid, inhibited, and relatively over-controlled and vulnerable"; while children who go on to become adult liberals are "self-reliant, energetic, somewhat dominating, relatively under-controlled, and resilient" (p. 1). The modern consensus seems to be that conservatism is the result of a "motivated social cognition," in other words, a view of the social world that springs from a psychic need—in this case a need "to reduce fear, anxiety, and uncertainty; to avoid change, disruption, and ambiguity" (Jost et al. 2003, 340; see also Jost 2006).

The relative lack of attention to the personality bases of liberalism is potentially instructive in that it suggests that for many researchers, conservatism is the aberration in need of explanation: the normal human condition is political liberalism, and those who do not subscribe to it must possess unfortunate and lamentable personality traits such as "psychological rigidity" (McClosky 1958, 42) or runaway "anxiety and uncertainty" (Jost et al. 2003, 340), a need for authority (Altemeyer 1981, 1996; Lakoff 2006), or a need for their group to be better than others (Pratto et al. 1994). Thus, there is a need to explain what is the matter with Kansas (Frank 2004) but not to explain what is the matter with, say, Massachusetts. Of course, conservatives and others have been quick to challenge many of the findings summarized above. And indeed it seems that prominent exemplars of American conservatism today, such as Rush Limbaugh, Sean Hanity, Newt Gingrich, and Donald Rumsfeld, are not accurately characterized as "submissive, timid, and wanting in confidence"; lacking "a clear sense of direction and purpose"; and being "uncertain about their values."

When research is restricted to those personality traits psychologists tend to identify as central—for example, the "Big Five" of extroversion, agreeableness, conscientiousness, emotional stability, and intellect/intelligence—results are less clear. Using an American sample, Mehrabian (1996) found that four of the five core personality traits are not significantly related to political ideology, and the fifth, intellect/imagination, is related to conservatism at only −.26 (see also Comrey and Newmeyer 1965). Caprara's (Caprara, Barbaranelli, and Zimbardo 1999; Caprara et al. 2006) large Italian sample shows a somewhat stronger relationship than this, with conservatives scoring significantly higher than liberals on the extroversion and conscientiousness factors and (like Mehrabian 1996) significantly lower on imagination. Mondak and Halperin (forthcoming) found self-reported conservatism to be negatively related to imagination/openness and positively related to both conscientiousness and emotional stability (see Whitaker [2006] for additional evidence of links between the Big Five personality traits and political views).

All told, empirical results on this matter therefore are somewhat inconsistent. Not only are individual relationships found to be significant in some instances and insignificant in others, but the direction of significant relationships is sometimes positive and sometimes negative. It is disconcerting, for example, that conservatives are in some studies found to be "submissive, timid, and wanting in confidence" and in other studies to be extroverted. Part of the problem may be the different manners of conceptualizing personality. Many psychologists prefer purer personal temperaments such as the Big Five, but others branch out to hybrid concepts such as right-wing authoritarianism and social dominance orientation. As noted by critics (see, for example, Ray 1985), several of the items used to tap these latter concepts seem to draw on political attitudes, suggesting that relationships ostensibly between personality traits and political views are actually relationships between political views and other political views.

For example, two of the commonly employed social dominance orientation items are "in getting what you want it is sometimes necessary to use force against other groups" and "we should strive to make income as equal as possible." And two of the right-wing authoritarianism items suggested by Altemeyer (1981, 1996) are "gays and lesbians are just as healthy and moral as anybody else" and "God's laws about abortion, pornography, and marriage must be strictly followed before it is too late." None of these four seems to directly tap a core personality trait; rather, all four seem to come closer to tapping political and social attitudes. Thus, any correlation between indices built on items such as social dominance orientation and right-wing authoritarianism on one hand and indices of political orientations on the other is conceptually suspect in the minds of many. To a certain degree, confusion on this matter is indicative of larger confusion on the separation between the personal and the political, an issue to which we hope to return later in this article.

> *All told, empirical results . . . are somewhat inconsistent. . . . It is disconcerting, for example, that conservatives are in some studies found to be "submissive, timid, and wanting in confidence" and in other studies to be extroverted.*

Personal temperament and interpersonal temperament

Less work has been done on the relationship between interpersonal (or social) temperament and personal temperament. Most of the research in this area measures interpersonal behavior by decisions made in laboratory games involving small sums of money. These games include the dictator game, in which one player (the dictator) is free to divide a sum of money with another player however the dictator sees fit; the ultimatum game, in which, in contrast to the dictator game, the receiving player now has the option of accepting or rejecting the allocator's proposal; the trust game, in which the money a player sends to the other player is tripled but then is placed entirely under the discretion of the receiving (trusted) player; and the Prisoner's Dilemma, in which cooperative play is rewarded assuming the other player cooperates as well. Thus, measures of interpersonal generosity, punitiveness, trust, and cooperation are possible. Personal temperaments are measured by a variety of diverse schemes from the Eysenck Personality Quotient to Myers-Briggs to type A/sensation-seeking/self-monitoring/ locus of control categories.

The results of these studies are as diverse as the approaches. Boone, De Branbander, and van Witteloostuijn (1999) found people with an internal locus of control, those with high self-monitoring, and those high in sensation seeking all tend to be slightly more likely to display cooperative behavior, particularly in multiple play games. Brandstatter and Guth (2002) conducted similar studies with a broader range of economic games, but the personality inventories they employed are more limited. They discovered that subjects claiming to be benevolent are more generous in dictator games (where the other player has no power) than they are in ultimatum games (where the other player can at least veto the proposal), but for the most part, the link to core personality traits is either untested or found to be absent. Finally, Swope et al. (2005), using the Myers-Briggs set of personality indicators, found no direct effects of any of the four categories of personality (orientation, perception, judgment, and attitude) on economic behavior, though they did find a small effect of personality on economic game play when the extroversion/introversion spectrum (orientation) is interacted with the feeling/thinking (judgment) spectrum. Individuals who are extroverted and tend to use feeling rather than thinking in their judgments are more cooperative in economic games.

Interpersonal temperament and political temperament

The connection between interpersonal behavior and political attitudes has likewise been the subject of less previous research than the possible connection between personal temperament and political temperament, and here again, the results suggest there may not be much of a connection. Early work by Mestelman and Feeny (1988) found suggestive evidence that, compared to liberals, conservatives are slightly more likely to free ride in a public goods game. (The public goods game has more than two players, and each player has the choice of contributing to a public fund or keeping their allotment. Money contributed to the public fund is multiplied but distributed back to all participants whether they contributed or not, so the optimal strategy from a selfish point of view is not to contribute but to take advantage of those who do contribute.) Using a German sample, Fehr et al. (2002) found a weak connection between party affiliation (but not ideological position) and trusting behavior.

And in perhaps the study most directly relevant to ours, Anderson, Mellor, and Milyo (2004), also using a public goods game, found "no significant differences in contribution for any one group of subjects" (Democrats, Republicans, liberals, or conservatives). These same scholars employed a trust game and (except for one special situation) reported similarly weak results across the various political groups. Their overall conclusion is that, contrary to conventional wisdom, liberals are not more likely to "play nice" than conservatives. All in all, a connection between political temperament and interpersonal temperament is not usually in evidence in these experimental studies.

Like the purported link between personal temperament and political temperament and the link between personal and interpersonal temperaments, this third possible link is found to be empirically weak. Previous research is quite inconsistent in findings, but one thing that can be said with some certainty is that neither the personal, the interpersonal, nor the political determines the other components. The human condition seems to be quite compartmentalized depending upon the context in which decisions are made. But the varying results from these previous studies as well as the fact that all studies focus on just two of the temperaments rather than all three encourage us to collect our own original data and to perform our own analyses.

Research Design

In this article, we take advantage of a unique data set that contains information on each subject's personal, interpersonal, and political temperaments, thus making it possible to tie together the whole package. The 299 subjects were a combination of Rice University students and other nonstudent subjects recruited from the Houston metropolitan area. Each was asked an extensive array of personality items, including batteries tapping the Big Five. They were asked a set of political items, including the Wilson-Patterson Inventory of political and social attitudes, party identification, and self-identified ideology. And they were asked to play a series of economic games in which they had to make decisions including whether to be generous and whether to be punitive. The results for each type of temperament individually are of interest, but our primary concern here is with the correlations across temperaments, from personal to interpersonal to political. We want to clarify the uncertainty present in previous research and to determine whether our overarching hypothesis (a negligible relationship across temperaments) is correct.

Findings

Table 1 provides correlations for the Big Five personality factors, self-interest versus generosity in experimental games, and the two measures of ideology described above. Not all of the subjects participated in the same set of economic games; our experimental measure of behavioral generosity comes from combining two distinct pools of subjects. The larger group of 211 was given a choice of how much money to withdraw from a common pool of funds and could choose any amount from $0 to $10. The modal choice was $5 with a second, less prominent peak at $10. The remaining 88 subjects were dividing $10 with another player in an ultimatum game where their choice was how much of the $10 to keep for themselves and how much to give to the other player. Again, as in the common pool withdrawal, the modal choice was to retain $5 with a second, much smaller peak at retaining $10. In the table we provide both the results divided by game type and the combined dollar score for both groups. Clearly, there is little evidence of any direct connection between personality and behavioral generosity. Pool withdrawal is modestly correlated with two of the Big Five personality measures, negatively with conscientiousness (with individuals scoring higher on

TABLE 1

PERSONALITY, INTERPERSONAL ECONOMIC CHOICES, AND IDEOLOGY

| | Self-Interest | | | | |
	Pool Withdrawal	Ultimatum	Combined	Ideology (Self-ID)	Wilson-Patterson Index
Big Five					
1. Extroversion	−.024	.012	−.120	−.097	−.086
2. Agreeableness	−.093	−.006	−.074	−.153*	−.116*
3. Conscientiousness	−.140*	.057	−.088	.012	.082
4. Emotional stability	−.008	.181	.026	−.021	.010
5. Intellect/imagination	.153*	.015	.126*	−.136*	−.133*
Ideology (self-ID)	−.051	−.031	−.053		
Wilson-Patterson index	−.051	−.018	−.053	.721*	
n	211	88	299	299	299

*Significant at the .05 level.

conscientiousness withdrawing modestly fewer dollars) and positively with intellect (with individuals scoring higher on intellect/imagination withdrawing slightly more dollars). Self-interest in the ultimatum game is very weakly related to the Big Five dimensions, and none of the correlations reaches statistical significance. When the two measures are combined, interpersonal self-interest is significantly related only to dimension five (intellect/imagination) where the modest positive relationship of intellect with selfishness is statistically significant.

Political ideology fares even worse. While consistently negative, indicating that higher levels of self-interest are associated with liberalism, the correlations for both self-described ideology and the Wilson-Patterson issue-based measure of ideology are small and fail to reach statistical significance. The correlation of personality traits with political ideology is a little more promising but still weak on the whole. Consistent with most all previous research, we find a negative relationship between intellect/imagination and ideological conservatism. Inconsistent with some previous research, we find no link between either conscientiousness or emotional stability and conservatism and we do find a negative relationship between agreeableness and conservatism.

One possible explanation for the general weakness of the correlations between personality and ideology is the presence of a nonlinear relationship. A particular personality factor, for example high intelligence, might be characteristic of both highly liberal and highly conservative individuals while generally less characteristic of moderates. Such a U-shaped relationship would be an example of a clearly predictive role for a personality factor but would nonetheless produce the sort of attenuated correlations that we see here. Exploring this possibility by fitting a variety of nonlinear models to the association between personality factors and ideology did not produce significant evidence of any sort of nonlinear relationship. Thus, the generally weak association between personality and directional ideology is matched by little association between personality and nondirectional intensity of ideological sentiment.

The Wilson-Patterson Inventory is a useful addition to self-described ideology in part because it allows a more fine-grained analysis of how personality factors might affect distinct subcategories of ideology and even individual issue positions. Table 2 provides the correlations between the previously discussed five personality factors and the thirty items that make up the version of the Wilson-Patterson Inventory used here.

None of the thirty individual items is significantly related to more than three of the Big Five factors, and in fact only one of the thirty (foreign aid) is significantly related to three factors. A little more than a third of the individual items exhibit no significant relationship to any of the Big Five personality factors. And this group includes such high-profile items as abortion, gay rights, capitalism, pacifism, nuclear power, living together, school prayer, and mercy killing. This is striking not only because many of these are viewed as deeply emotional hot-button issues but also in light of the association of many of these issues with fundamental personal traits such as religiosity and the fact that several of these are among the most genetically heritable items in the Wilson-Patterson Inventory. Clearly people's strong emotional reactions to these items stem at least in part from very deep sources, but the standard Big Five model of personality is not tapping any of this variation.

Viewing the table down the columns is also informative. Factors 3 and 4 (conscientiousness and emotional stability, respectively) are notably weak predictors of individual issue positions with only three significant correlations in their collective sixty potential relationships, precisely what we would expect simply by chance at the .05 level of significance. Factor 2 (agreeableness) provides the most evidence of association with individual issue items, showing a significant relationship with thirteen of the thirty Wilson-Patterson issues. Higher levels of agreeableness are associated with opposition to the death penalty, segregation, and evolution and are also associated with higher levels of support for women's liberation, foreign aid, gun control, property tax, and labor unions. Factor 5 (intellect/imagination) yields eight statistically significant correlations, including a positive association between higher levels of imagination and a lack of support for astrology and the moral majority.

Overall, the results in Tables 1 and 2, while not unexpected based on previous research, are still counterintuitive. Most people would probably agree with the characterization that an outgoing, agreeable, conscientious, emotionally stable, and intellectually open person would be substantially more generous in their decisions than a withdrawn, uncaring, sloppy, emotionally unstable, and closed-minded person. Similarly, as the pejorative descriptions of political conservatism quoted earlier make clear, it has been suggested that generous people are typically liberals (those with at least modest opposition to policies such as the death penalty), but again our data provide no support for any such relationship. The lack of a substantial significant association here between personality or ideology on one hand and behavioral generosity on the other is particularly stark given that this is a controlled experimental behavior. The failure to find clear associations between personal attitudes and behaviors in previous studies has often been attributed to the complexity of contextual impacts on individual behavior; in real-world behavior,

TABLE 2

DETAILS OF THE RELATIONSHIP BETWEEN PERSONALITY AND IDEOLOGY

	Factor 1: Extroversion	Factor 2: Agreeableness	Factor 3: Conscientiousness	Factor 4: Emotional Stability	Factor 5: Intellect/Imagination
Wilson-Patterson (Yes = 1, ? = 2, No = 3)					
Death penalty	0.031	0.224*	-0.074	0.020	0.124*
Astrology	-0.029	-0.041	-0.099	0.042	0.166*
X-rated movies	-0.058	0.138*	0.087	0.040	-0.045
Modern art	-0.022	-0.033	-0.019	-0.006	-0.028
Women's liberation	0.122*	-0.166*	-0.070	0.035	0.053
Foreign aid	-0.147*	-0.330*	0.035	0.017	-0.119*
Federal housing	-0.123*	-0.155*	-0.015	-0.038	-0.012
Democrats	0.021	-0.187*	-0.100	-0.004	0.031
Gun control	-0.135*	-0.140*	-0.075	0.021	-0.057
The draft	0.075	0.100	0.046	-0.079	0.033
Abortion	-0.061	0.001	0.073	0.085	-0.080
Property tax	-0.008	-0.159*	0.073	-0.013	-0.098
Gay rights	0.017	-0.075	0.051	0.103	-0.047
Liberals	-0.021	-0.159*	-0.016	-0.002	0.018
Immigration	-0.033	-0.081	0.117*	0.019	-0.137*
Capitalism	0.055	0.013	0.029	0.019	-0.016
Segregation	-0.032	0.144*	-0.025	0.127*	0.038
Moral Majority	0.120*	-0.030	-0.090	0.089	0.176*
Pacifism	-0.033	-0.081	0.092	-0.029	-0.090
Censorship	0.004	-0.074	-0.044	0.104	0.125*
Nuclear power	0.002	0.078	0.055	-0.008	-0.112
Living together	-0.058	0.036	0.062	0.027	-0.016
Republicans	0.022	0.143*	-0.029	0.018	0.055
Divorce	-0.037	0.072	0.113	0.044	-0.135*
School prayer	0.104	-0.024	-0.112	0.007	0.083
Labor unions	-0.043	-0.175*	-0.043	0.028	0.031
Socialism	-0.035	-0.056	-0.053	-0.019	-0.120*
Busing	0.109	0.004	-0.042	-0.060	-0.015
Evolution	-0.074	0.128*	0.166*	0.037	-0.075
Mercy killing	-0.034	0.087	0.079	0.006	-0.109

*Significant at the .05 level.

the large array of varying contextual cues may in fact severely attenuate any relationship between personality and behavior, but here experimental control reduces both the volume and variation in context and should allow any effects to be clearly discernible.

The lack of a substantial significant association here between personality or ideology on one hand and behavioral generosity on the other is particularly stark given that this is a controlled experimental behavior.

As was the case with personality and behavioral generosity, personality and ideology are only modestly related. The findings are quite similar for both self-identified ideology and the issue-based Wilson-Patterson index (not surprising given that they are positively correlated with each other at .72). Both show a modest but statistically significant correlation with factor 2 (agreeableness) and with factor 5 (intellectual openness). As both liberals and conservatives would probably expect, agreeableness, a personality factor partially associated with the desire to please others, is more evident in liberals than in conservatives. For example, one of the items included in the agreeableness scale is "I have a soft heart," something that liberals would generally agree is a positive trait of liberals and conservatives would agree is a negative trait of liberals.

The association of liberalism with relatively high levels of self-described intellect and imagination is more contentious. Liberals will have no problem accepting the validity of this finding, but conservatives will undoubtedly be less pleased. This factor is sometimes labeled simply as openness both to reduce its association with the volatile issue of variation in intelligence and to suggest that it in fact measures openness to new experience as opposed to quality of brain power. The fact is, however, that at least in the reduced form used here, factor 5 is clearly a measure of intellect and imagination rather than openness to new experience. Items such as "I have excellent ideas," "I am quick to understand things," and "I use difficult words" clearly illustrate a focus on intellectual capability and imagination rather than simple tolerance for ambiguity. On the other hand, as these are all self-descriptions, conservatives could be forgiven for pointing out that this might reflect little more than a tendency toward self-serving intellectual pomposity among self-described liberals.

While the two positive associations are interesting, it is important not to miss the larger picture. Both of the correlations are quite weak, and there is no significant association for the other three facets of personality. The lack of a relationship for factor 3 (conscientiousness) is surprising. Both liberals and conservatives would probably agree that conscientiousness is a characteristic more closely tied to conservatism than to liberalism, and while the direction of the relationship is correct, the correlation is small and far short of significance. The correlation for factor 1 (extroversion) is in the negative direction, as might be expected from some of the pejorative descriptions of conservatism cited above, but again the correlation is weak and far short of statistical significance. The weakest relationship with ideology is factor 4 (emotional stability), and this places our findings clearly at odds with the previous pejorative descriptions of conservatism. Emotional stability or the lack thereof appears to be shared equally across the ideological spectrum, and we find no evidence to support the strong assertions in previous discussions that conservatives are more emotionally vulnerable than liberals.

Taken together, all of this suggests a surprisingly weak relationship between personality, interpersonal behavior, and political ideology. Neither personality nor broader political ideology offers much predictive power when applied to simple controlled experimental observation of behavioral generosity. The relationship between personality and political ideology is similarly weak.

Neither personality nor broader political ideology offers much predictive power when applied to simple controlled experimental observation of behavioral generosity. The relationship between personality and political ideology is similarly weak.

Discussion

Empirical evidence of substantial interpersonal generosity has eroded the emphasis on rational self-interested behavior in both economics and political science. These findings, consistent with our findings here (recall that retaining half of the $10 is clearly the modal behavior in both of our experimental settings), simply cannot be explained by a model of self-interested, cognitive maximization. The attempt to account for these experimental findings has led to an explosion of concern across the social sciences and beyond for an understanding of the evolution of cooperative social behavior in humans. If the impetus toward self-sacrificing behavior has been encoded deeply within the human brain, one might expect to find it expressed organically in fundamental variation in personality. In contrast, if socially conscious self-sacrifice is largely culturally constructed, one might expect to find it encoded in more intellectually abstract cognitive organizational structures such as ideology. Those favoring a nature-plus-nurture view would likely argue that prosocial behavior is in fact embedded interactively in both our fundamental personality and our cognitively elaborated ideologies. Despite the obvious importance of understanding the genesis of self-sacrificing behavior, little empirical work in political science has been directed at understanding the relationship between this behavior and either underlying personality traits or overarching ideological frameworks.

The findings here hold out little hope for any of these hypotheses. Deeply encoded, stable personality traits offer little predictive purchase on self-sacrificing prosocial behavior, and ideology fares no better, though as might be expected and as Mondak and Halperin (forthcoming) reported, personality seems to do much better in predicting political behaviors such as getting up to speak on a political issue. Our view as sketched above differs from the general view in several important regards. First, we view ideology as being no less deeply encoded in the genes and brains of humans than personality. Furthermore, we are not harnessed to a conception that yields clear centrality to personality as an explanatory variable on the basis of its presumed unique deep encoding. Placing both personality and something as presumably abstract as ideology abreast of each other in terms of their level of biological encoding, and hence temporal priority, allows for an alternative view of the sources of interpersonal generosity. Rather than arising from either of these deeply encoded temperaments, interpersonal generosity may arise from a conceptually distinct third deeply encoded temperament. If, as we have suggested above, each of these distinct realms of human nature originates at a similarly deep level, then there is no reason to suppose that they must be closely correlated. Some degree of overlap in the physiological systems in which they are instantiated would suggest that modest correlations may exist. This is quite different than a model that builds interpersonal behavior out of biologically encoded personality and then, in turn, builds culturally elaborated ideology out of some combination of both personality and interpersonal behavior.

References

Adorno, T., E. Frenkel-Brunswik, D. Levinson, and R. Sanford. 1950. *The authoritarian personality*. New York: Harper.
Altemeyer, Bob. 1981. *Right-wing authoritarianism*. Winnipeg, Canada: University of Manitoba Press.
———. 1996. *The authoritarian specter*. Cambridge, MA: Harvard University Press.
Anderson, Lisa R., Jennifer M. Mellor, and Jeffrey Milyo. 2004. Do liberals play nice? The effects of party and political ideology in public goods and trust games. Unpublished Working Paper, College of William and Mary, Williamsburg, VA.

Bachner-Melman, Rachel, Christian Dina, Ada H. Zohar, Naama Constantini, Elad Lerer, Sarah Hoch, Sarah Sella, Lubov Nemanov, Inga Gritsenko, Pesach Lichtenberg, et al. 2005. AVPR1 and SLC6A4 gene polymorphisms are associated with creative dance performance. *PLoS Genetics* 1:394-403.
Block, Jack, and Jeanne H. Block. 2005. Nursery school personality and political orientation two decades later. *Journal of Research in Personality* 39:395-422.
Boone, Christopher, Bert De Branbander, and Arjen van Witteloostuijn. 1999. The impact of personality on behavior in five Prisoner's Dilemma games. *Journal of Economic Psychology* 20:343-77.
Bouchard, T. J., Jr., and Matt McGue. 2003. Genetic and environmental influences on human psychological differences. *Journal of Neurobiology* 54:4-45.
Brandstatter, Hermann, and Werner Guth. 2002. Personality in dictator and ultimatum games. *Central European Journal of Operations Research* 10:191-215.
Caprara, G. V., C. Barbaranelli, and P. G. Zimbardo. 1999. Personality profiles and political parties. *Political Psychology* 20:175-97.
Caprara, G. V., S. Schwartz, C. Capanna, M. Vecchione, and C. Barbaranelli. 2006. Personality and politics: Values, traits, and political choice. *Political Psychology* 27:1-28.
Carmen, Ira. 2007. Genetic configurations of political phenomena. *Annals of the American Academy of Political and Social Science* 614:34-55.
Comings, D. E., R. Gade-Andavoluy, N. Gonzales, S. Wu, D. Muhleman, H. Blake, M. B. Mann, G. Dietz, G. Saucier, and J. P. MacMurray. 2000. A multivariate analysis of 59 candidate genes in personality traits: The Temperament and Character Inventory. *Clinical Genetics* 58:375-85.
Comrey, A. L., and J. A. Newmeyer. 1965. Measurement of radicalism-conservatism. *Journal of Social Psychology* 67:357-69.
De Waal, Frans B. M. 1982. *Chimpanzee politics: Power and sex among apes.* London: Jonathan Cape.
———. 1996. *Good natured: The origins and right and wrong in humans and other animals.* Cambridge, MA: Harvard University Press.
DeYoung, Colin G., Jordan B. Peterson, and Daniel M. Higgins. 2005. Sources of openness/intellect: Cognitive and neuropsychological correlates of the fifth factor of personality. *Journal of Personality* 73:825-58.
Fehr, Ernst, Urs Fischbacher, Bernhard von Rosenbladt, Jurgen Schupp, and Gert G. Wagner. 2002. A nation-wide laboratory—Examining trust and trustworthiness by integrating behavioral experiments into representative surveys. *Schmollers Jahrbuch* 122 (4): 519-42.
Frank, Thomas. 2004. *What's the matter with Kansas?* New York: Metropolitan Books.
Jost, John T. 2006. The end of the end of ideology. *American Psychologist* 61:651-70.
Jost, John T., Jack Glaser, Arie W. Kruglanski, and Frank J. Sulloway. 2003. Political conservatism as motivated social cognition. *Psychological Bulletin* 129:339-75.
Lakoff, George. 2006. *Thinking points: Communicating our American values and vision.* New York: Farrar, Straus, and Giroux.
McClosky, Herbert. 1958. Conservatism and personality. *American Political Science Review* 52:27-45.
McCrae, Robert R., and Paul T. Costa Jr. 1999. A five-factor theory of personality. In *Handbook of personality*, 2nd ed., ed. Lawrence A. Pervin and Oliver P. John. New York: Guilford.
Mehrabian, Albert. 1996. Relations among political attitudes, personality, and psychopathology. *Basic and Applied Social Psychology* 18:469-91.
Mestelman, Stuart, and David Feeny. 1988. Does ideology matter? Anecdotal experimental evidence on the voluntary provision of public goods. *Public Choice* 57:287-94.
Mondak, Jeffery J., and Karen D. Halperin. Forthcoming. A framework for the study of personality and political behavior. *British Journal of Political Science.*
Pratto, F., J. Sidanius, L. M. Stallworth, and B. F. Malle. 1994. Social dominance orientation: A personality variable predicting social and political attitudes. *Journal of Personality and Social Psychology* 67:741-63.
Ray, John J. 1985. Defective validity in the Altemeyer Authoritarianism Scale. *Journal of Social Psychology* 125:271-72.
Shils, Edward A. 1954. Authoritarianism: Right and left. In *Studies in the scope and method of the authoritarian personality*, ed. Richard Christie and Marie Jahoda. Glencoe, IL: Free Press.

Swope, Kurtis J., John Cadigan, Pamela M. Schmitt, and Robert S. Shupp. 2005. Personality preferences in laboratory economics experiments. Working Paper, Department of Economics, Ball State University, Muncie, IN.

van Gestel, S., and C. van Broeckhoven. 2003. Genetics of personality: Are we making progress? *Molecular Psychiatry* 8:840-52.

Whitaker, Eric. 2006. Personality and political orientation: A reanalysis of an age-old question. Unpublished paper, Department of Political Science, University of Nebraska–Lincoln.

QUICK READ SYNOPSIS

The Biology of Political Behavior

Special Editors: JOHN R. HIBBING
and
KEVIN B. SMITH
University of Nebraska–Lincoln

Volume 614, November 2007

Prepared by Herb Fayer, Jerry Lee Foundation

DOI: 10.1177/0002716207307213

Testosterone and Aggression in a Simulated Crisis Game

Rose McDermott, University of California, Santa Barbara;
Dominic Johnson, Princeton University; Jonathan Cowden,
University of California, Santa Barbara; and Stephen Rosen,
Harvard University

Background   This study investigated the impact of testosterone on aggression in a crisis simulation game.

- The authors found a significant positive relationship between levels of testosterone and aggression.
- Men were much more likely to engage in aggressive action than women and more likely to lose their fights as well.
- The implications of the proper origin of aggression suggest different strategies for intervention; if social conditions are responsible for violence, then changing certain situational or institutional factors can reduce the incidence of death and destruction.
- However, if genetic predispositions and biochemical hormones play a decisive role, ethical intervention becomes more difficult to imagine.

Testosterone   While it may be difficult to prove a direct relationship between testosterone and criminality, certain aggressive behaviors that can be exacerbated by high levels of testosterone tend to get men in trouble with the law.

- Prison studies, for example, show that high-testosterone men commit more violent crimes against other people, as opposed to property crimes, and act out more than lower-testosterone men.
- Men convicted of domestic violence also possess higher levels of testosterone and display greater physical violence than healthy controls.
- Testosterone also correlates with sensation seeking.

NOTE: The study looks at these hypotheses:

- Younger males will have higher testosterone and show greater aggression and older females will have higher testosterone (and lower estrogen) and show greater aggression.
- Individuals with higher levels of testosterone will be more likely to engage in aggressive action than those who possess relatively lower levels.

Results   The following results came out of this study:
- *Testosterone and age:* The authors found a significant negative relationship between age and testosterone levels.
- *Testosterone and aggressive action:* Individuals with higher initial levels of testosterone were more likely to make an unprovoked attack on their opponent.

Discussion The findings in this study confirm several of the original hypotheses.
- Women clearly display a contrary dynamic to that of young men (who were more belligerent); however, *older* women are much more likely to engage in unprovoked attack than younger women.
- There is support for the hypothesis of a relationship between testosterone and aggressive action. However, there were no *within*-sex differences, so we do not know if aggression was driven by testosterone or by some other gender-specific factor.
- The authors did not find the expected relationship between testosterone and aggressive action.

Genetic Configurations of Political Phenomena: New Theories, New Methods

Ira H. Carmen, University of Illinois

Background In this article, the author presents a new theory—sociogenomics—to replace the shopworn conceptions of yesterday's political science.
- He shows how social scientists can use the tools of molecular biology to flesh out the genes coding for baseline political attitudes/behaviors.
- The theory and methods of sociogenomics will serve to synthesize the social sciences with the natural sciences in a broader consilient framework, so that the laboratory of Darwinian investigation can become the laboratory of Aristotelian investigation.
- This article will engage the central issue for political science in our time: how can we construct an overarching paradigm for the grand purpose of at long last ending the internecine squabbles among those of us who believe in the scientific pursuit of things political?

NOTE: The waters are as murky as ever. The empiricism of behavioralism steeped in the premises and biases of social psychology and attitudinal inference has long since come under challenge from the deductivism of rational choice—steeped in the premises and biases of the economic marketplace and Rawlsian philosophy. The core thesis of this article is simply that these competing paradigms fail because they are not scientific *enough*.

Q
R
S

Genetics

Approximately thirty genes have been isolated in nonhuman species that, if isolated in *Homo sapiens*, would provide important information as to our political behavior repertoires.

- One notes fifteen gene-related sequences in the human with clear political implications.
- It is easy to spot the importance of the neurotransmitters serotonin and dopamine in influencing sociality.
  - A certain genetic promoter controls the serotonin transporter function.
  - A high correlation involving serotonin was reported for harm avoidance, especially worry, pessimism, fear of uncertainty, and fatigability.
  - Rather like serotonin, dopamine is one of those brain chemicals that needs to be at equilibrium in the typical case, or personality problems and worse arise.
  - Dopamine overload correlates with highly risky behavior: too much gambling, too much sex, too much drinking.

NOTE: Of course, it would be wrong to assume that "pure types" are forever gene-driven, that nothing will counterbalance their established mind-sets. Still, these efforts are corollary to the fundamental role of genetics in politics.

God Gene

Perhaps the oddest, and certainly one of the most controversial, DNA sequences is Hamer's inaptly dubbed "God gene."

- Some people display a greater sense of "self-transcendence" than others, what Hamer calls a sense of spirituality.
- Spirituality, he says, "provides a numerical measure of people's capacity to reach out beyond themselves."

The Challenge

Ultimately, "The challenge is to link genes and their products into functional pathways, circuits, and networks" (Loomis and Sternberg 1995, 649).

- A proliferating literature in political science stresses the need to address decision making as a neuroscientific phenomenon.
- Experiments conjoining genetic and cranial parameters are needed.

The Amygdala

The amygdala is a complex, socially relevant processing center, citations to which are just now beginning to appear in the political science literature.

- We now know through functional MRI amygdalar screenings that inhibited infants grow up generally to be "avoidance" adults, while uninhibited infants grow up generally to be novelty-seeking adults.
- To say that we need to appreciate the genetic mainsprings of amygdalar function is a gross understatement, though we have learned recently that the *stathmin* gene is highly expressed in the lateral nucleus of the mouse amygdala, and when this gene is knocked out, subjects do not respond either to learned or innate fear.

The Future   Access to the human genome, taken as a whole, provides parsimonious entrée to the investigation of complex traits of which human social behavior—human *political* behavior—is a prime example.

- Complex traits arise from a battery of genes acting together.
- Genes are no longer treated as static entities frozen in time.
- Some genes can be slipped into or out of animal models to pin down precise behavioral manifestations.
- Researchers scan the genome in search of precursor DNA chromosomal locations.
- At a higher level of magnitude, new theory also inspires new methods, and in this case, the breakthrough procedure of choice is called the microarray gene expression technology.
  - Microarrays have led to startling new genetic discoveries in nonhuman subjects.
  - Genes that exhibit different alleles in different people hold the secret to phenotypic variation.
- Eventually, political scientists working with biological scientists can commence to control for the role of each gene one by one, folding in as well interspecies and pedigree data.

Balancing Ambition and Gender among Decision Makers

Christopher W. Larimer, University of Northern Iowa;
Rebecca J. Hannagan, Northern Illinois University; and Kevin B. Smith,
University of Nebraska–Lincoln

Background   Political theorists have recognized a paradox underlying the exercise of political power: citizens do not trust leaders perceived as desiring power, but those not desiring power are, by definition, unlikely to become political leaders.

- Political leaders who take up office as a burden of public service are viewed as more legitimate and trustworthy than those who are perceived to pursue power as an individual prize to be won.
- Overt ambition for power is clearly a political liability.

NOTE: This article builds a conceptual framework to explain why a universal predisposition to mistrust certain types of leaders might exist, what traits would trigger this mistrust, and how people would behaviorally respond.

Gender   Two potential reasons are forwarded to explain gender differences.

- Socialization, that is, that a system of gender-specific behavioral expectations or roles are institutionalized (invariably to the advantage of men and the disadvantage of women).
- There are innate psychological differences between males and females, products of evolved responses to differing adaptive problems (notably, though not exclusively, reproduction).

NOTE: Males are more competitive, physically aggressive, risk-tolerant, status-oriented, and oriented toward dominance. Given this, there is a high probability that a "big man"—a leader with negative ambition—is indeed going to be a male.

Ambition

If negative ambition is a particularly male trait, reactions to ambition may be mediated by gender.
- Ambition in female decision makers may not prompt such severe leveling mechanism responses as those in males.
- Female policy makers could conceivably even benefit from ambition if it is seen as a type of leveling mechanism itself.
- The female candidate may actually have an advantage because negative ambition is so stereotypically male.
- Women who are successful in gaining office and keeping it are often those who present themselves as having a clear and deliberate message and represent themselves as being as "independent a decision maker as any man, but more caring and trustworthy."

Hypotheses

The authors tested three types of hypotheses.
- The first concerns inferences about ambitious decision makers.
- The second type of hypothesis concerns the choices people will make in selecting a decision maker for a group.
- The third type of hypothesis concerns the reaction to unfair allocations.

Conclusions

The findings of this study have significant implications for the study of trait inferences and mass political behavior.
- First, the authors provide a theory and empirical support for why the trait of ambition is important for candidate evaluation.
- Second, they show that judgments of fairness and the behavioral consequences of those judgments are less about what people get from a decision maker and more about a specific set of decision-maker traits.
- Third, their argument has important implications for research on gender stereotypes and representation.

An Evolutionary Model of Racial Attitude Formation: Socially Shared and Idiosyncratic Racial Attitudes

Thomas Craemer, University of Connecticut

Background

A growing body of research in political science and social psychology has uncovered evidence of a "split personality" among Americans when it comes to racial attitudes.
- People appear to voice different attitudes publicly than privately when given the opportunity to express their views anonymously.
- This discrepancy is often interpreted as a social desirability effect among white Americans who engage in self-monitoring.

- Differences between implicit and explicit attitudes are often interpreted as a result of self-monitoring in response to a new, problack norm of "political correctness."
- At present there is no theoretical model that could account for the emergence of a discrepancy between individual attitudes and social norms.
- This article provides a simple theoretical model of racial norms evolution that is based on a few simple assumptions about neural organization and social communication.

Attitudes

There is a two-by-two classification of attitudes:
- implicit idiosyncratic,
- explicit idiosyncratic,
- implicit socially shared, and
- explicit socially shared.

NOTE: Three of the above were considered in this study (implicit idiosyncratic, implicit socially shared, and explicit socially shared).

Model Assumptions

The theoretical model of racial norms evolution combines two assumptions of neural organization with one assumption about social communication processes.
- The first of these assumptions holds that perceptions of internal body states ("chemistry" or idiosyncratic attitudes) and perceptions of external stimuli (socially shared attitudes) are processed in different (yet interconnected) areas of the brain.
- The second assumption holds that both idiosyncratic and socially shared attitudes can become automatic through attitude rehearsal, that is, Hebbian Learning (frequent simultaneous activation of neurons leading to faster signal transmission).
- The third assumption of the model holds that social communication can produce social norms by virtue of a random evolutionary process first described by Kimura (1983) as "random drift."

Approach

This article investigates the possibility that random norms evolution may help us explain the otherwise puzzling observation that people adjust their views to powerful social norms.
- If we assume that social norms are simply an additive function of individual attitudes, no systematic differences should occur between average idiosyncratic and average socially shared attitudes.
- In contrast, if we assume that an individual's socially shared attitudes will differ from idiosyncratic ones due to the norms-generating effect of social communication, we would expect the two sets of attitudes to differ substantially.
- Simulations based on the random norms evolution model hold idiosyncratic attitudes constant while allowing for changes in socially shared attitudes due to random persuasion among neighbors.
- The simulation results are surprisingly similar to the observed college student experiment described in this article. No systematic racial bias is observable at the level of implicit idiosyncratic attitudes (implicit closeness),

while racial groups significantly differ in their explicit racial attitudes (explicit closeness). Further implicit socially shared attitudes display a universal prowhite and antiblack bias (racial priming).

- As a maximally parsimonious baseline model, the random racial norms evolution model suffices to produce considerable similarity between observed and simulated racial attitude data.
- Due to its parsimony, the model of racial norms evolution presented here may serve as a null model against which more complex models can be tested in the future.

Q
R
S

Neuroendocrine Mechanisms, Stress Coping Strategies, and Social Dominance: Comparative Lessons about Leadership Potential

William D. Anderson and Cliff H. Summers,
University of South Dakota

Background   This article broadly focuses on the likely neuroendocrine and neurochemical foundations for extreme leadership and subordination phenotypes.

- The concern is with leaders, followers, the creation of social dominance hierarchies, and traits and behaviors that drive individuals to leadership.
- The article addresses two extreme but useful cases of leadership and followership—social dominance orientation (SDO) and right-wing authoritarianism (RWA).
- The article diagrams likely neuroendocrine and neurochemical profiles for these dominance/subordination phenotypes.
- The article suggests two potentially fruitful directions for research.

Biology and Leadership   The human personality traits most closely related with dominance and leadership—confidence, initiative, and extraversion—also have heritable hormonal and neurotransmitter antecedents.

- Among the potential hormones or neurotransmitters that might be studied, testosterone has received the most attention.
- Important other hormones—cortisol, for example—and neurotransmitters such as serotonin also likely influence leadership and subordination emergence and persistence.
- The mechanisms causing changes in concentrations of these hormones and neurotransmitters in the blood and brain appear to be caused by a confluence of genetic predisposition and environmental or social stresses.

SDO and RWA   SDO and RWA, coupled with perceived threat or stress, have proven to be strong predictors of political attitudes and behaviors.

- After the 9/11 terrorist attacks, Crowson, Debacker, and Thoma (2006, 746) found that both SDOs and RWAs were more supportive of restrictions on rights and the use of aggression in U.S. foreign policy.

- Moreover, SDOs and RWAs evince a preference for conservative over liberal political candidates.
- High SDOs emphasize group-based dominance and superiority.
- Individuals with higher SDO scale scores hold hostile worldviews and are prejudiced against those in identified out-groups.

NOTE: Taken together, the elements of the high-SDO leadership profile suggest predominately male individuals who lack a moral center and who disproportionately manipulate followers—even to those followers' harm—to achieve political and social ends.

RWA People   RWAs are "followers who have submissive attitudes toward established authorities, show a general aggressiveness toward persons 'targeted by those authorities,' and adhere to social conventions."

SDO People   SDOs fit the profile of impulsive, proactive individuals that produce fits of unrestrained severe aggression but not affiliative or cooperative behavior.

Next Steps   The above suggested that dominance and subordination—or leadership and followership—have clear biological foundations. Hormone and neurotransmitter profiles for SDOs and RWAs are provided, and a series of potential research steps are offered to test the veracity of these suggested profiles.

- The first step to testing the hypothesized neurochemical profiles for SDOs and RWAs is to understand the basal neurochemical profiles for highly dominant, highly submissive, and healthy dominance–submission profiles.
- Although the tests suggested provide some elucidation of the neuroendocrine profiles that differentiate high SDOs and RWAs, a focus only on peripheral chemical messengers—such as androgens and glucocorticoids—is only preliminary.
- Real understanding of these behavioral phenotypes requires some measure of the subject's brain neurochemistry.
- Such an approach will allow us to make even stronger inferences about the neurochemical foundations for leadership, dominance, subordination, and any resulting political and social behaviors.

The Political Consequences of Perceived Threat and Felt Insecurity

Leonie Huddy, Stanley Feldman, and Christopher Weber,
Stony Brook University

Background   This study explores political reactions to threat and how a sense of security interacts with threat to influence support for national security policies.

- Personal threat increases one's sense of vulnerability and motivates individual action designed to minimize personal risk.

- Threat not only drives protective individual behaviors, it also promotes support for protective government policies. These include support for increased surveillance against current and potential Arab immigrants to the United States and policies that promise increased domestic safety.
  - But some individuals are able to maintain a sense of security even in the face of threatening events. This sense of security may undercut their need for protective personal and government policies in response to threatening events.

NOTE: The authors further explore the link between threat and support of national security policy by examining the extent to which it depends on a person's degree of felt security.

Adult
Attachment

Numerous scholars have explored the likely evolutionary advantage of adult attachment under conditions of threat.
- Adult attachment could improve human reproductive fitness through the process of kin selection by promoting the protection of those with whom one shares similar genes.
- Adult attachment could be a simple outgrowth of humans' protracted developmental period in infancy in which attachment is needed to protect offspring and stimulate complex social and cognitive skills.
- Adult attachment may foster long-lasting romantic and parenting relationships that may improve the fitness of one's offspring.

Hypotheses

This research closely examines whether a sense of felt security provides a buffer against threatening events and reduces the need for government action to maintain a sense of safety.
- In essence, the authors test whether perceived threat coupled with a feeling of insecurity promotes support for policies that enhance domestic security but may reduce civil liberties, and leads to increased support for overseas military action.
- The authors supplement past findings with recent psychological insights from attachment and terror-management theories on the importance of felt security in dealing with stressful events.
- The authors focus specifically on the degree to which the political effects of threat depend on a sense of insecurity.
- The authors contrast the origins of felt security with other reactions to the 9/11 terrorist attacks and expect security to be less influenced by the details of the immediate event than anxiety and depression because it is based on a long-standing sense of secure attachment.
- Consistent with the predictions of attachment theory, the authors also expect felt security to moderate the influence of threat on anxiety.
- The authors examine whether a sense of security moderates the desire to bolster self-esteem through an increase in American patriotism and heightened denigration of outsiders, consistent with the expectations of a blended attachment–terror management approach.
- Finally, the authors evaluate whether felt security decreases the political effects of perceived threat on support of national security policy.

Conclusion   The current findings demonstrate that the greatest impact of threat is con-
                centrated among individuals who had difficulty maintaining a sense of secu-
                rity in the months following the terrorist attacks of 9/11.
                • Drawing on psychological attachment theory, the authors suggest that
                  feelings of security are a long-standing individual characteristic that may
                  derive from early childhood attachment experiences.
                • Attachment theory indicates that most adults achieve a secure attach-
                  ment, and this, in turn, improves their ability to deal with stress through
                  imagined or real proximity to attachment figures.
                • The authors uncover suggestive evidence consistent with attachment theory
                  that felt security was not greatly affected by the terrorist attacks of 9/11 and
                  was much less affected than other reactions such as anxiety or depression.
                • Felt security helped to minimize feelings of anxiety and mitigated the
                  need to elevate feelings of symbolic patriotism to cope with threat.

A Dual-Edged Sword: Empathy
and Collective Action in the Prisoner's Dilemma

John A. Sautter; Levente Littvay, Central European University;
and Brennen Bearnes

Background   Researchers guided by evolutionary psychology have theorized that in an
                iterated Prisoner's Dilemma, reciprocal behavior is a product of evolutionary
                design, where individuals are guided by an innate sense of fairness.
                • Results suggest that an empathetic disposition does not lead to a higher
                  rate of cooperation but interacts with environmental conditioning to pro-
                  duce either a highly cooperative or highly uncooperative personality type.
                • Evolutionary theory posits that group-level selection gives humans a
                  propensity for cooperative behavior in the absence of selective incentives
                  by equipping the human mind with prosocial emotions.
                • Some people get more satisfaction than others out of political participa-
                  tion or paying attention to civic issues.

                NOTE: The Prisoner's Dilemma framework is ideal for a test of prosocial emo-
                tional disposition in an incentive-based game because it is simple enough for
                those first exposed to it in an experimental setting to comprehend, yet theo-
                retically sophisticated enough to allow a rich interpretation of the results.

Evolution and   Evolution has cultivated a multitude of personality traits that vary among
Empathy   humans.
                • Whether an individual is more of a rational calculator or an empathetic
                  altruist, both would have played an important role in collective success in
                  humans' distant past.
                • Geneticists have found important links between genes and behavior.
                  • Studies of autism, violent behavior, and other asocial disorders indicate that
                    genetic inheritance is an important determinant of patterns of behavior.
                • Prosocial personality traits have also been connected to an individual's
                  genetic makeup.

• It is likely that genetic inheritance of behavioral traits affects the preferences that individuals form for cooperative social behavior.

NOTE: Empathy is arguably one of the most important socioemotional experiences because it provides the impetus and mental processes involved in "the effort to understand the internal mental and emotional events of other human beings" (Rosenberg 1990, 8).

Hypotheses There are two empathetic hypotheses presented in this article.
• A more robust empathetic psychological disposition will lead to higher rates of "punishment" (or mutual defection) in the face of defection by an opposing player.
  ◦ The study shows that a participant's empathetic disposition was a significant predictor of defection in retaliation to the opposing player's second-stage defections.
• Empathy will predict more forgiving behavior during a period when the opposing player attempts to reestablish mutual cooperation.
  ◦ Here the study indicates that even marginal levels of empathy led to more defection in the final rounds of the experiment.

Conclusion Judging by this experiment, empathy seems to have a bipolar nature.
• Higher rates of empathy tended to have two contrary effects by either making an individual more likely to defect or more likely to cooperate but not to converge toward the median level of cooperation as the majority of participants in this experiment.
• Contrary to the hypotheses originally being tested, it is not that empathy has a simple positive linear relationship with a desire for egalitarian outcomes; rather, an empathetic emotional disposition likely cultivates a sensitivity to social decisions, which, depending on an individual's social conditioning, leads to a more intense display of cooperation and defection.

Personality and Emotional Response: Strategic and Tactical Responses to Changing Political Circumstances

Jennifer Wolak, University of Colorado at Boulder;
and George E. Marcus, Williams College

Background In this article, the authors investigate what role personality has in the operation of the systems of affective intelligence.
• The authors first consider whether personality affects the activation of emotional response.
• They explore the degree to which citizen attitudes like openness to information and compromise are explained by personality characteristics and subconscious emotional response.
• They consider the implications of these results for our normative understanding of democratic citizenship.
• Thus, this article considers the personality roots of emotional response.

Emotion's Use	When confronted with familiar friends or foes, people rely on an appraisal system that uses variations in the emotions of enthusiasm and anger to deliver assessments of the situation and guide habitual routines to manage such recurring events. • These feelings guide our reliance on existing habits. • As anxiety increases, people become more attentive to the immediate circumstances and rely on expressly deliberative strategies rather than continued reliance on habitual responses. • Preconscious affective appraisal systems provide a potent dual capacity, distinguishing the situations when previously learned routines are suitable from the contexts where greater attentiveness and consideration are needed.
Citizenship	The practice of good citizenship has deeper roots than personal issue preferences and socialized views of citizenship. • While good citizenship can be learned, some are perhaps more predisposed to support such principles than others. • Personality differences can drive candidate evaluations and party preferences. • People's willingness to extend rights to disliked groups can also depend on personality. • Authoritarian predispositions combine with perceptions of threat to influence views on civil liberties and race. • Dogmatism associated with authoritarianism can limit political tolerance. • Personality differences have also been shown to influence people's levels of political engagement. • Individual differences in the need to evaluate help explain political activism and opinionation. NOTE: These accounts suggest important individual differences in reactivity to political signals. In this study, the authors select three dimensions of citizenship that are central to most accounts of democratic citizenship. First, people become citizens when they turn away from the mundane affairs that consume their lives and shift their attention to some political issue that commands their attention. Second, once they become attentive, people need to speak up and become active citizens. And third, once engaged by a political conflict, they have to determine whether to engage in compromise, to seek some middle ground that might resolve the dispute by mutual accommodation, or to remain steadfastly loyal to the cause.
Personality Effects	The authors focus on four personality characteristics: neuroticism, extroversion, openness, and authoritarianism. • Those who are more neurotic may be more likely to seek out information to ease their feelings of anxiety, but to the extent to which neurotic individuals feel not just anxiety but also hostility or distress, neuroticism may instead close the door to consideration, discouraging consideration of compromise and political action. • Extroversion and openness to experience, however, will likely have a positive relationship with citizenship behaviors of learning and compromise. • Authoritarianism is a personality trait associated with support for social conventions and respect for authorities.

Personality and The next considerations are the effects of personality on three citizenship
Citizenship behaviors—the willingness to learn more about the issue, interest in political
participation, and consideration of policy compromise.

- Anxiety prompts greater interest in learning more about the policy issue, confirming prior affective intelligence findings.
- There are significant direct effects of personality on citizenship behavior beyond any contribution via emotional engagement.
- Here, the authors find effects for neuroticism only in the condition of when people confront a familiar and affirming issue position, where those high in neuroticism express a heightened desire to learn more about the policy.
- For those who see reassuring policy change, levels of extroversion are also positively associated with a willingness to learn about public policy.

NOTE: Thus, personality plays a modestly greater role when subjects are in a reassuring familiar context and a lesser role when in the confrontational disturbing condition, as we find significant interactions with neuroticism and extraversion and this treatment condition.

Conclusion Overall, the authors found modest evidence that the activation of the emotional surveillance system depends on personality differences, where the joint interaction of extraversion and neuroticism heightens anxiety responses.

- In the practice of citizenship, they found mixed evidence of the influence of personality traits.
- When it comes to matters of compromise and political participation, traits tend to propel people along particular deliberative paths.
- The effects of traits depend on both the citizenship behavior and the nature of policy threat.

NOTE: Overall, while the authors found some influence of personality traits in the triggering of emotional response and the practice of political citizenship, neither is determined by these prior predispositions.

Personal, Interpersonal, and Political Temperaments

John R. Alford, Rice University; and John R. Hibbing,
University of Nebraska–Lincoln

Background Research in behavioral genetics and elsewhere increasingly indicates a biological basis for the manner in which people behave in personal, interpersonal, and political situations, but this biological basis does not mean behavior in these three very different contexts is correlated.

- This article tests for the degree to which personal, interpersonal, and political temperaments are related.
- As expected, the overall correlations are quite low—standard personality traits do not predict political attitudes, and neither political attitudes nor personality predicts the extent to which subjects are generous in interpersonal situations.

- Behavior is partially biological, but the systems involved in shaping political behavior seem to be largely, but not completely, distinct from those involved in shaping personal and interpersonal behavior.

The Three Temperaments

This article argues that the behaviors of an individual are not influenced solely by the personal temperaments traditionally studied by psychologists but also by reasonably distinct interpersonal and political temperaments that operate alongside personal.

- Personal temperaments are predispositions (e.g., fastidiousness) that can manifest themselves even when other people are not present.
- Interpersonal temperaments are predispositions (e.g., extroversion) that are at least dyadic in that they involve at a minimum one person in the immediate social environment.
- Political temperaments (e.g., conservatism) are those that apply to the governance of large-scale social life—life beyond one's immediate social environment—and involve the norms, mores, and statutes that govern large-scale social life: norms and statutes that do not only apply to people well known and close by but also unknown and far away.

Temperament Links

There are three possible links among these temperament categories:
- the link between the personal and the political,
- the link between the personal and the interpersonal, and
- the link between the interpersonal and the political.

NOTE: This article looks at each of these links and the available research.

Key Results

Individuals' preferences for the conduct of their personal lives are only weakly predictive of their preferences for both large-scale societal organization and behaviors in concrete, small-scale social situations.

- The real message is that people's personal behaviors are quite different from the behaviors they advocate for society as a whole.
- To the extent that political and interpersonal temperaments do not correlate with personal temperament, these areas of study must be undertaken with separate approaches, theories, and expectations.

Discussion

The findings hold little hope for any of the current hypotheses.

- Deeply encoded, stable personality traits offer little predictive purchase on self-sacrificing prosocial behavior; ideology fares no better.
- The authors view ideology as being no less deeply encoded in the genes and brains of humans than personality and are not harnessed to a conception that yields clear centrality to personality as an explanatory variable on the basis of its presumed unique deep encoding.
- Placing both personality and something as presumably abstract as ideology abreast of each other in terms of their level of biological encoding, and hence temporal priority, allows for an alternative view of the sources of interpersonal generosity.
- Rather than arising from either of these deeply encoded temperaments, interpersonal generosity may arise from a conceptually distinct third deeply encoded temperament.
- If each of these distinct realms of human nature originates at a similarly deep level, then there is no reason to suppose that they must be closely correlated.

STATEMENT OF OWNERSHIP, MANAGEMENT, AND CIRCULATION
P.S. Form 3526 Facsimile

1. TITLE: THE ANNALS OF THE AMERICAN ACADEMY OF POLITICAL AND SOCIAL SCIENCE
2. USPS PUB. #: 026-060

3. DATE OF FILING: October 1, 2007

4. FREQUENCY OF ISSUE: Bimonthly
5. NO. OF ISSUES ANNUALLY: 6
6. ANNUAL SUBSCRIPTION PRICE:

Paperback cover:	Institution	$	600.00
Paperback cover:	Individual	$	91.00
Hardcover:	Institution	$	678.00
Hardcover:	Individual	$	134.00

7. PUBLISHER ADDRESS: 2455 Teller Road, Thousand Oaks, CA 91320
   CONTACT PERSON: Emily Koberling, Circulation Director
   TELEPHONE: (805) 499-0721

8. HEADQUARTERS ADDRESS: 2455 Teller Road, Thousand Oaks, CA 91320

9. PUBLISHER: Sage Publications Inc., 2455 Teller Road, Thousand Oaks, CA 91320
   EDITORS: Dr. Phyllis Kaniss, University of Pennsylvania, Fells Institute of Goverment
   3814 Walnut St., Philadelphia, PA 19104
   MANAGING EDITOR: Julie Odland

10. OWNER: The American Academy of Political and Social Science, 3814 Walnut St.
    Philadelphia, PA 19104-6197

11. KNOWN BONDHOLDERS, ETC.
    None

12. NONPROFIT PURPOSE, FUNCTION, STATUS:
    Has Not Changed During Preceding 12 Months

13. PUBLICATION NAME: THE ANNALS OF THE AMERICAN ACADEMY OF POLITICAL & SOCIAL SCIENCE

14. ISSUE FOR CIRCULATION DATA BELOW: SEPTEMBER 2007

15. EXTENT & NATURE OF CIRCULATION:

		AVG. NO. COPIES EACH ISSUE DURING PRECEDING 12 MONTHS	ACT. NO. COPIES OF SINGLE ISSUE PUB. NEAREST TO FILING DATE
A.	TOTAL NO. COPIES	2704	2582
B.	PAID CIRCULATION		
	1. PAID/REQUESTED OUTSIDE-CO, ETC	1359	1334
	2. PAID IN-COUNTY SUBSCRIPTIONS	0	0
	3. SALES THROUGH DEALERS, ETC	19	19
	4. OTHER CLASSES MAILED USPS	0	0
C.	TOTAL PAID CIRCULATION	1378	1353
D.	FREE DISTRIBUTION BY MAIL		
	1. OUTSIDE-COUNTY AS ON 3541	84	94
	2. IN-COUNTY AS STATED ON 3541	0	0
	3. OTHER CLASSES MAILED USPS	0	0
E.	FREE DISTRIBUTION OTHER	0	0
F.	TOTAL FREE DISTRIBUTION	84	94
G.	TOTAL DISTRIBUTION	1462	1447
H.	COPIES NOT DISTRIBUTED		
	1. OFFICE USE, ETC	1242	1135
	2. RETURN FROM NEWS AGENTS	0	0
I.	TOTAL	2190	2099
	PERCENT PAID CIRCULATION	94%	94%

16. NOT REQUIRED TO PUBLISH.

17. I CERTIFY THAT ALL INFORMATION FURNISHED ON THIS FORM IS TRUE AND COMPLETE.
    I UNDERSTAND THAT ANYONE WHO FURNISHES FALSE OR MISLEADING INFORMATION ON
    THIS FORM OR WHO OMITS MATERIAL OR INFORMATION REQUESTED ON THE FORM MAY
    BE SUBJECT TO CRIMINAL SANCTIONS (INCLUDING FINES AND IMPRISONMENT) AND/OR
    CIVIL SANCTIONS (INCLUDING MULTIPLE DAMAGES AND CIVIL PENALTIES).

Emily Koberling

Emily Koberling   Date   9/10/2007
Circulation Director
Sage Publications, Inc.